KT-529-858

Anorexia nervosa and bulimia: how to help

SECOND EDITION

Marilyn Duker and
Roger Slade

Open University Press
Buckingham · Philadelphia

Open University Press
Celtic Court
22 Ballmoor
Buckingham
MK18 1XW

email: enquiries@openup.co.uk
world wide web: www.openup.co.uk

and
325 Chestnut Street
Philadelphia, PA 19106, USA

First published 1988
Reprinted 1990, 1992, 1994, 1996, 1997, 2000

First published in this second edition 2003

Copyright © Marilyn Duker and Roger Slade 2003

All rights reserved. Except for the quotation of short passages for the purpose of criticism and review, no part of this publication may be reproduced, stored in a retrieval system, or transmitted, in any form or by any means, electronic, mechanical, photocopying, recording or otherwise, without the prior written permission of the publisher or a licence from the Copyright Licensing Agency Limited. Details of such licences (for reprographic reproduction) may be obtained from the Copyright Licensing Agency Ltd of 90 Tottenham Court Road, London, W1P 0LP.

A catalogue record of this book is available from the British Library

ISBN 0 335 21203 4 (pb)   0 335 21204 2 (hb)

Library of Congress Cataloging-in-Publication Data
Duker, Marilyn.
    Anorexia nervosa and bulimia : how to help/Marilyn Duker and Roger Slade. — 2nd ed.
        p. ; cm.
    Includes bibliographical references and index.
    ISBN 0-335-21204-2 (hb.) — ISBN 0-335-21203-4 (pb.)
    1. Anorexia nervosa—Treatment. 2. Bulimia—Treatment. I. Slade, Roger. II. Title.
    [DNLM: 1 Anorexia Nervosa—psychology. 2. Bulimia—psychology. 3. Anorexia Nervosa—therapy. 4. Behavior Therapy—methods. 5. Bulimia—therapy. Wm 175 D877a 2002]
    RC552.A5 D85 2002
    616.85′2606—dc21

                                                                    2002074927

Typeset by Graphicraft Limited, Hong Kong
Printed in Great Britain by Biddles Limited, Guildford and Kings Lynn

With love to our children
Naomi, Raphael, Nathaniel and Morwenna

Contents

Acknowledgements

We would like to acknowledge and to thank the many sufferers who over the years have shared their problems, their struggles and their recoveries with us. It is their stories that are woven into this book.

Introduction

This book is for anyone who wants to help a person who is anorexic or bulimic, and sufferers will also find it valuable. It is based on the 'starvation whirlpool' theory which we presented first in *The Anorexia Nervosa Reference Book* and outline here in Chapter 2. We show in detail how this theory applies in the practical task of providing help.

We consider anorexia nervosa and bulimia, and excessive exercising not as separate problems but as different physical and behavioural manifestations of the same 'anorexic', or food/body controlling, style of thinking. While it is essential to understand the nature of the condition, this on its own is not enough. A helper needs to know how to talk to a sufferer in a way that is likely to be constructive rather than exacerbate his or her problem, and we illustrate ways in which this may be achieved.

The book as a whole reflects the change there has been in the division of responsibility in caring for sufferers, and the tensions that continue in this respect. The change has occurred partly as a result of conceptual developments such as the starvation whirlpool theory, and partly as a result of growing medical consensus about physical aspects of the condition. For it is now generally appreciated that anorexia nervosa/bulimia and preoccupation with exercising belong to the same order of problems as drug addiction and alcoholism, and that like these it is a condition in which the individual's actions produce physical and psychological changes that are entrapping.

Here we strike a balance between the role of medical and other helpers. Unlike those who offer a social analysis and pay scant regard to physical dangers, we insist the helper asks for and responds to medical information, and indicate where the need for such information and further help will arise. On the other hand there is no need for treatment to be exclusively a medical preserve. Often those who are medically trained have neither the human skills nor the necessary time to address the root of the problem. So we give encouragement and guidance to those who are prepared to take on the main task of providing sufferers with appropriate help; an approach that moves in the direction, long established in the case of alcoholism and drug abuse, of non-medical agencies sustaining a therapeutic role.

It is essential that the helper is attuned to the particular complexities that are presented by anorexic illness in its various manifestations. Established psychotherapy techniques can be helpful, but we have not provided a basic account of these. Rather we have indicated when they may profitably be used, and the kind of pitfalls there can be in using them.

Information about weight is given in percentages of average expected body weight (AEBW), this being the quickest way of ascertaining the degree of physical and psychological change, and, with this, the margin of physical safety and likely associated behaviour. For example, when any person's weight has fallen to 65 per cent AEBW his or her condition will be physically dangerous, behaviour will have become very rigid and communication problems will be severe. All of these aspects have implications for the way help is best provided in each individual case.

Straightforward weight measurements are still sufficient to indicate the level of concern that is needed. Whilst it is true that bodies can vary in the degree to which their potential energy reserves are held in the form of fat or muscle, fat plays a very important part in the body's chemistry, and particularly in its reproductive function. It is not possible to lose fat and retain muscle, or alter the proportions of fat to muscle without incurring some of the consequences that will be discussed in this book. This is particularly so at weights below average.

Weight can be calculated as a percentage of a person's AEBW by dividing current weight by AEBW and then multiplying this by 100, as follows:

$$\frac{\text{Current weight}}{\text{AEBW}} \times \frac{100}{1} = \text{n}\%$$

The average expected body weight (AEBW) for any individual is calculated on the basis of their age, height and gender. Tables showing average weights for men and for women are given in the Appendix. Also indicated in the tables are the 65 per cent AEBW levels where weight loss itself is hazardous.

These tables can be used to calculate, for example, that a healthy weight for a 23-year-old woman whose height is 5 ft. 6 in. (1.68 m) would on average be 60 kg (9 st. 6 lbs). Should this same young woman currently weigh 45 kg (7 st. 1 lb.) then, using the above formula, it can be calculated that she would at this point weigh only 75 per cent of her AEBW:

$$\frac{45 \text{ kg}}{60 \text{ kg}} \times \frac{100}{1} = 75\%$$

The above process, which compares a person's weight to a standard, is limited in that it works only for those people who come from populations that are the same or similar to the population from which the standard AEBW was derived. It cannot be used for international comparisons of groups with very different physical characteristics. If this is likely to be a problem then the preferred measure is the body mass index (BMI).

The BMI does not work by comparing weights to a standard but instead uses a statistic that has been found to vary with changes in weight but not changes in height. It is a measure of weight therefore that is independent of a person's stature. The result for each person is a single index figure. It is also corrected for age and gender. The measure is obtained by dividing weight in kilogrammes by height in metres squared (i.e. height multiplied by itself).

$$\frac{\text{current weight in kilograms}}{\text{height in metres}^2} = n$$

So the calculation of the BMI of the above 23-year-old woman, at a 60 kg weight level, would be as follows:

$$\frac{60 \text{ kg}}{1.68 \text{ m}^2} = 21.3$$

The range of BMI figures that is theoretically possible is subjected to classification, so that the significance of the single index figure can be understood. Thus it is also necessary to know that, for instance, the normal weight range for women is between 19.1 and 25.8 and for men is between 20.7 and 26.4, and likewise, for instance, to know that the BMI figure produced in the following calculation signifies that the same 23-year-old is to be classified as severely underweight.

$$\frac{45 \text{ kg}}{1.68 \text{ m}^2} = 16$$

In relation to anorexia nervosa/bulimia, however, the use of the BMI in turn is not without practical difficulties. Should a helper want to know, for instance, what an approximate healthy weight would be for a 23-year-old woman who is 5 ft. 6 in. tall, in AEBW terms the answer comes back in kilograms, or stones and pounds – specifically 60 kg, or 9 st. 6 lbs. Bathroom scales measure in kilograms, or stones and pounds, so all concerned will know directly what this means. The answer therefore has immediately intelligibility. Likewise if a helper were to ask what 80 per cent of that same woman's AEBW would be, the answer again would be in the familiar unit of measurement – i.e. 45 kg or 7 st. 1 lb. – straightforward and instantly comprehensible. Further calculations are not needed, nor further knowledge about classifications.

The index figure the BMI calculation produces is not immediately intelligible in this way. It is not possible to know what the figure means in terms of the person's weight on the scales until it is translated again into that unit of measurement which was used in the first place. With the BMI it is always necessary to make conversions. Nor is it possible to know what a particular index figure means in relation to any other index figure without knowing how the indices generally have been classified. Thus the BMI calculation is less direct. It has to be interpreted, or decoded, before it can be used.

With the AEBW it is also possible to work in rough approximations. As a rule of thumb, for instance, for adult females 1 per cent AEBW is likely to lie between $1^1/_4$ and $1^1/_2$ lbs. If a helper finds that between appointments a sufferer gains or loses one pound, it will be obvious that this is a bit less than 1 per cent AEBW, while a 1 kg (2.2 lbs) shift will be a bit more than 1 per cent AEBW, which, as the helper will know, at certain points will have physical or psychological significance. While this may seem crude, it does enable a helper quickly to double check calculations, and mistakes to be avoided.

By way of comparison, for the same 23-year-old female, the equivalent of 1 per cent AEBW is 0.213 points on the BMI scale. It is of course entirely possible to become familiar with any form of measurement. Arithmetically, however, it is always easier to calculate in terms of whole numbers.

It is a particular feature of the food/body controlling lifestyle that all computations and calculations become overridingly important. Given this and the fog of misinformation that hangs over the problem in general, as well as how easy it is inadvertently to play into the psychopathology of the illness, complexity of measurements is best avoided – as indeed is any other possible decoy to helpers using their eyes and ears in obtaining a full sense of how a sufferer is.

For these practical reasons we have chosen to continue to use percentages of AEBW.

The term 'anorexic' is a misnomer meaning 'without appetite'. As it occurs here it is used broadly to refer to the person whose food intake is persistently inadequate for his or her daily energy requirements, who is currently restricting successfully, who is generally low weight and/or exercising excessively. The term 'bulimic' will refer to the person whose weight may be normal or near normal but whose attempts to maintain food and body control recurrently fail; whose hunger cyclicly manifests itself in bulimic ('ox appetite') eating.

Girls and women still present as the majority of cases of this illness. Available series in the mid-1980s gave the incidence of male to female sufferers as between 1:20 and 1:10. Most recently it has been estimated that at least one in six or seven cases is male. Without menstruation as an indicator of change men can become very thin without attracting attention, medical or otherwise. Male sufferers can also be exceedingly reluctant to admit to needing help for a problem that has become associated with females. It is generally acknowledged that the incidence of the illness in males is under-reported.

The book divides into three parts. Part I is concerned with the nature of the illness and the different forms it takes. It shows the way theories and ideas influence treatment, and the problems inherent in certain approaches. In Part II we give a picture of the illness at different stages. We indicate how family circumstances and social and cultural values combine in the development of the condition, and how all of these contribute to its remaining hidden. This part enables would-be helpers to get to know more fully the people they are aiming to help, as well as to reflect perhaps upon their own background and values. In Part III we describe appropriate responses to the particular problems that are likely to arise in each of four weight bands.

Though each example here is a real sufferer in a real situation, the names used in all illustrations are fictitious.

The approach to help that we offer is one that we developed during the decade and a half prior to the first edition of this book. It combines our academic research, our practical experience of providing therapy, care and education for sufferers and their families, and the learning we gained from contact with a network of professionals and sufferers. Our work has continued since then and our hope is still, with this second edition, that many more people may be helped.

Roger Slade and Marilyn Duker

Part I

one

Beginning to unravel the problem

There can be few conditions that have generated as much interest as anorexia nervosa/bulimia, but where effective help remains notably sparse. It is an interest that, as its incidence increased, grew dramatically over the last decades of the twentieth century. Books and articles on the subject, internet postings, programmes of all kinds continue to proliferate. Dissertations are penned, and conferences convened. Across continents residential centres open their doors, groups and organizations spring up, new therapies are devised. Yet little of this activity has much practical or lasting significance for so many who find themselves having to cope, day in and day out, with the relentless stress this illness creates. Desperate people find there are few places to go with their particular difficulty. Self-help organizations generally make no claims to be able to intervene therapeutically. Groups are limited in their ability to help. Medical centres readily become overloaded. Information organizations, in common with general practitioners, have few places to which to refer those who contact them. The need for skilled help remains.

This can seem surprising. It was noted early on that the condition usually occurs in sections of the community where people usually obtain the help they need. Even as incidence has increased, this is a pattern that tends to endure. Sufferers typically come from homes that are respectable, often middle-class and usually relatively affluent. Younger sufferers have parents who are responsible and caring people who tend to move in circles where social and professional contacts with the caring agencies are plentiful. Those who are older move in the same circles themselves.

The question of providing help is not exactly straightforward, however. There is no particular consensus over who has the necessary therapeutic expertise. While hospital treatment programmes for low-weight anorexics that involve restoring the emaciated sufferer to normal weight can attract criticism from inside and outside the medical profession, there is also reason to be concerned about therapists who insist that keeping track of changes in a client's weight and monitoring symptoms such as vomiting, where this is used as a form of food control, is peripheral to 'real' therapy. It is also difficult to provide help for people who do not actively seek it.

A few may speak out, sometimes to obtain help for themselves, but perhaps more often in the hope of helping others. There are those, as the internet revealed, who are defiant in defence of their anorexic lifestyle. There are many more who stay quiet. Far from seeing themselves as in need of help, those caught up in anorexic illness feel better when they are skinny, losing weight, confident they can get rid of the calories one way or another, fine when food is controlled. For these people, none of this is a problem. Other people's anxieties are the problem. Hence requests for help are more likely to come from relatives and others who are close.

Even when sufferers have become aware that their food/body controlling way of life is limiting and ultimately destructive, they are still unlikely to make any attempt to obtain help. It would be weak, in their view. They ought not to need help. If there is a problem, they believe they should be able to sort it out for themselves. 'Help is for losers.' Because of the distress it causes them they are more likely to seek help when they become bulimic, but, equally, are likely to consider such behaviour does not deserve help. Compared with other people's more tangible, more obvious pressing problems they see their own difficulties with food and weight as unreasonable and unjustified. Hopeless, disgusted and ashamed at the methods they use to control the ingestion or absorption of food, ashamed at their 'laziness', at their failure to do enough exercise, at their 'not getting things done', and experiencing themselves thus as out of control, those who have become bulimic shy away from making their problem public. They can feel they are beyond help. It may be only their suicidal despair that eventually brings them to the point of seeking the help they need.

Mysteriousness

Much that has been written on anorexia nervosa/bulimia conveys an air of mystery, though this is mistaken and unhelpful. All the main characteristics of this illness have already been investigated in considerable detail and a great deal of information is available. There is no reason to await further basic research before setting about the task of helping a sufferer. Academic disputes are likely to continue because the condition, particularly in its low-weight stages, is remarkable for the way it challenges well-worn ways of thinking. Such disputes are largely the result of the personal and professional reasons which those involved have for disregarding sections of the relevant information. The commitment to 'objective' science leads some to ignore the moral aspects of the sufferer's view of food and body control. Others, convinced they have found the meaning of the symptom, overlook well-established physiological facts about the effects of undernutrition and/or persistent physical activity. Many more, sure that hard work, competitiveness and willpower are valuable in their own right, are unwilling to see that these qualities in a sufferer are part of what has caused that person to become ill.

Leaving professional knowledge and differences of opinion aside, it still remains true that for those meeting anorexia nervosa/bulimia for the first time the condition is baffling and frustrating. It is this that makes it so difficult to channel the concerned interest the problem generates in a way that benefits sufferers, or members of their families who can be stressed almost to breaking point by the illness. However much solicitude those close to a sufferer might initially feel, this rapidly becomes diffused in the mounting tension created by persistent food avoidance and increasing weight loss, by the intensifying preoccupation with repetitive exercising or by the intractable, chaotic, bulimic mess. Though there may at first be an abundance of goodwill, sooner or later it gives way to a sense of helpless impotence and downright anger.

It is not hard to find reasons for the bafflement. Explanations of the food/body controlling behaviour that marks anorexic illness sometimes seem to contain outright contradictions of the everyday experiences of those who live alongside a sufferer. While there is wide academic agreement for instance that lack of a clear sense of self is central to the problem, that those caught up in the condition have a very fragile notion of their own being,[1] the experience of those who are close to them is that sufferers are iron-willed and dominating. Certainly this is true where food control and exercise regimes are concerned. They are definite and demanding about what they will or will not tolerate in relation to domestic arrangements and routines. These must be totally clear and predictable to support their control. As anxiety and tension mount over the rigid refusal to eat or to eat adequately and over the uncompromising commitment to physical activity, relatives and others who are close are unlikely to look beyond the intransigence they meet on food or exercise-related matters as they judge the food/body controller in their midst as having 'a strong personality'.

The bafflement that anorexia nervosa/bulimia create runs deeper, however, than contradictions between academic explanations and personal experience. Coming across the illness for the first time, people generally, in a very fundamental sense, do not know what kind of problem they are facing. They often make certain assumptions, ordinary, everyday assumptions that in so many ways seem perfectly reasonable; but it just so happens that these hinder rather than help an understanding of the sufferer's behaviour.

The difficulty in understanding usually becomes clear once an individual has developed definite physical symptoms, that is, the key symptoms usually associated with the use of the term 'anorexia nervosa' of extreme weight loss and endocrine 'shut down': obvious in female sufferers as menstruation ceases, but in male sufferers less so since decreased testosterone and gonadotrophin levels do not result in such evident change. Until this point has been reached, others can be unaware that there is anything that needs to be explained. It is only when sufferers become so thin their emaciation can no longer be ignored that the need for understanding emerges. The tendency is then to assume that their condition must fall into one of two categories. Either it must be the result of something having gone wrong with the way their body is working – as when a person has tuberculosis, or cancer, or a gastric ulcer – or it must be the result of something they are doing to themselves.

Similarly, those who regularly, and sometime massively, overeat and vomit may be seen as over-indulgent and greedy. Or where, using laxatives or vomiting, they have varying patterns of eliminating even very moderate amounts of food, they may be seen simply as 'not trying', or as 'failing to make any attempt to improve' their behaviour. Either way, those who believe 'self-discipline is really what's needed here' fail totally to understand sufferers' experience as they endure, or battle against, bulimia.

The illness as a category problem

Classifying an event is usually the first step in deciding what to do about it – in this case deciding what kind of help is appropriate. The distinction between physical illness and deliberate action is particularly important here because the responses people make are so very different. Generally we do not see ourselves as having the same kind of choice over events such as physical illness as we feel we have over the things we do. So, where something is thought to be the result of an individual's action, ideas of personal responsibility tend to be invoked, and sometimes also blame. But where an event is classified as physical illness, ideas of personal responsibility and blame have usually been considered unwarranted and unnecessary.

The difficulty where anorexia nervosa/bulimia is concerned is that it does not fit straightforwardly into either of the above categories. Rather it is a mixture of both. It is akin to alcoholism and drug addiction in this respect. The problem belongs to a different or third category in which a person's actions are constrained and have progressively become so as a result of physical and psychological changes that are self-induced. There are a number of reasons why bulimic aspects of the illness may be more easily recognized as having this kinship. Food binges are similar to episodic bouts of drunkenness. The urgency that can accompany them, and the meticulous and ritualistic attention to detail that can be involved in their preparation, is characteristic of 'fixing' generally. Anorexic food restricting and restless exercising is, meanwhile, 'a horribly complicated tangle that people can get themselves into when their behaviour upsets the conditions under which their body and brain usually function'.[2] Those who work with alcoholism can find themselves fending off similar assumptions that alcoholics are either the passive victims of a disease or susceptibility not yet fully understood, or that they are entirely responsible for their own fate. To inhabit the middle ground in these issues takes skill and practice on the part of a helper.

The impossibility of containing anorexia nervosa/bulimia either in the category of physical illness or that of deliberate action is not simply an academic problem. It is an experience lived out painfully by the sufferer's family. It is a common experience for parents and partners to find themselves constantly thrown between irritation and anxiety. Either they get involved in angry scenes at what seems to be a stubborn refusal to eat, or they are nagged by the fear that they have someone here who really might be ill, and, if it is not the sufferer's fault therefore, they ought to be more caring. Such is the confusion over which position to adopt, they end up completely at a loss to know how to respond.

> I knew my daughter was getting too thin and I suggested she ought to see the doctor. I was worried about her health. But there again she was very lively and busy. She had a demanding job, and said she felt fine. So I tried not to worry. But I found myself getting very angry when she always refused to eat proper meals. She'd say she wasn't hungry, then I'd find she'd eaten other food I'd planned for another meal. She'd be so convincing if I said anything, I'd end up thinking I was the one who was unreasonable. But she was so thin there was always that worry. You don't know what to think. You end up confused.

A bulimic's flatmate records a similar experience:

> For ages I didn't know what was wrong. Some days she'd be so energetic and organized and helpful. Then she'd disappear into her room and only come out in her dressing gown to snap at us. I didn't realize she was bingeing like mad. It was only when she took an overdose we found out what had been going on. I felt terrible then about all the times I'd been so angry with her for being so inconsiderate.

A difficulty for those close to anyone successfully restricting food and/or controlling through exercise is the total, rigid consistency they are faced with. (As long as they are *not* eating, or as long as their binge/elimination rituals remain undisturbed, the behaviour of those who are bulimic will be consistent too.) From this there springs another level of confusion, as this parent's comment shows:

> She is *so* rational. Her opinions seem reasonable, very clearly thought out – you're convinced there can't be anything mentally wrong with her. But then she'll also seem very obsessive. So obsessive, it's hard to believe *that's* quite so rational.

And another's, likewise:

He's been so convincing about this business of being fit. He gives lots of thought to what he eats – and how important it is to be healthy, and you can't argue with that, can you? But when he's here, my kitchen's not my own. And the distances he cycles when he's not! Well, I think . . . really, he goes so far each day, it can't be right. The distances . . . they're getting to be . . . well, Olympic.

Differing interpretations of behaviour can frequently be one of the sources of the tensions and conflicts that develop within the family over the sufferer's problem with eating. One father felt very sympathetic and was sure his daughter was ill and needed help and, amongst other things, contacted various helping organizations, but her mother was equally convinced that the daughter was deliberately attempting to break up the parents' marriage. In another case, while the girl's mother felt her daughter was not to blame for her emacia- tion, her father was sure she was avoiding having to take her final exam- inations at university. Either parent may take either position. But, embroiled as they are in the day-to-day task of coping with the behaviour, they are unlikely to be aware of the extent to which their differences of opinion may be organized around two opposing views of the nature of anorexic illness, neither of which is sufficiently elaborate to gain any leverage on the problem.

The physical illness category

Once clear physical emaciation has developed there is generally pressure on all sufferers to see a doctor, though a girl or young woman whose periods have stopped will usually be obliged by her family to do so, and, as a consequence of this particular physical symptom, probably the sooner. But although the doctor may make sure that anorexia nervosa is correctly dia- gnosed, and that there is no other physical condition that might have caused these symptoms, the consultation does not resolve the practical problem, or the confusion over what to do about them.

A sufferer's physical appearance at low weight can be quite alarming, particularly when the point is reached where urgent medical care is needed. Medical training does not immunize against bafflement in this instance, while bias in favour of entirely physiological explanations gets in the way of understanding the difficulty. There are doctors still who can admit they find it hard to believe such dramatic and life-threatening emaciation, accompanied as it is by endocrinological changes, does not have a biological cause. It can also seem deeply implausible that someone from a comfortable home, who has a good family background, should be suffering from something so straight- forward as malnutrition. As one general practitioner said:

I know the family well. Her father's a solicitor, and very well connected. And Elizabeth's a highly intelligent and cultured young woman, and very charming. I can't believe she would be so stupid, or so lacking in common sense as to do this deliberately.

It is as a consequence of this puzzlement that classic low-weight anorexia nervosa has been actively researched by the medical profession for well over a hundred years. With each new advance in physical medicine the issue is reopened and more research undertaken. Amidst numerous auto-biographical accounts of the illness, the popular press flags that 'there is ongoing research into the parts genetics, oestrogen and serotonin might play'.[3] So the general public is informed of whatever current efforts are being made.

Yet, overall, the medical opinion that prevails is that the physical symptoms at low weight are those of a healthy person whose body is adjusting to the effects of persistent undernutrition. The physiological picture presented here is much the same as that produced by major calorie depletion from any cause.

Where a person who is not physically mature becomes anorexic – and children at least as young as 8 have been identified as sufferers – there is the risk of permanent damage if their underfeeding persists in that they may not reach their full height. Where sufferers are physically mature, or nearly so, before they begin to restrict their food intake, and because typically they also eat food that is of high nutritional quality, albeit in minimal amounts, starvation does not usually stunt growth or leave the legacy of physical disorders associated with dietary deficiencies that it can do when it occurs as a result of famine and other disasters. A particular exception to this is loss of bone mass, or osteoporosis. This can occur in thin, chronic food restricting and/or exercising women who do not menstruate at all for many years. It can occur likewise in males whose testosterone levels are lowered as a result of their self-starvation and/or excessive exercising.

As with starvation in any other situation, anorexic starvation symptoms also remit when adequate nourishment is taken again consistently. Even osteoporosis can improve with high calcium and vitamin D intake, if this is coupled with the readjustment of the endocrine system and a nearer normal level of protein in the person's diet. This ability to recover the original physically healthy state has, from a medical point of view, provided perhaps the strongest evidence that food restriction is the primary cause of the anorexic's weight loss, however drastic this may have been.[4]

Doctors thus find themselves in the same position as any other concerned person in relation to the low-weight sufferer. All the evidence suggests that the starved state is self-imposed, yet in the absence of political or religious dogma, or any other clearly comprehensible intention, the extreme behaviour and the sufferer's imperviousness to its life-threatening nature can seem peculiarly unintelligible. It creates an intellectual discomfort in the observer which, as it persists, is a powerful stimulus to continuing medical research. Meanwhile investigations into an anorexic's physical state offer no challenge to the way he or she is controlling food intake. Indeed such investigations can draw attention away from the fact that a person is food avoiding or engaged in relentless activity, and effectively disguise the significance of falling weight from the attending hospital staff.

I went into hospital about six months after my periods stopped, into a gynaecological ward just to see if there was anything wrong. I wasn't worried myself. I knew I wasn't eating, and all that mattered was to keep that up. They didn't find anything, and no one mentioned anorexia. Then later I went in again for pains in my stomach. Still no one said anything. They said I was OK, and discharged me. Except that time there was one doctor. He was quite young. He saw me afterwards sort of casually on my way out and said had I thought I might have anorexia. I said no, but I knew I did. But if I had check-ups it kept my parents happy. They felt better if they thought I was doing something to help myself.

The deliberate action category

In many ways it seems the most natural thing to extend an ordinary purposive account of human behaviour to anorexia nervosa to explain the sufferer's actions. Many people restrict the amount of food they eat, and do so for a variety of reasons without any suggestion that they are ill. So at an ordinary common-sense level it seems likely that an anorexic too might have a particular aim in mind in consistently refusing food. In relation to female sufferers for instance, it has been suggested that self-starving could be simply a way of gaining attention, or objecting to the female role, or committing slow suicide, or getting at her mother.

It is with the idea that there is some underlying purpose to anorexic behaviour that, for most people, the whole issue is likely to rest, particularly if they never come face to face with the problem. Those who do meet the condition, however, soon discover that, for all its apparent plausibility, this common-sense approach quickly breaks down. Although sufferers seem to be actively and purposefully creating their symptoms by severely restricting their food, they are quite at a loss to explain their utter preoccupation with regulating in this way. Where they do offer reasons, such as not wanting to be fat, or lazy, or 'an unhealthy slob', their reasons seem wholly inadequate to explain their persistence in taking this self-regulation to such extremes.

> He's lean alright. All you can see is muscle. But he's still horribly underweight, and totally pernickety about food. He can't stop. Every waking moment he's calculating what he can and can't eat, and what he's got to burn off to be healthy – so he says.

Similarly, in the words of a student nurse reporting to the ward's care team:

> It's hopeless. She wouldn't have it. She just went on saying she wasn't going to drink this stuff because she didn't want to get fat. She insists she's fat enough already, and she's really disgusted at being so fat. She pinched together the skinniest bit of flesh on her ribs to show me. You can count every one of her ribs. Her bones are sticking through her skin!

She can't be more than four and a half stone (28.6 kg) and she's there lying on the bed because she's too weak to sit up. It just doesn't make sense!

The nurse here had been trying to encourage the emaciated girl – who, at this point, was in fact 25.4 kg (4 st.) and 57 per cent of her AEBW – to take the liquid food that had been prescribed.

As these accounts show, anorexic behaviour lacks the flexibility that is usually associated with voluntary action. Sufferers seem to be choosing to restrict food intake. They seem to have strong personal preferences and great determination to act on these, yet at the same time appear to be completely unable to alter course, even though their starved state is upsetting people they would rather not upset, like their parents or partner, their children, or friends. They are unable to alter course even when they are so emaciated they are in danger of dying. Thus, although there are ways in which food restricting behaviour looks as though it could be understandable, those who come face to face with the problem find that, in practice, it is totally unintelligible.

Recognizing the condition that is anorexia nervosa

The formal medical criteria for recognizing anorexia nervosa contain information of two kinds, first, information relating to the physical symptoms of undernutrition, or starvation, and second, information relating to the sufferer's distinctive attitude towards food and body control.

The importance of the 'anorexic attitude'

Where a person is evidently underweight or emaciated it is essential for the doctor to detect the presence of the particular 'anorexic attitude' for a positive diagnosis of anorexia nervosa to be made. The condition cannot and *must not* be confirmed on the physical picture alone. If the characteristic anorexic style of thinking is not present, if there is not that distinctive anorexic set of beliefs, then the patient's emaciation is not the result of anorexia nervosa and other causes for the low weight or emaciation must be sought, and treated.

The 'anorexic attitude' is, in the various sets of medical criteria, identified as involving a 'studied and purposive' avoidance of food[5] and a steadfast and 'implacable' attitude[6] in 'pursuing a low body weight and then maintaining it'.[7] It is identified as engagement in an 'active refusal' to eat enough to maintain a normal weight and/or in 'determined, sustained effort' to prevent ingested food from being absorbed.[8] It is an attitude, or state of mind, that demonstrates itself in the 'relentless pursuit of thinness'.[9] These original sets of criteria thus include all the forms of food elimination generally swept under the heading of bulimia, and cover the use of all forms of physical activity or exercise.

The descriptions of the anorexic attitude effectively distinguish under-weight or emaciated sufferers from other groups of patients who may have substantial weight loss without organic cause. They enable anorexics to be differentiated by their distinctive mindset from those who have become emaciated because they are profoundly depressed, for example, and physically so slowed down that it is too much effort for them to get meals, or even to eat when someone prepares and serves meals for them. It differentiates them from anxious people who have a neurotic fear that food will stick in their throat or give them stomach pains, and from schizophrenics who believe falsely that, for instance, the food they are being offered is poisoned, and so avoid it.

There is a difficulty, however. For words such as 'studied', and 'active', and 'determined' are usually associated with the idea of being autonomous, effective, self-directed as a human being. They describe characteristics usu-ally attributed to those who are, in themselves, well integrated and whole. Accurate though these descriptions are therefore, and essential to the diagnosis of the problem, they are also an important source of confusion. They under-line the persistent uneasiness there is about the justification for saying that the person who is anorexic is ill.

These criteria need to be understood in relation to the context in which they are designed to work. They are practical tools used in a medical setting in which there is an identified patient, usually with clear physical symptoms, and parents or other relatives expecting some action to be taken. In this situation, if the patient looks particularly skeletal, or if emaciation has actu-ally become life-threatening, it seems an academic quibble to point out that the distinguishing attitudinal characteristics here are not in themselves unusual; or that in terms of these characteristics appearing to indicate self-directed and autonomous behaviour, the anorexic style of thinking suggests normality rather than abnormality.

The difficulty there is in defining the anorexic attitude in ways that suggest sufferers are people who are functioning fully – who can connect the things they think, and say, with subsequent practical decisions about the things they do – is a difficulty that becomes apparent as soon as physical thinness becomes less alarming. Once some weight has been gained, attitude or thinking is not usually seen as cause for concern. Thus many parents and relatives, and, not uncommonly, medical and other professionals too, are inclined to view the problem as cured as soon as a normal or near-normal weight has been achieved. This is a mistake, however.

Weight gain alone does *not* constitute recovery. If weight is all that has changed, if there has been no parallel alteration in attitude or beliefs, there will be no change in the determination to pursue thinness. Body-controlling activities will persist. Food restriction will be re-established or a progression made to alternative means of control or, when this seems to fail, to finding some means of obliterating the subsequent feelings of despair (see Chap-ter 3). Some shift in attitude, some change in thinking, is essential if a sufferer is to begin to move away from food/body control.

From the point of view of providing appropriate help, there are two good reasons why it is important to be able to identify sufferers by their attitude or state of mind, and to distinguish them without relying on the presence of physical symptoms. First, if there is the premature assumption, either on the part of the sufferer or the helper, that a recovery has been achieved simply because lost weight has been regained, then support will be readily abandoned or therapy broken off at the very point where continuing help is most needed (see Chapter 13). Secondly, to recognize and confront the problem at an early stage – i.e. at that point where thinking has become classically anorexic or food/body, but changed or 'hardened' beliefs are only just beginning to result in weight-restricting and/or other controlling behaviour – is the most effective way of shortening the length of time a person ultimately spends caught in the illness.

Once anyone has been drawn into the condition it is very difficult for them to extract themselves from the set style of thinking it generates and from the consequent self-destructive lifestyle. Since the problem is one that endures for years, the possibility of recognizing attitudinal symptoms early is worth serious consideration.

Distinguishing the food/body control that is characteristically anorexic

Distinguishing sufferers by their characteristic attitude, and in the absence of other symptoms, can be achieved informally or formally. Both ways involve a much finer discrimination of this attitude than appears in the published medical criteria.

Informal observation

Informally the anorexia nervosa sufferer can be characterized as someone for whom maintaining control over his/her food intake and body shape is the highest priority: the task in life that takes precedence over every other. As sufferers are anorexic they will succeed in establishing and keeping that control – whatever form it takes. As they are bulimic they will try, but fail repeatedly and spectacularly. This will be observable in numbers of ways. In any situation where there is a choice to be made they will always take the option that involves non-eating, or that enables exercise. This may for a time be implicit, as when there is an apparent preference to walk or run to work rather than take the car, or do homework rather than go with the family to see grandmother. What the person in question knows, and the rest of the family does not know, is that walking to work takes longer than going by car, so there is no time for breakfast. Similarly, by arranging to do homework, the sufferer can bypass the meal grandmother always serves. Later this avoidance will become more explicit, as perhaps when tension mounts within the family because the refusal to visit grandmother is so persistent, or because it just happens that 'I'm never hungry at Grandma's', or the insistence is, 'I'll go as long as I only have to have a cup of tea', or on condition that the visit does not coincide with a mealtime.

The following conversation with a sufferer, who at the time was 78 per cent of her AEBW, shows similarly the importance placed on food/weight control and how this overrides every other issue.

Bea: The trouble with going out with Joe is I drink too much beer.
Helper: Are you worried you might have a drink problem?
Bea: Oh no! It's not the alcohol that worries me. It's the calories in the stuff . . .
Helper: But if you're drinking that much aren't you afraid you might get into a sexual situation you can't handle?
Bea: No, it's not that. I'm not worried about him wanting to sleep with me. Just as long as I don't put on any weight.

Dedication to the pursuit of thinness is illustrated in the exclamation made by the despairing husband of his emaciated wife: 'Oh, yes. If there were low-calorie water, she'd be having that!' Where rigorous physical exercise routines are essential to a sense of control, then these, equally with food regulation, will take precedence over all other considerations.

Careers mistress: I'm surprised at the choices you've made. Were those universities the ones that were offering the courses you wanted?
Ella [who habitually swims at least two miles every day]: I wasn't too concerned about the courses I suppose. I went on what sports facilities they have. The only ones I was interested in were the ones with a swimming pool on the campus, so I can get there between lectures. I've got to have my swim every day.

The advantages of restricting food are illustrated in the following comment made (before the reunification of Germany) by a young woman who also used swimming as routine exercise: 'Not eating is much more reliable than exercise as a means of keeping control. What happens if my work suddenly takes me to East Germany and there's no swimming pool in the town?'

Anorexic food/body control can be further distinguished by the way it functions in continually creating and establishing a sense of 'self'. From this springs the characteristic statements sufferers make, such as: 'I'm all right as long as I've got my eating under control. That's just how I am. If I don't manage that, everything goes haywire', and 'I'm fine when I don't eat. That's when I can get a few things done.' Equally, 'I have to exercise. I'm not me unless I exercise' (see Chapter 8).

Hence characteristic anorexic control is also distinguished by the strongly polarized perception sufferers have of the consequences of their maintaining or not maintaining it. Their entire idea of 'self' changes according to whether or not control, as they alone judge it, is being achieved. This is evident in the above statements, but the consequences are wider still. For a move from not eating to eating, from being in control to being out of control, involves a similar move in relation to every other distinction, such as whether they are being a success or a failure academically, or at work, or whether they are a good or bad member of their family: 'I'm disturbing to the whole family when I eat. I'm uncontrolled and horrible, completely self-obsessed, and it upsets them so much. But when I don't eat I can manage all right. Then I can be thoughtful and sensitive, and behave properly.' Sufferers may be able to avoid upsetting people, keep up with academic or other work and generally do the things normally expected of them, but only if they are able to maintain their meticulous food and body regulation. Whatever their form of control, its success or failure switches them, so their whole being is either 'good', or 'bad'. Where eating is erratic or chaotic, then they are on a switchback, flung to and fro between the 'good' self and the 'bad, horrible, monstrous, greedy' self, between controlled starving and uncontrolled binge-eating.

Formal measures

Anorexic attitude can also, as we have said, be differentiated by more formal means. One psychological test, widely used in the literature, was created by selecting a series of statements, mostly about food, that were almost always endorsed by a group of anorexia nervosa sufferers but seldom endorsed by members of a non-anorexic control group. When applied to other groups a high score in this test is quite effective in selecting individuals who to this extent think like an anorexic.[10]

Formal measures of this kind make it possible to survey many different groups relatively easily. Results have shown that a significant proportion of the population as a whole thinks in this way, but that the proportion varies according to the interests and occupation of particular groups. Early in the 1980s, in a British technical college, 6.3 per cent of the women students were found to be high scorers on this test, but the incidence varied from almost 10 per cent of those on beauty therapy courses, and 7.2 per cent on secretarial courses, to 0 per cent on building and engineering courses.[11] Among half of the total number of pupils in a British ballet school, 16 per cent were high scorers as compared with only 5 per cent in a similarly aged group of girls attending an ordinary private school.[12] Meanwhile, in a highly competitive American dance school, a figure of 37.7 per cent was recorded.[13]

People who appeared from the results of this test as having extreme attitudes to food/body control form a very mixed group. When those from the above technical college who had high scores were interviewed, for example, it appeared that 17 per cent were 'normal dieters'. The rest revealed abnormal preoccupation with weight and food intake; 39 per cent indulged in self-induced vomiting and 18 per cent in laxative abuse. Notably, according to those sets of medical criteria that require there to be very substantial weight loss before a diagnosis of anorexia nervosa can be made, only 7 per cent were deemed to be sufferers.

It would seem from this that tests which focus on attitudes to food and weight are not always accurate in discriminating those with anorexia nervosa.

This is especially so in the case of those, both male and female, who are concerned about thinness and body shape because they are involved professionally and otherwise in dance, modelling, acting or entertainment, competitive sports and other body regulating pastimes. But the distinction can be made in different ways.[14] Other psychological measures reveal that whereas anorexia nervosa sufferers are driven to resolve their deep sense of personal inadequacy by rigidly controlling their food and body, the dancer or athletics enthusiast who is not anorexic will have good things to say about herself or himself that relate to abilities other than the capacity for maintaining various degrees of self-starvation (see Chapter 6) or the capacity to maintain a particular body shape. The non-anorexic person is *not* totally dependent for his or her sense of self-worth on the ability to control food, manipulate weight, or define body shape.

Even allowing for the subtleties of formal measures, there seems to be little doubt that in the population as a whole there is a large pool of people who are dependent for their sense of self on establishing or maintaining rigid regimes of food control and exercise, though they do not all have the frank physical symptoms of undernutrition at any one time. For anyone who does not have a firm sense of self, food/body control is a very potent 'remedy' (see Chapter 8), but also a hazardous one. It is highly effective in creating a sense of self where this is lacking because it sets in train a series of personality changes that are readily entrapping (see Chapter 2). Furthermore, these changes are likely to go unnoticed wherever there is a prevailing value system within which they signify success. This is why the early consequences of food restricting and persistent exercising can be so insidiously dangerous.

The similarities between anorexia nervosa and bulimia

Anyone setting out to help will find those who are bulimic, as they talk about themselves, sound surprisingly similar to the anorexic. They make the same kind of statements about themselves and about their world, because, quite simply, food and weight are the central preoccupation for both. A comment like 'Even that half pound matters. Not putting it on means everything to me. I'd have felt terrible if I'd gained even that. It'd have been much better to have lost half a pound' (about 0.25 kg) could be made by either, whatever level their weight, 'whether five stone or fifteen'. They make the same statements and express the same fundamental beliefs about themselves. 'I'm just despicable when I go out of control. I'm disgusting. I'm better when I don't eat. Everything would be fine if I never had to eat at all.' The main difference is that while bulimics are confronted each day with demonstrations of their failure to control their self and their food, anorexics who are rigorously food controlling, exercising, persistently underweight and losing weight are succeeding; as are those who, as thinness becomes synonymous with absence of fat, will maintain weight, or even a weight increase 'just as long as it's muscle, *not fat*'.

It is because these 'lifestyles' are different consequences of the same need to create and maintain a sense of self that it is possible here to approach the task of providing help for anorexics and bulimics conjointly. The physical hazards are different in each case, and helping strategies will necessarily vary (see Part III). But whatever the current or persistent pattern, effective therapy is that which carefully attends to the need to identify and develop the self that is not pivotal upon food/body control. Whether sufferers are in an anorexic or a bulimic state, or phase of the illness, this involves enabling substantial changes to take place in their beliefs about themselves.

Some medical and other objections to taking the two conditions as one problem

Not everyone is happy to accept the view that the picture presented by persistent starvers, relentless exercisers, binge–vomiters, laxative or diuretic abusers is simply the consequence of the kind, or kinds, of control to which they are currently or overridingly subjecting their body. For it appears to treat as identical conditions whose consequences result in their physically looking very different from each other.

Emaciated, endocrinologically altered, 'evidently anorexic' sufferers who organize their whole life around non-eating present quite a different physiological picture from normal-weight bulimics. Either instead of, or as well as, periodic starving, bulimics attempt to regulate by preventing the absorption of the food they have eaten. They use self-induced vomiting or quantities of laxatives as their way of redeeming the lapses into eating, of re-establishing a sense of control. They usually maintain a weight nearer an average expected for their height, age and gender than those who starve or restrict. Females will probably be menstruating normally or at least intermittently. Some who endure cycles of stuffing and starving may at times, or protractedly, be overweight or actually obese, but their anorexic attitude will still be absolutely intact. Often there is nothing in the physical appearance of those in bulimic 'mode', however, to give the slightest clue that they have any problem at all with food, or weight. Muscle-bound exercisers, male and female, organizing their calorie intake with rigid intensity in pursuance of their particular physical activity or sport, present a different picture again: a stringy leanness, or hard muscularity that is spare or, at the opposite pole, massively over-developed. Either way continuous 'training' is demanded to keep 'in shape' or to develop it. Endocrine function is likely to be disturbed, and physical injury is commonplace, as is damage where steroids and other drugs are used to increase muscle, and achieve 'enhanced performance'.

The idea that a sufferer's physical state is simply a consequence of the form of control currently or overridingly used tends to create uneasiness because, amongst other things, it involves abandoning the possibility of discovering a specific physical cure. It is unlikely that such radically different pictures as presented by the low-weight anorexic and the normal-weight bulimic could have a common organic cause.[15] Meanwhile, as intense pre-occupation with burning calories and with obtaining a taut physique readily elude the name of illness, those whose bodies are evidently over-exercised are generally seen to need no cure at all.

The approach adopted here might also be considered by some to ride roughshod over important psychological differences. The superior, aloof, austere and rigid anorexic is markedly different from the impulsive, change-able, guilt-ridden and confused bulimic. The 'focused', highly committed, self-asserting body trainer and the tightly presented fitness devotee, assured, coolly authoritative about 'all things healthy', are different again. Yet while it might seem odd to treat such apparently different personalities as stemming from the same problem, many of the differences are the effect, rather than the cause, of the condition. Personality is the dependent, rather than the independent, variable.

With sustained and successful food restriction, as with alcoholism and drug addiction, the individual's personality is changed often beyond recognition. Those close to a sufferer will be aware of this. As one father said bitterly, jerking his head towards the emaciated girl who sat looking distant and superior, 'That's not my daughter. I don't known who it is, but it's not my daughter.'

In academic circles the idea of running together such extremes of con-trolled and impulsive behaviour can meet resistance because it confounds those theories of personality development which might be used to explain anorexic behaviour. Nor is it particularly congenial to sufferers to be grouped together in this way. The concern to maintain control over food and body is central. However they are described, sufferers share the same preoccupations and the same fears.

There must be no possibility of an exerciser being 'lazy', or 'a slob'. Muscle provides visible insurance against imperfection. 'There mustn't be a gram of fat. It's flab. You just don't have it, or you're worthless. Just low-life.' From the position the controlling anorexic has attained, there is no wish to countenance the possibility that control might fail. 'I'm never going to get like that. I don't ever want to be like that' is the starving anorexic's typical shuddering comment about the bulimic. Because successful food restriction is so crucially important, among those persistently working to sustain it there is no wish to have its value diminished by their being associated with people whose eating is so 'out of order', who have such 'unaesthetic' and 'unacceptable' methods of regaining control. Hence, unsurprisingly, a sufferer who had consistently maintained her anorexic lifestyle for many years dis-missed a newly published autobiographical account[16] focusing on the bulimic phase of the illness as 'just a dirty story'.

Meanwhile those who are bulimic, who stuff and starve, purge, vomit, use diuretics in their desperation and who are convinced that, if only they could achieve total control over their food, weight, body shape then all their problems would be solved, are generally not very happy to be told that their cherished ambition, even if they attained it, is not a viable one.

Put very simply, bulimia is the anorexic's nightmare and anorexia is the bulimic's dream. It is for this reason that the suggestion that anorexia nervosa and bulimia are different stages of the same condition is unwelcome news to all concerned.

References

1 Bruch, H. (1978) *The Golden Cage*. London: Open Books, 39; Crisp, A. (1980) *Anorexia Nervosa: Let Me Be*. London: Academic Press, 65; McLeod, S. (1981) *The Art of Starvation*. London: Virago, 64.
2 Slade, R. (1984) *The Anorexia Nervosa Reference Book*. London: Harper and Row, 83.
3 Brewis, K. (2001) Wasting away, *The Sunday Times* Magazine, 23 December, 30–40.
4 Isaacs, A.J., in P. Dally and J. Gomez (eds) (1969) *Anorexia Nervosa*. London: Heinemann Medical Books, 202.
5 Russell, G.F.M. (1970) Anorexia nervosa: its identity as an illness and its treatment, in J.H. Price (ed.) *Modern Trends in Psychological Medicine*. London: Butterworth.
6 Feighner, J.P., Robins, E. and Guze, S.B. (1972) Diagnostic criteria for use in psychiatric research, *Archives of General Psychiatry*, Chicago, 26: 57–63.
7 Crisp, A.H. (1977) The differential diagnosis of anorexia nervosa, *Proceedings of the Royal Society of Medicine*, London, 70: 686–90.
8 Dally, P. (1969) *Anorexia Nervosa*. London: Heinemann Medical Books, 11.
9 Bruch, H. (1978) op. cit., ix.
10 Garner, D.M. and Garfinkel, P.E. (1979) The Eating Attitudes Test: an index of the symptoms of anorexia nervosa, *Psychological Medicine*, Cambridge, 9: 273–9.
11 Button, E.J. and Whitehouse, A. (1981) Subclinical anorexia nervosa, *Psychological Medicine*, Cambridge, 11: 509–16.
12 Szmukler, G.I., Eisler, I., Gillies, C. and Hayward, M. (1985) The implications of anorexia nervosa in a ballet school, *Journal of Psychiatric Research*, Oxford, 19(2/3): 177–81.
13 Garner, D.M. and Garfinkel, P.E. (1980) Socio-cultural factors in the development of anorexia nervosa, *Psychological Medicine*, Cambridge, 10: 647–56.
14 Weeda-Mannak, W.L. and Drop, M.J. (1985) The discriminative value of psychological characteristics in anorexia nervosa. Clinical and psychometric comparison between anorexia nervosa patients, ballet dancers and controls, *Journal of Psychiatric Research*, Oxford, 19(2/3): 285–90.
15 Slade, R. (1984) op. cit., 22–8.
16 Roche, L. (1984) *Glutton for Punishment*. London: Pan Books.

two

A path through the theories

The way people approach the task of help is inevitably influenced by the theories they hold. There are many theories, each with different implications for the helper and different possible consequences for the sufferer. One person may insist weight must be increased before psychotherapy can be attempted. Another may adopt exactly the opposite strategy. Still another may prefer to concentrate on changing the pattern of family relationships and avoid dealing directly with the sufferer at all. Thus a potential helper coming anew to the problem might be forgiven for thinking that almost anything might be tried in the hope of providing help.

Yet while the range of authoritative ideas might seem daunting, only a relatively small number of distinctions need be made to render the whole field manageable and enable the newcomer to weave a path through the theories. Likewise many of these theories can seem awe-inspiring in their sweeping analysis of, say, child development, or Western culture or feminist politics. But hardly any provide information that is sufficiently finely textured to make it possible for helpers to engage in a practical way with the sufferers they are meeting.

Two types of theory

As we saw in Chapter 1, the central dispute has in the past been over the physical symptoms of the low-weight anorexic and whether or not these really are the result of self-induced starvation. From there the debate moved to the psychological effects that starvation brings about, and whether and to what extent these explain why sufferers continue to refuse to eat adequate amounts. On this issue, theories or explanations of the condition tend to fall broadly into two categories, the divide occurring over the question of the significance that is to be given to the psychological effects of starvation.

In the one category are those explanations of anorexia nervosa/bulimia that build on the evidence that underfeeding and low weight themselves produce dramatic psychological changes. For where food intake is reduced and body weight falls, some experiences are removed, others are altered, and certain experiences are induced that are not available to people who are adequately fed. These changes are important and will be considered in some detail later in this chapter.

In the other category are those explanations that ignore the psychological consequences of restricting food intake and rest instead on the idea that there is a coherent pattern in anorexic food control which should be interpreted as a whole. The general view here is that refusal to eat is something the individual may be carrying out in pursuit of a particular purpose; or it may be behaviour that carries some meaning, but a meaning that is being expressed in terms of a metaphor. Either way these explanations carry the assumption that, if the meaning or purpose that lies behind the behaviour is discovered, the whole self-starvation episode will be understood.

The kinds of explanation in this second category have great resilience. Ideas of purpose and intention are, after all, a normal part of our understanding of each other's actions and in general they work very well. They have an immediate intelligibility that the idea that psychological change can be induced by food restriction does not. It is not universally well known that persistent undernutrition and low weight can create dependence.[1]

Theories and how they relate to what is seen as needing explanation

This distinction between explanations that encompass the psychological consequences of starvation and those that do not has the effect of dividing the theoretical literature because, in a very fundamental way, it influences the interpretations that are placed on the sufferer's actions. It influences what helpers will actually see in the sufferer, and consequently their view about which aspects of her or his behaviour need explaining and which do not.

One of the characteristics of the illness that can be used to illustrate this is anorexic restlessness, or hyperactivity. A bright-eyed, alert liveliness was the distinctive demeanour that first enabled the discrimination of these particular emaciated patients from others who were suffering from wasting diseases, such as abdominal tuberculosis, that were prevalent in the nineteenth century. These active, alert (i.e. anorexic) patients would survive if they were fed. The others, despite feeding, would succumb to their infectious diseases.

Those whose theoretical position does not acknowledge the effects of undernutrition may see such hyperactivity as the key indicator to the meaning of the whole starvation episode. For instance, where extreme thinness is construed as a way of achieving freedom from a sexual stereotype,[2] a girl's incessant exercising, as she attains this, could be interpreted as her enjoyment of physical activities otherwise denied by the constraints of fashion or convention within the female role. But where it is acknowledged that hyperactive behaviour is entirely to be expected in all people who are underweight and continuing to deprive themselves of food, irrespective of their gender, the situation will tend to be construed differently. The helper who knows that anyone who gets hungry and thin is typically ceaselessly active, while mindful of possible later diversions into 'sport' or 'fitness', at this point will be able to see the restless activity otherwise as a symptom that will recede with adequate nourishment and increase in weight.

Another symptom that can be quite differently understood, depending on the perspective from which it is viewed, is the overwhelming and continual preoccupation with food that is found in low-weight anorexia nervosa. In this instance the two different ways of understanding this symptom lead to quite different ideas about the way in which the anorexic's symptoms generally are created.

Some theorists, ignoring the effects of underfeeding, are inclined to see anorexic preoccupation with food and eating as evidence of fixation at an earlier stage of development, sometimes referred to as the oral stage, where food and hunger dominate thought processes. This perception has set in train a search through theories of child development to find reasons why sufferers should want, or need, to return or regress to this earlier stage. A view that has been advanced, to take but one example from the many that have sprung from this tradition, and with the focus on female sufferers, is that the anorexic is someone in whom the early experience of mothering engendered both strong positive and strong negative feelings and that, during adolescence, when she is engaged in a struggle for autonomy, these strong feelings re-emerge and she conducts her struggle in the same terms as she did in early childhood, investing food with the same symbolism as it acquired then. It is a symbolism that is inappropriate at this later stage but nevertheless determines her responses.[3] The assumption in this argument is that the regression the anorexic manifests at low weight in her total preoccupation with thoughts of food is achieved entirely through psychological processes. It is assumed that her progressive reduction in food intake is merely a by-product of the way she is confronting the developmental tasks of adolescence.

Yet the fact is, whatever the series of events, or actions, or accidents that have brought about a person's starved state, it is this very state that actively alters that person. Total preoccupation with thoughts of food is found in anyone who is underfed, and this in itself is efficacious in bringing about personality change. The end result of the sufferer's food control would be much the same, therefore, whether it was the consequence of psychological regression or not.

The practical significance of the theoretical divide

As the understanding of the condition determines the kind of help that is provided, so the helper's view about the way anorexia nervosa works is of great practical importance. Those whose theoretical perspective takes into account the psychological effects of starvation will see anorexia nervosa as a gradually intensifying state of incapacity in which different processes are at work at different stages. This is a view that, as we will show here, provides the helper with a set of ideas concerning the sufferer that are flexible and differentiated enough to meet that person exactly where she or he happens to be as – in the long course of the illness – weight, behaviour and subjective experiences change.

The approach that ignores the inevitable psychological consequences of starvation is, on the other hand, likely to be more fixed. For instance, only one interpretation of the symbolic significance of the refusal of food may be permitted. Being limited, it will be less fitted to the considerable variations and changes in experience that can occur within the condition. This is not to doubt that those working with such a psychodynamic model may be highly subtle and sophisticated in their ability to tease out feelings hidden by unconscious defences. But they may not appreciate that it is not so much a problem of unconscious defences that they are meeting in the low-weight anorexic as the characteristic attenuation or blanking out of feelings and emotions that is found in all underweight and starving people.

Those who have a theoretical preference for placing interpretations on anorexic behaviour and attributing it with unconscious meaning are usually, and often justifiably, opposed to medical intervention and generally very liberal in their sentiments. Yet, for reasons that will become clear, sufferers are not only characteristically vulnerable to being taken over by other people's views: they can also experience interpretations of their behaviour as very oppressive.[4]

Of the two types of theory broadly outlined we will concentrate on those which recognize the psychological effects of starvation, for in our view they generally provide a better fit with the fine detail of the illness. However, to acknowledge that starvation has psychological as well as physical consequences is not to imply that the low-weight sufferer must therefore be made to gain weight before therapy can begin. Weight is not irrelevant, as will be evident in the chapters that follow. But being able to help a person to emerge from this illness does not depend on weight being immediately restored, unless, of course, current weight loss is severe enough to endanger his or her life. Then some weight gain must be the first goal – even if only enough to make the situation safe (see Chapter 11).

The psychological effects of starvation

There is a range of psychological changes that are created by consistent food restriction and weight loss. The detail of these changes we will look at here. Physical hazards will be considered in Part III.

Intellectual change

First, and perhaps most important, is the way persistent underfeeding restricts thinking. This impairment is progressive, but it is reversible. It disappears when weight returns to a level that is within the normal range for height, age and gender, and when food intake then is consistently adequate for that level to be sustained.

The more severely underfed people become, the more altered is their thinking. In the early stages the changes will be quite subtle but detectable none the less in certain areas. It is a helper's awareness of the specific deficits that, in practice, is therapeutically useful – much more useful than just knowing, in general, that starvation diminishes mental capacity.

Undernutrition impairs intellectual functioning by gradually reducing the capacity for complex thought. As starvation progresses and weight falls, thinking becomes simple: people who are underfed have fewer and fewer available categories in which to place their experiences, and the sets of categories available to them are distinct, and highly polarized. For these people there are no moderate positions, no in-between stages. They cannot conceive of grey areas, or respond to situations in a graduated way. Everything divides into good or bad, acceptable or unacceptable. As the shades of grey in situations progressively disappear, so the subtleties and complexities of life disappear too. It is not only the world that is seen this way. Those whose weight is low, and who are in an underfed or starved state, understand themselves too from within this black-and-white, everything or nothing mindset.

When food intake is consistently restricted, the higher mental functions such as the capacity for abstract thought are the first to disappear. Case histories often reveal that the problem initially became apparent when sufferers found they were unable to cope with mathematical ideas, and this happened long before any of the more obviously anorexic symptoms began to show. As impairment intensifies the ability to engage in other complex activities gradually diminishes. There is no longer any capacity to be imaginative, or creative, or to meet complicated or challenging situations.

For instance, being with even quite a small group of people will be too much to cope with, and will increasingly be avoided. The number of interactions that take place in a group readily confuses and overwhelms people whose intellectual capacity is impaired by their underfed state. It becomes impossible for them to follow what is happening. Indeed they may barely manage to cope with the presence of just one other person.

As cognitive impairment intensifies, every aspect of life will need to be totally predictable and organized well in advance. The ability to respond spontaneously to an unforeseen event completely disappears. Relationships which have been difficult become even more problematic. The capacity to cope with frustration is reduced. Hence established sufferers are characteristically very isolated, very set in their own precise routines. It takes little to upset or offend them. It takes little for them to respond in a panicky or harsh, even violent, way. In a sufferer's company others typically describe themselves as 'walking on egg shells'.

As thinking becomes more polarized as a result of persistent inadequate feeding, the range of ideas that can be encompassed grows narrower too, and the remaining mental capacity is increasingly taken up with thoughts of food. Hunger ensures that food, and everything to do with food, becomes a total preoccupation. This change is normal when people are underfed. It need not necessarily involve sensations of hunger, but the complete preoccupation with food will certainly be clear in the person's behaviour.

> She's lost a lot of weight, and she won't eat more than a mouthful of anything. She says she's not hungry and spends all her time poring over cookery books. She'll prepare a meal any time I ask, but she won't eat any of it. I even found a scrap book she'd made full of pictures of food cut out of magazines. It's obvious, food's on her mind all the time.

The ability to concentrate also diminishes as weight falls. This is a change sufferers will notice themselves as they find it harder to read or focus attention on their job, or on studying. Where food restriction persists and the sufferer becomes extremely emaciated, many more brain functions also begin to fail. Memory will deteriorate, as will the capacity to control the movements of the body. Sufferers who are low weight will notice their own clumsiness. Those who become more severely emaciated are more markedly accident prone. The lower a person's weight, the more generally disorientated they will feel, and the more out of touch with reality (see Chapter 5).

Sexuality

Sexual feelings diminish when food intake is consistently reduced over a long period. This reflects the hormonal change that takes place in both males and females as weight falls. After a certain point the secretion of reproductive hormones is inhibited and, from an endocrinological point of view, the underweight and/or underfed person is held in the equivalent of a pre-adolescent bodily state. Endocrine shut-down in women is evident in their ceasing to menstruate. While consequences of this shut-down are not so obvious in men, male sufferers do report that, as they lose weight, they stop having wet dreams. It needs to be acknowledged, of course, that in human beings the relationships between the secretion of reproductive hormones and sexual interest is not a simple one, because cultural and other factors play their part. But nevertheless the inhibition of hormone secretions does have its effect and starving people, male or female, typically have very little interest in sexual activity.

Moods and feelings

Feelings and emotions also become attenuated in the person who is undernourished. Whatever is felt – be it love, sadness, hatred, pleasure, anger, jealousy – it will be felt less energetically. As weight loss progresses, all emotion dwindles further. This creates a sense of detachment, of being anaesthetized, removed, far from the rest of the world, being above all the ordinary turmoil of living. It is this that creates the anorexic's characteristic haughty attitude; the aloofness; his or her distant superiority.

Starvation also induces a state of elation or euphoria, a feeling of well-being or 'high', sometimes referred to as a 'fasting high'. This is a psychotropic, or mood-changing, effect that occurs quite predictably whenever people consistently cut back on the amount of food they eat. Depending upon the individual's weight and the extent to which food is being restricted, this is a change that can begin to take place quite rapidly. A person whose weight is quite average for his/her age and height can begin to feel high, or elated, within as little as 24–48 hours.

In physiological terms starvation, i.e. going without food for more than half a day, is perceived by the body's internal monitoring system as hunger stress. This results in the secretion of adrenalin which, as well as creating the keyed-up effect noticeable in the underfed person's wider open eyes, faster heart rate and deeper breathing, also mobilizes reserves of glycogen in muscle to provide more blood glucose. Where there is the continued presence of adrenalin in the bloodstream, it acts on the brain and causes it to secrete endokinins. These are chemicals closely related to morphine and have similar tranquillizing and euphoric effects. At the same time, metabolites (such as ketones) which are produced by the breaking down or metabolism of fat also act on the brain and can create an odd and lightheaded experience.

The brain has receptors for morphine-like substances (endorphins) which are also produced by the body when it is stressed by vigorous exercise. (It is the presence of these receptors which makes human beings susceptible to chemicals of this kind when they are administered as a drug or as medical pain relievers.) This is how an individual can come to derive a particular pleasure, or sense of well-being, from strenuous exercise. It is how, by further stimulating the body's production of endorphins, hyperactivity itself acts as its own spur in anyone who is excessively dedicated to running, dance, cycling, working in the gym, walking, going up and down stairs, or any other such persistent or repetitive movement. It is also how, with the 'floating', detached experience it induces, the sleeplessness that accompanies hunger and hyperactivity becomes woven into the process. It is not unusual for underfeeders and those who 'must be active' to be in a sleep-deprived state.

It is thus that anorexic illness can be viewed as an addiction to food/body control. Sufferers occasionally refer to themselves as 'starvation junkies' or as needing their 'exercise fix'. There are psychiatrists too who acknowledge the anorexia nervosa/bulimia sufferer as dependent on the biological states that result from starvation, as 'hooked' on recurrent fixes of internally generated brain chemicals.[5] The view, whether in relation to food restriction, exercising, inadequate rest or persistent sleep-avoidance, is one that has always been more easily accommodated by those aware of the process of addiction.

In a fixed or high state, sufferers experience hyperacuity: the enhanced sensitivity to light, sound, colour and other external stimuli that occurs with increasing hunger – birdsong is louder, grass greener, light more intense – and they will be hyperactive. This will be clear from their extreme restlessness, the constant 'need to be on the go', and from their disturbed sleep patterns. Far more movements have been recorded during sleep in underweight sufferers than in people who are normal weight.[6] Because they are so thin, they do not have the normal muscle bulk to prevent blood vessels being pinched between their hip bone, for instance, and the bed. As cramp persistently sets in, so they continually change position. Typically they get up very early, and may routinely run at this time.

The way they experience these psychotropic effects as pleasing, and as validating their food restriction, is clear in this early account.

> Fanny became more and more preoccupied with her inner experiences, the delight over the new intense sensations which seemed to prove she was on the right road. Her hyperacuity to sound led to continuous arguments with her brother for playing records too loud, and she felt that people were shouting at her. Her hypersensitivity to light was so severe that she wore sunglasses all the time, even inside the house.[7]

'Positive' experiences like these are further validated by other intense and highly valued physical sensations such as being completely empty of food and being actually physically lighter. This also provides sufferers with the evidence they need that they are 'fine', that they are still in their 'good' category, still 'on the right road' (see Chapter 9).

Theories that build on the psychological effects of starvation

In considering the ways in which the psychological effects of starvation are used theoretically, it becomes immediately apparent that sometimes, and in some places, the changes that starvation and/or underfeeding create are construed as highly desirable and good, while at other times and in other places these same changes are construed as destructive and bad.

Those attempting to work with anorexia nervosa/bulimia sufferers meet distraught families, and increasingly incapacitated clients/patients, some less and less able to function because of their increasing emaciation, others more and more disturbed by the severity and the violence of the rollercoaster they are on as they lunge between non-eating and chaotic, non-stop bingeing, or frenetic physical activity and total 'indolence'. Constantly faced with the amount of visible distress this creates, helpers in this position unsurprisingly employ theories that focus on the hazardous aspects of undernutrition and persistent exercising. They use theories that acknowledge the compulsive quality of food restricting or bingeing and the natural tendency of these activities to intensify.

There are, at the same time, other groups that place a positive value on food restriction. The ideas they employ may not always have the stature of academic theories, but they are often quite sophisticated. They are also widely influential at a popular level. The practical point here is that helpers who recognize that food restricting and persistent exercising can be hazardous are likely to find that the perceptions they are working with run in direct opposition to the very positive views about these activities that are held by others than themselves.

The conflicting values that surround food and body regulation become particularly apparent as soon as an evident anorexic regains a small amount of weight. Others' anxieties tend to subside and, as this happens, the helper's account of the difficulties that are created by continued inadequate eating and by a persistently maintained underweight state ceases to carry conviction. The support from relatives and friends, which the helper needs to enable him or her to work effectively with the sufferer in continuing to confront the problems that emerge with any weight gain (including feeling safe about further weight gain), at this point often ebbs away (see Chapter 13).

Starvation as avoidance of sexuality

A theory that has been particularly influential focused on the loss of sexual interest that accompanies falling weight. The view was that the adolescent, confronted with the need to establish a sense of self in the face of resurgent sexuality and the social pressures that occur at this time, achieves comfort in starving specifically because this switches off sexual feelings. With no desire to be involved in sexual relationships, a major component of this identity crisis was removed. Since sufferers are endocrinologically in a pre-adolescent state at low weight, they are, so it was held, in the position of being 'regressed': a state here achieved by physiological processes, and for which the term 'psychobiological regression' was used.[8] It was further suggested that, at low weight, sufferers would be unlikely to be aware of their rejection of sexual maturity and adulthood as being the reason why it was so important for them not to return to a higher weight level – a level at which their endocrine system would readjust, and their adolescent sex drive return – so, again within the terms of the theory, because of their lack of awareness they were described as 'phobic' about eating and weight gain.

Curiously, however, though it used the term 'psychobiological', the theory largely ignored many of the physiological processes which are known to have psychological effects. To this extent it seems strange that it had the influence it did in medical circles. Rooted as it was in Freudian psychology, it focused on the fact that starvation reduces sexual interest and gave scant attention to other changes wrought directly by the processes of underfeeding and over-exercising.

Sea changes as they occur in the wider culture put such theorizing into a different perspective, however. The labyrinthine mechanisms of ego psychology are likely to seem odd and indirect to people used to taking direct action to change the way they feel, if that is what they want to do. The effects of underfeeding, starvation and rigorous exercise take their place among the plethora of techniques and drug substances that remove people from mental states that are unwelcome to them.

Overall the theory is misleading, not only because of its over-emphasis on sexuality and avoidance of adulthood but, far more importantly, because it represents anorexia nervosa as a coherent episode the nature of which becomes clear once the point, or the value, of low weight has been explained. Indeed, great stress is laid on the idea that weight loss is 'adaptive': that is, it enables the ego to establish a new equilibrium by solving certain developmental problems. This is mistaken. Anorexia nervosa is not a steady state. It is not an equilibrium, but its very opposite. It is a gradually intensifying form of incapacity with, consequently, a possible fatal outcome.

The starvation whirlpool

To appreciate how anorexic illness works it is necessary to focus on the intellectual and emotional changes that occur as an underfed state develops, and in particular on the way these changes gradually affect the capacity to choose and make decisions, and the way they affect the nature of the decisions that are made – including the decisions not just to maintain but to intensify food/body control.

Decision making

Sustained food restriction progressively constrains the number of categories of ideas any underfed or increasingly starving person has to work with, so that – as this process takes place – varied and graduated responses give way to a few rigid certainties. As cognitive complexity is thus diminished, so increasingly all choices and decisions come to be made between extreme, or polarized, positions. The lower weight falls, the greater difficulty a person has in grasping the possibility of there being any moderate position on any issue.

These intellectual changes affect every aspect of experience, and consequently every aspect of a person's existence. Quite ordinary comments made to someone who is constrained in this way, therefore, will inevitably be construed by that person in polarized terms. This is how it is that, where the anorexic is concerned, other people are either 'doing their best to make me fat', or 'totally supporting me in being controlled about my weight'; how other people, indeed 'the whole world', is either 'entirely for me' or 'entirely against me'.

Yet these intellectual or cognitive changes would not help create the illness that is anorexia nervosa in all its various dimensions were it not for the way sufferers value the alternatives facing them. Apart from the admiration and respect they earn for being seen to be in control, they also experience a sense of relief. This is a relief at being freed from a profound and overwhelming sense of confusion and ineffectiveness previously endured (see Chapter 8). They experience their altered cognitive state as 'being able to think more clearly'. They do not see that their thinking has become polarized. Constrained as they are, they do not see that they have only two categories available to them. They only experience the ease with which they can now make their judgements. They only perceive the 'effectiveness' with which they can now make choices, and decisions, and they interpret this as following from their 'greater clarity of mind'.

Food preoccupation and the idea of self

Because, like all underfed or starving people, they are beset by thoughts of food and eating, as food restriction or avoidance progresses everything becomes construed in terms of food and its regulation, including the idea of self. This is how, as weight falls and thinking becomes increasingly polarized, the self-starver comes to have a more definite sense of who she or he is. It is how self comes to reside in food/body control.

The polarized categories sufferers are working with also affect the attitudes they have and the values they hold. These too become increasingly hardened, rigid, effectively set in stone. As these attitudes are applied to self, sufferers then *must* be effective. There has to be *total* certainty in relation to the regimentation of food and body. Standards are absolute. Failure comes to have unbearable implications for self-respect, for the ability to accept self. To lose control is to become absolutely unacceptable, utterly despicable, completely loathsome. Others will notice this.

> Since she's had this anorexia there seems to be no middle way with her. Either she's absolutely fine, or everything's absolutely terrible. She's so excessively smug and superior at times, she's quite insufferable. Then she'll be disgusted with herself, saying she's worthless, an abject failure. She loathes herself. Says she's no right to be alive.

For a sufferer who is 'in control', to eat even the most minute quantity of food that is not part of that control regime is to be catapulted from a position where self is acceptable – though still in every respect under the obligation to strive – to a position where that self is completely and totally unacceptable. Just the prospect of this happening can cause extreme panic. Self-worth rides the same switchback where a sufferer is swinging between stuffing and starving.

The condition naturally intensifies

The polarized thinking that is induced by restricting food, together with these particular values, create a whirlpool momentum. As the consequences

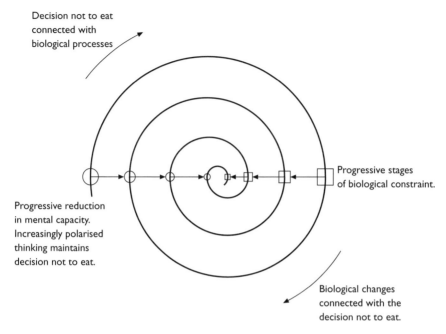

Decision not to eat connected with biological processes

Progressive stages of biological constraint.

Progressive reduction in mental capacity. Increasingly polarised thinking maintains decision not to eat.

Biological changes connected with the decision not to eat.

Figure 1: The Whirlpool, showing how the decision to go on self-starving/exercising is made from a position that is physically and psychologically different from the position where the decision was made to begin. (Reproduced from *The Anorexia Nervosa Reference Book*. London: Harper and Row 1984.)

of underfeeding affect the way those who are restricting or avoiding food think about eating and not eating, and as they affect the view they have of themselves, the decision not to eat rebounds on them. Each series of changes exacerbates the other, so gradually they are sucked in. The more polarized thinking becomes, the more the decision not to eat is reinforced. Weight falls further, and the cycle continues. As sufferers become less fed, the easier it is for them to 'choose' not to eat. The more emaciated they are, the more clearly this decision appears to them as being the only decision possible. So they spiral downwards in the way that will eventually bring them to the point of physical collapse[9] (see Figure 1).

It is the whirlpool motion that explains how it is that, at any present moment, decisions to restrict or control food intake may be deliberate and reasoned, and yet how over time the dynamic relationship between the decisions that are made and the changes they bring about draws sufferers into a situation that runs away with them. It shows how the decisions to continue starving and to continue 'being active', or exercising, are necessarily made from a different position from the decision to begin. In this 'pull' lies the compulsive quality of the condition: the way sufferers' choices are no longer entirely free.

THE HENLEY COLLEGE LIBRARY

It is important to appreciate just how different this process is from the usual state of affairs. The human body is regulated by negative feedback systems that maintain it in a steady state (homeostasis), so that decisions today are likely to be made broadly from within the same physiological state as they were yesterday. Much of the continuity, the balance, in human behaviour rests upon this baseline of physical stability. Positive feedback of the kind that occurs in the whirlpool of starvation destroys this stasis, and moves behaviour to extremes.

The whirlpool concept illuminates the insidious nature of the illness. For anorexia nervosa moves in the same way as the whirlpool moves – slow, creeping, almost imperceptibly at first, then intensifying, spinning faster and faster as it obtains its own momentum. As its gathering force draws the sufferer in, and into an ever-tightening spiral, its dynamic demonstrates clearly the way the condition becomes life-threatening.

It is the starvation whirlpool as it affects the totality of experience that is the theoretical basis of the approach to help that is presented here. Polarized thinking and the personality changes the whirlpool creates play a significant part in confounding many treatment approaches. It will become clear in the following chapters how a special understanding of this dynamic is needed, and particular strategies in relation to it.

Positive ideas about food and body regulation

Theorizing about food/body regulation in what appear to them to be negative or unfavourable terms can make sufferers quite angry. As one girl said, 'They all keep on about what I lose by refusing to eat. But they never say anything about what I gain. They just don't know.'

Fasting

The state of altered consciousness induced either by underfeeding or by total starvation can be highly rewarding and in this respect has its place alongside the use of alcohol, solvents and drug substances of all kinds. There are relatively few people who do not use one or another of these ways of altering experience at some time. Going without food, intentionally or unintentionally, also plays a part in maximizing the desired effects from the alcohol or drugs taken.

A popular literature exists that extols the use of self-starvation. Here first-hand accounts can be found in which food restriction is positively interpreted as a way of inducing altered consciousness, though in this context the word 'fasting' is used. In one such account, for example, the speaker – a male – refers to his 'consciousness fast' and expresses the opinion that:

Where we are 'now' is a space that is controlled by the ingesting of food . . . It is a drug. It induces a state of reality which we are prone to call real, simply because this is where we are at . . . You go into an internal system during a fast which allows for another, and as valid, a reality which is virtually uncharted.[10]

Another describes his fast as taking place in 'a beautiful mountainous area' where there was a 'loose knit, spiritually oriented community' that fasted as part of 'yogic practice or their own interpretation of it'. He describes himself during his fast as:

Immensely energetic, immensely alert, a very, very high state, very stimulated . . . a sense of being elated by the intellectual context of what you're saying and what you feel. When I say that fasting works as a stimulus I mean that there's a wild euphoria that is continuous and pervasive.[11]

For those familiar with anorexia nervosa/bulimia this mental state will have a very familiar ring. Contrary to the notion that it is 'virtually uncharted', however, a very clear map can be drawn of this 'reality', as we will show in Chapter 5.

Dieting, slimming and exercising

Pointing out the way food restricting, like over-exercising, can be used 'for kicks' or 'because you like the buzz' can, in some circles, serve to marginalize this activity. Its being associated with esoteric subcultures or alternative lifestyles may cause some to look askance. But the positive evaluation of semi-starvation is more central than this, more pervasive, and in this respect more insidious.

One of our major social values lies in the idea of taking personal responsibility and in 'making something of yourself' (see Chapter 7). Nor is there a secret about food/body regulation being a highly acceptable strategy for achieving this. The message that to feel better about yourself you lose weight is clear in the following 'problem page' reply which – given the whirlpool that such 'weight watching' can lead into – is also alarming. (The italics are ours.)

Question: Where can I find therapy? I've asked my GP but he just smiled and said, 'We all have excesses.' He's not joking. I'm sixteen stone (101.6 kg), my nails are bitten to the quick, I drink much too often, can't sleep and cry endlessly. I've tried hypnotism, acupuncture, pills, potions *et al.*, so therapy seems the only answer.

Answer: Start with Weight Watchers. *Success with weight loss will build up your self-esteem, and your self-esteem will help you to have success, and that in turn increases your self-esteem, and hey presto! the vicious cycle is turned into a benevolent one.* You see, therapy only means a kind of help and self-help is one of the best.[12]

Popular magazines available at supermarket checkouts advertise articles with such titles as 'Help a chubby child lose weight and gain confidence'.[13] Unsurprisingly, the message gets through to children too.

Under the headings of fashion and health there is a vast array of reading and other material encouraging us to improve ourselves by dieting or slimming, by 'removing toxins', by taking more exercise, going on a fast, getting into shape, improving shape, but its purpose is not just cosmetic, nor just about fitness or vitality. For male and female alike, the encouragement is also in 'not letting oneself go', in meeting the obligation not to become physically flabby and slow, or mentally flabby either, but to 'make something of oneself by one's own personal effort'. Subtle or not so subtle, the message is imbued with cultural ideas and cultural values. Hence the idea of self-help can also carry a notion of self-reform.

Many of the strategies for this kind of self-improvement can be quite extreme. Although some caution has developed with increased awareness of anorexia nervosa, and of 'eating disorders', there have nevertheless been popular diets suggesting that it is 'medically safe' to live on 200 calories a day. While other diets or slimming plans may set out to be rather more moderate, the generally promised result is that those who embark on those courses of self-improvement where food quantities are carefully calculated, and types of food carefully categorized, or who self-improve through exercise, will feel more alive, cleansed, purified, good, more finely tuned, or toned, more self-confident, more active, more effective. An informed professional, experienced in working with sufferers dependent upon the psychotropic effects of underfeeding, has described it as 'both eerie and frustrating'[14] to see advertising slogans stating: 'Fasting is the way to clearer thinking and more energy.'

Activities that embody some of society's most cherished values acquire a status that makes it difficult to see what is happening. In this case little attention is given to what it is precisely that brings about the sense of confidence, the feelings of well-being, self-esteem and goodness. Many people who rigorously restrict food intake, who persistently exercise, who eat 'all the right food' as they body control, certainly feel better about themselves, but, contrary to the way they may judge themselves, their feelings are not entirely a result of their moral goodness. Rather they are the result of these activities setting in train that series of psychological and physical changes described above, changes that in certain circumstances can have very unhappy consequences.

It is the use of two different sets of words for the same actions that ensures that moral values and beliefs are not compromised by the suggestion that the activities might be hazardous. 'Self-starvation' may be dangerous, but a 'fast' is purifying. 'Slimming' or 'going on a diet' are associated with positive ideas, but to 'maintain a state of semi-starvation' is to present the same activity in a way that is much more negative. Likewise, coaching or training that is 'intensive' draws easy support and being put through a routine that is 'punishing' invites the murmur of approval, but the idea that this might also be self-harming overuse of the body, that it might be exercising as a form of fixing or an activity-binge, is more difficult to take on board. Again, in any context, it is hard not to be in favour of 'healthy eating'. 'Undernutrition', on the other hand, just may strike a chord as being rather more dubious. The different terms effectively insulate approved activities from valid criticism, and the possibility of reappraisal. It is not easy to suggest that sometimes increased clarity of thought and greater self-confidence might be better described as mental simplicity and restricted capacity for choice.

Though medical approval may be used as a marketing strategy, many diets contain no warning of possible dangers. When cautions are given, the emphasis is on physical health. There is generally no information about the nature of the experiential changes these activities can create, or how it is possible to become hooked on 'feeling good' or 'being right' in this way. The assumption that a person will know when to stop losing weight, or be able to stop exercising, is dangerously naïve. People who manage to lose a substantial amount of weight will neither think in the same way, nor experience the same emotional state, nor the same perception of their bodies as they did when they started to restrict their food intake.

Not everyone now takes the question of stopping weight loss so lightly, however, as a group of researchers found when studying potential anorexia nervosa in a top London ballet school.

> We were impressed both with the pressures towards maintaining a slim figure and with the forces brought into play to reverse the process of weight loss when this became abnormal. The matron reacted strongly to girls with a marked drop in weight and insisted that it be regained promptly. Friends were similarly concerned. The result, in all the cases we saw, was positive and further deterioration was averted.[15]

There are similarities that might be drawn between the matron's role here and that of the religious superior, or novice master or mistress in a monastic order. In communities like these, which have centuries-long experience of fasting, it is usually allowed only under the direction of such a supervisor who will ensure the fast has an end, and that normal eating is resumed under vows of obedience. Yet the experience of starvation is such that, whether it is taking place in the context of religion, sport, the performing arts or anywhere else, its effect may be far less easy to manage than the presence of institutional failsafes suggests; its real outcome far less benign.

Those who, from dieting, fasting, 'cleansing', exercising, go on to become anorexic and/or bulimic are generally those who have had difficulty in establishing a sense of who they are and who also believe they ought, through their own personal effort and self-discipline, to make something of themselves. In these respects they are quite similar to many other people who do not proceed into the starvation whirlpool. Yet once established it is this whirlpool motion that creates most of the incomprehensible behaviour (psychopathology) that is found in anorexic illness. Thus the idea that the rest of the population can be encouraged to diet and exercise with impunity is nothing but a comforting fiction.

Professional objections to the idea of starvation effects

Apart from pervasive ideas and cultural values, the informed helper is likely to meet resistance of a different kind to the assertion that underfeeding/ starvation effects play a crucial part in creating the symptomatology of anorexia nervosa and its counterparts. This resistance exists at a theoretical level and stems from important traditions in psychiatry, the social sciences and feminism. These traditions are not to be dismissed lightly. For apart from their theoretical pedigree, the differences of opinion they create reach right down to the practical discussion, in clinics, hospitals and other therapy centres, about how each particular sufferer might be helped.

People trained in the social sciences can find it hard to accept that part of the problem has a straightforward basis in the consequences of starvation. Familiar with the very many occasions when inappropriate and over-extended physical explanations have been offered for complex human behaviour, they can be ill-inclined to change their approach in the case of anorexia nervosa or bulimia unless they have actually had to grapple with the problem. It is usually only then that they become more receptive to other notions.

Those working in a Freudian tradition also have difficulty in recognizing the importance of the biological aspects of starvation. Freud's insights brought about a reallocation of symptoms as between physical and psychological causes. As a result of his ideas, symptoms such as slips of the tongue, for example, and some forms of paralysis which had previously been thought of as having purely physical causes were recognized to be psychological in origin, their reasons and purposes having been repressed. So the suggestion that behaviour which seems meaningful is largely due to physiological change is a backward step for anyone of a Freudian persuasion. Thus those who use this approach tend to offer over-inclusive psychological accounts for some symptoms that are better explained biologically.

Feminists meanwhile are likely to see the problem of helping anorexics in the context of the whole historic struggle of women to regain control over their own bodies. For them it is an example to set alongside the issues of legitimacy, contraception and access to medical care for specifically female complaints. To accept that the effects of starvation play an important part in creating anorexia nervosa too easily seems to allow or condone coercive refeeding programmes, a course which, given the predominance of men in positions of power within the medical profession, tends to take the form of a classic male/female confrontation for control over a woman's body.

Our concern here is not to deny the usefulness or the validity of any of the above views so much as to question whether they are appropriate or sufficient when applied to this particular illness.

The idea of illness

To acknowledge that underfeeding itself creates a vortex that readily draws in anyone, male or female, who values its effects is to bring theorizing about food control down to an almost prosaic level. It also emphasizes the importance of directing attention in therapy to the detail of the sufferer's experience in the present, in this moment of time (see Chapters 12 and 14).

Because of its whirlpool nature, the condition must be expected to intensify. There is no need to search for exotic customs, religious practices, esoteric or otherwise, or literary analogues to cast some light on the meaning of a sufferer's actions. Persistent food restriction creates its own extremes, and, sooner or later, its own processes of fragmentation. To explain anorexia nervosa as the struggle of the creative artist, or as the pinnacle of spiritual experience, or as the principled gesture, is not only to be less than honest about the physiological and psychological effects that underlie the process of self-starvation. It is also directly to mislead sufferers. Rather than enabling them to gain the courage to begin the slow, difficult course of moving away from their compulsive and potentially lethal control, investing this control with meaning is likely to reinforce their attachment to their style of thinking by applauding their 'focus', or their 'commitment', or their 'success' (see Chapter 9) and, most certainly, it will prolong their confusion. It will also confuse other vulnerable onlookers.

The fact that the effects of undernutrition have their own dynamic also gives anorexia nervosa/bulimia some of the characteristics that are usually associated with the idea of illness. It can be identified as a distinct segment of a person's life, though, as with drug or alcohol using, a segment of a particular and usually lengthy kind.

There can be objections to calling it an illness, and in particular a mental illness, on the grounds that to do so separates sufferers from the rest of the population and hides the many similarities that exist between their preoccupations and those of others who do not have such distressing symptoms. It can be argued too that to distinguish sufferers as ill also serves to prevent, or stifle, political action to change the pressures and expectations that are generally experienced both by women and by men in a patriarchal society. Accepting that the extremes which are characteristic of the illness are explained by its process is, however, not so much to separate sufferers from their environment as to make it easier to see how their ideas about food and body control grow out of the ordinary values and beliefs that they share with their family, colleagues, friends, communities. It makes it easier too, as will be shown in Part II, to see how the everyday ideas concerning the importance of hard work, self-restraint, personal responsibility, commitment and success are swept into the whirlpool of psychological change, and how it is starvation that pushes these ideas to the point where they become unrecognizable in their extremity.

References

1 Slade, R. (1984) *The Anorexia Nervosa Reference Book*. London: Harper and Row, 70–6.
2 Orbach, S. (1978) *Fat is a Feminist Issue*. London: Hamlyn Paperbacks, 166–7.
3 Eichenbaum, L. and Orbach, S. (1982) *Outside In Inside Out*. Harmondsworth: Pelican, 89.
4 Bruch, H. (1961) Conceptual confusion in eating disorders, *Journal of Nervous and Mental Diseases*, Baltimore: 133; McLeod, S. (1981) *The Art of Starvation*. London: Virago: 139–40, 142–3.
5 Szmuckler, G.I. and Tantam, D. (1984) Anorexia Nervosa: starvation dependence, *British Journal of Medical Psychology*, Cambridge, 57: 303–10.
6 Crisp, A.H., Stonehill, E. and Fenton, G.W. (1971) The relationship between sleep, nutrition and mood: a study of patients with anorexia nervosa, *Postgraduate Medical Journal*, Basingstoke, 47: 207–13.
7 Bruch, H. (1978) *The Golden Cage*. London: Open Books, 14.
8 Crisp, A. (1980) *Anorexia Nervosa: Let Me Be*. London: Academic Press, 86.
9 Slade, R. (1984) op. cit., 68–83.
10 Ross, S. (1978) *Fasting*. London: Pan Books, 93–4.
11 Ibid., 5, 24.
12 *Cosmopolitan*, London, April 1981.
13 *Living Magazine*, London, March 1987.
14 Welbourne, J., Personal communication.
15 Szmuckler, G.I., Eisler, I., Gillies, C. and Hayward, M. (1985) The implications of anorexia nervosa in a ballet school, *Journal of Psychiatric Research*, Oxford, 19(2/3): 177–81.

three

Control by any other name

There are strong pressures in favour of an authoritarian response to the low-weight sufferer who continues to restrict or refuse food and is persistent in exercising; in favour of insistence that exercise is curtailed and some weight gained. Thus strategies to which parents are driven out of desperation, doctors may also put in hand in the belief that these are the best solutions to an intractable problem. In this chapter we will show how it is that such an approach is unlikely to have the desired effect. Meanwhile the reasons why many medical authorities continue to believe that it is still their best option will be discussed in the final part of Chapter 4.

The suspicion that a person might be anorexic can create an uncomfortable nagging worry in any onlooker. But a definite diagnosis of anorexia nervosa arouses stronger emotions, particularly in sufferers' parents. Their feelings range through fear and horror to disbelief and despair, though often most prominent is anger, and a sense of betrayal, spurred by the realization that their daughter or son has become so emaciated as a result of deliberate and systematic food avoidance. As one outraged father said:

> I'm appalled by this! How could she let us down like this? She knows what she's doing. She's said to us straightforwardly that she's quite truthful about everything else . . . but she'll lie her head off over food. How can she behave in this way? How can she go on doing this to herself? It's so stupid!

The situation is not quite so simple, of course, for, as we have seen, the decision to continue cutting down on the amount eaten is influenced by the effect that consistent food restriction itself has upon a person's thinking and experiencing. But the idea that anyone can display such remarkable self-control without being truly responsible for it requires a degree of information and understanding about the way anorexia nervosa works that few people actually have when they meet the condition for the first time.

The more emaciated sufferers become, the more intense the feelings of those trying to help. As well as worries about the person's physical health, the sight of an increasingly skeletal body is disturbing. Strong physical revulsion combined with anger and fear, and the urgent sense that something *must* be done, often accompany attempts to reassert authority over sufferers at low weight. Asserting authority or moral control is also precisely the kind of action that responsible parents are expected to take. Parents who are seen to behave in this way receive strong social approval. This is equally matched by the disapproval they can receive when their offspring's behaviour is considered to be out of hand.

'How could you let her get so thin?' and 'Why don't you stop her?' are simple questions, ones that friends, neighbours, other family members often ask, but in a way that parents sense as blaming. They feel very criticized by such remarks. They also feel the more painfully inadequate as a daughter's (or son's) increasingly emaciated appearance proclaims ever more clearly their own incapacity to exercise proper authority, and their failure to care.

> We were worried enough. Carol was looking really awful by then. It'd got to the point where we didn't dare mention food for the row there'd be. But what made it more unbearable was all the criticism. People would just come up and say, 'Why are you letting her do it? You're her mother, aren't you? Surely you've got *some* say?' There was no question. I was to blame.

Many young people are legally minors when they first become anorexic, and this can make an authoritarian response to their stubborn refusal to eat seem reasonable. But where sufferers are legally adult, parents can still actively attempt to influence their behaviour in quite an authoritarian way. Certainly, in the crisis that occurs with progressive emaciation, parents frequently respond in a way that would generally be thought of as more appropriate for a much younger person. This is how, when the condition does gain hold during teenage years, it can begin to appear as a form of parent/ teenager conflict over autonomy, even though it does not originate in this way.

In the face of what seems a wilful disregard either for their own health or for their parents' concern, an authoritarian approach to those caught up in this illness can seem justified. Yet where a sufferer has adult status there is often a different conflict, as the following account illustrates.

This anorexia began when she was 15 and it was reasonable then to insist she went to the doctor. But she's 22 next month, and I don't see I've got the right to insist now. Sometimes I try to encourage her to see the people at the hospital. We might get as far as making an appointment, but she doesn't keep it. She says it's pointless. They were no help before. She'll lie in bed all day drinking nothing but water, or disappear out walking. You don't know what to do for the best. You just – well, you feel hopeless.

Exerting moral control is not a new response. Well over a hundred years ago Sir William Gull, the English physician who first named the condition 'anorexia nervosa', wrote that 'patients should be fed at regular intervals and surrounded by persons who could have moral control over them', and he cited relations and friends as being 'the worst attendants'.[1] When, more than a century later, the same attitudes surface in such remarks as 'If she were mine I'd give her a damned good thrashing and just make sure she got a few good meals inside her', and 'You've just got to let her know that if she doesn't get a grip on herself you'll do it for her', it seems clear that very little has changed. Professional helpers are not immune from feelings of anger either, as those who become involved with sufferers find. In a context of scarce resources anorexics have been publicly criticized by members of the medical profession, for instance, for taking up hospital beds.

The easy assumption that falling weight stems from a sufferer's failure to 'get a grip', or from lack of authority on the part of parents, or partners, or professional helpers, rests on a fundamental misunderstanding of the condition. For the adamant refusal to eat adequate amounts of food, the persistent exercising and the emaciation that follows grow out of a sufferer's already excessive commitment to some of society's most cherished moral beliefs (see Chapters 6 and 7). Indeed, the sad irony is – as has been illustrated by the staunch philanthropy of some sufferers that has come into the public eye – those who become anorexic are people who have more willpower, more determination, more active conscience than most. Without the characteristic ability to get such a grip they would not have become sufferers in the first place.

The dangers of authoritarian intervention

If alarm over appearance and physical health were not in themselves reasons enough for suggesting that low-weight self-starvers should at least be encouraged, if not explicitly made, to eat and gain weight, it could be argued that the psychological consequences of their starved state, with the difficulties in communication these create, should be sufficient justification for adopting a course of immediate weight restoration. It might be seen as a waste of time to attempt to talk to a sufferer whose intellectual capacity is so constrained. But though, in face of all these difficulties, it may seem a good idea to respond to deliberate food avoidance by insisting on refeeding and restoring weight, if this is the first or only response it is unlikely to have the desired effect. This is something many families learn to their cost. By the time they come to seek help they will often have tried every possible means of persuasion, from plying a sufferer with tempting food and offering rewards such as holidays abroad to blunt demands to eat and threats to withdraw treats and pleasures. 'We've done everything – pleaded, pressured, cajoled, *everything* in the hope of making her come to her senses.'

Not only are coercive measures unlikely to work. They can also make matters worse. They can assist in moving sufferers from straightforward, anorexic self-starvation to other forms of food restriction and body regulation. Those who, for whatever reason, fail to maintain rigid control may turn to induced vomiting, using laxatives, or both in their desperation to rid themselves of food they have eaten.

> I was really thin (71 per cent AEBW) and my A-level exams were coming up, and that was when everyone started getting at me. I had to go and see the headmistress. My mother asked her to talk to me. Then my father put on the pressure. He's a vet. They spelled it out. I *must* put on weight because it would be professionally embarrassing for daddy to have a daughter who was anorexic. It took them a long time to realize I was still avoiding meals. But they never stopped pushing. I *must* sort this thing out before university. I did put on weight by the time I took the exams, but after that my eating got more and more odd. I weighed about seven and a half stone (47.6 kg) (78 per cent of this person's AEBW) by the time I started university in the October. I tried to cut down on my food to get my weight lower. I did a lot of yoga, and keep fit, and trampolining, but after that first time my weight dropped I could never manage it again. I never seemed to be able to get back to that strict routine. It was when I found I couldn't do it I started to make myself sick. That's got more frequent ever since.

While sufferers whose weight has been restored may seem to be cured, the reality is that where they turn to purging and/or vomiting they are in a worse position than they were before. For these methods of control are from a medical point of view more dangerous than self-starvation. Vomiting and the use of laxatives and/or diuretics, which reduce body fluid and therefore weight, disturb the biochemical balance of the body. Each time an imbalance is created, the body adjusts to achieve the biochemical equilibrium necessary to maintain the functioning of vital tissues, such as conductive tissue in nerve and muscle, and of vital organs such as the heart and kidneys. The body does this at the cost of losing certain chemicals, particularly potassium. Where such an imbalance is caused regularly there is gradual adaptation to the constant change. A consequence of the process of adapting to the continual use of laxatives is that progressively greater quantities are needed to achieve the same effect. This, together with the anorexic need for certainty that weight will not be gained, can sometimes result in a sufferer taking as many as 50–100 Senokot tablets a day.

Though adjustments and adaptations in body chemistry will take place, the position of anyone regularly eliminating in these ways is physiologically precarious. There is a risk that the body, at any time, may suddenly cease to be able to make the necessary adaptations. When this happens, because vital organs are involved, a 'pack of cards effect' is likely to take place so that deterioration is very rapid and can be fatal. A chronic anorexic, for example, who was living at between 65 and 70 per cent AEBW and had been a permanent laxative user for seven years, was very efficient at work. Being so efficient she was promoted. She felt inadequate to cope with this. Her control tightened, which produced another 3.2 kg (7 lbs) weight loss. She caught tonsillitis at this point, after two days suffered kidney failure, and three days after that, in spite of being admitted to an intensive care unit in a teaching hospital, she died.

Strange though it may seem, therefore, and particularly perhaps to a sufferer's beleaguered relatives, in its earlier stages pure starvation is to be preferred to the later complications of vomiting and purging. This is not only so from a medical standpoint but also from the point of view of the communication which is the prerequisite of effective help. Certainly, while a person is low weight, the task of communicating can be a difficult one. Even so, talking is far more straightforward when a person is suffering merely the psychological consequences of starvation than when thinking and feeling is complicated by the biochemical disturbances created by persistent vomiting and purging. Where biochemistry is thus disturbed there are more possible variables where moods and feelings are concerned, and more variables generally for a helper to take into account in terms of a sufferer's behaviour and perceptions of self. The speed of mood changes too can be bewilderingly swift. All of this ensures a less predictable experience from which sufferers have to attempt to learn about themselves, and the tangled confusion will be too complex to unravel unaided (see Chapter 13).

It is not only as a result of family pressure that a sufferer's eating pattern may change from straightforward starvation to other forms of control. Recourse to vomiting, purging or the use of diuretics can be a response to being coerced into eating in hospital. Alternative ways of controlling food intake can be learned directly from other anorexic patients, or from nursing and other staff who are themselves undeclared fellow sufferers. Though the illness isolates, sufferers can also collude, or push, as one girl recalled: 'I just said I was sure I'd eaten too much, and this older woman we were with, she knew! She just came back, quick as a flash with: "Well, you know what to do about that then, don't you?"' Another admitted he made himself sick 'on booze, food, whatever. You get rid of it. We all do. Regular thing. Don't want to get lardy, do we?' Such is the hold the anorexic attitude can obtain, activities previously kept private, secret, felt as 'disgusting' and 'shameful', become overt, apparently acceptable, inviting, used subtly or otherwise to convey complacent pride.

The anorexia nervosa/bulimia board game

Self-starving, purging and/or vomiting and rigorous physical activity are, broadly, the patterns of behaviour compatible with the ideas of control that are a sufferer's central preoccupation. These three patterns give a range of possibilities for action. Depending on their previous experience, and on the circumstances they find themselves in, sufferers move among these possibilities in much the same way as a player moves around the squares of a board game. At its most simple, the anorexia nervosa/bulimia board has four squares (see Figure 2).

Those who are low weight or emaciated will for the most part remain in Square 1, but tend to make routine excursions into Square 2, or because control fails. Unplanned eating forces movement between Squares 1 and 2. It may also be spurred by starvation-induced hyperactivity.

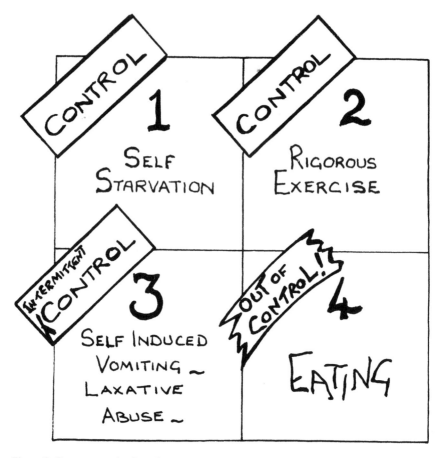

Figure 2: Squares on the board

My aunt made me eat a meal with them. But my sweater had large pockets, so I managed to hide the potatoes and some of the ham, but I had to eat loads. I could feel myself panicking in case they said anything about what I'd left on my plate. I was scared they'd stop me running, but they didn't, and I ran as far as the Toll House which was an extra mile. I felt better then.

The pattern here is the same, irrespective of gender, as one male reported of himself: 'I constantly think I'm overweight, and go into cycles of hardly eating and madly exercising.'[2]

Some, perhaps through sport, dance or another activity intensely pursued, begin their anorexic career in Square 2 and again for the most part will remain there. This square is often where male sufferers join as 'players' on the board. 'The harder he exercised, the more he went on about the percentage fat he'd got, it had to be lower, and the more often he *had* to go to the gym.'

Those in this square may not specifically reduce food intake. As eating is performed in support of their all-absorbing exercise, in support of food-burning or muscle-building regimes, calorie intake can seem reasonable, organized, apparently sufficient. Whether the avowed interest, however, is in being fit, or building muscle, or avoiding fat, in terms of quantity and kinds of food they allow themselves, they are rigidly controlled. Like any other anorexic there is nothing such an exerciser will *not* know about food, how it can be used as a body regulating substance, whether it is 'good' or 'bad'. Their food management will be very exacting and time consuming, absolutely calculated, dominated totally by what is 'right' in relation to the requirements of exercise, or their sport.

In this square sufferers may not look underweight, nor be underweight in terms of measurement on the scales. Where muscle has been developed, weight may be above average for height, age and gender. For where ideas of excellence and perfection coalesce around leanness or muscularity, and fat is at the opposite pole, so muscle bulk can inversely become the imperative. Hence, whatever level their weight, the bodies of those males or females in Square 2 will generally be lacking an appropriate proportional amount of fat tissue, and their preoccupation with 'self-regulation' will be absolute. Hardened muscle and 'fitness diets' readily camouflage anorexic thinking and psychological change.

Accidents and injuries are common among those who persistently over-use their bodies. Should such an occurrence interrupt or compromise their exercise routine, then, being unable to justify eating, which their exercising would permit them to do, and yet with 'self-improvement' through body control still their overriding concern, they are likely to move into Square 1, or attempt to straddle Squares 1 and 2. Since reports such as the following are commonplace, unsurprisingly, exercisers can end up in wheelchairs.

He is nursing a knee injury, but is still putting in four weight-training and four aerobic sessions a week. He has gained two stone in muscle but still wants to improve. 'I'm never content. The more I work out, the more faults I find with myself.' He keeps finding fault with his diet too. Four days into a rigorous detox diet he says, 'I'm dying to eat bad food, it's amazing how strong that craving is.'[3]

Some may land on Square 3, but the reduced ability to be physically active brought about by the biochemical imbalances that follow from vomiting and laxative/diuretic use can make Square 3 less congenial for those whose control routines demand exercise, though muscle-bound male models report that it is 'common to use diuretics to eliminate body fluid prior to a photo shoot'.[4] Some exercisers, unable to train 'properly' as a result of temporary injury, or because they are more permanently crippled, not uncommonly resort to coaching others.

Square 4 is where sufferers land whenever eating occurs in a way they experience as being out of control, or indeed whenever any other form of body regulation is felt as having failed. This square they try to avoid at all costs. If they slip, or are pushed, into Square 4 they will make every effort to escape from it just as soon as they can. It is this that can result in their landing in Square 3.

> I'd managed not to eat anything for five days. I'd kept to black coffee, and fruit juice, but then my control went. I knew I was going to have a binge. The feeling just grew and grew. I couldn't stop it. I'd started stuffing myself before I'd even got through the checkout. Then in the car I just went through the lot. All the biscuits, bread, bars of chocolate, shoving it down as I drove home. Then straight up to the bathroom and got rid of the lot. It was a relief, but I was still angry with myself for giving in. I was determined I wasn't going to eat again.

Sufferers whose starvation regime has crumpled, or is felt to have been destroyed, move around the board, often quite rapidly, using whatever resources are available to regain their preferred position.

> My mother-in-law came over because Derek (the speaker's husband) was coming home. It would have been all right if he'd been there but he wasn't. She made this meal and I had to eat it with her. I tried to get rid of it, but I couldn't bring it all back up, not even with drinking salt water. I panicked. I had to pick Derek up from the station, and there wasn't much time. I could still feel this lump in me. We got back from the station, then I said I had to go out. I had to get to the fitness centre, and I still took a handful of Ducolax when I got back, just to make sure.

Wherever a sufferer moves on the board, the preoccupation is the same. Food/body control is central. It is *the* imperative. As one man put it: 'I'm always on a diet; I can't eat sweets or (drink) alcohol; I'm at the gym four times a week. It requires a lot of discipline and sacrifice, but it's a matter of priorities and what's important to you.'[5] Again the attitude is central, typical of any sufferer. Though each pattern of behaviour tends to produce different physical symptoms and involve apparently different lifestyles, in terms of mindset all may be considered forms of anorexia nervosa (see Chapter 1). It is important to recognize that those caught up in anorexic illness are by no means always distinguishable by their extreme thinness.

Progression around the board

There is a characteristic progression in the condition that takes place as a sufferer shifts between the restricted options. This progression occurs because some of the moves on the board are difficult to reverse. Classically self-starvation and/or excessive exercise mark the beginning of the illness, though this is not absolutely invariable. There are those who see themselves as having 'gone for the quick fix' that vomiting and laxative use provide, and therefore as having got into the problem via Square 3. It is also possible to have arrived in this square so speedily as to be unaware of having been previously in any other square. So desirable are the effects of dieting and exercise, it is difficult for many to see that these specific effects are those which place people in Squares 1 and 2, or therefore to see that these are part of a larger board. So though they may have landed in these squares, they would not necessarily have experienced themselves as 'wrong', or 'ill'.

Having generally joined the game in Square 1 or Square 2, however, sooner in some cases, later in others, the mode of control changes and the 'player' begins to land on Square 3.

> I was (while at boarding school) put back on the diet designed to 'build me up'. This time the supervision was stricter, and it became more difficult for me to pass my butter ration to someone else, to pour Ovaltine down the sink behind the matron's back, or to dispose of extra food by means of the lavatory. But . . . I soon found out that if I swigged a mouthful or two of the laxative *cascara sagrada* from the medicine cupboard, I could get rid of the obnoxious feeling of weight and fullness which had been forced upon me.[6]

The move into Square 3, for many sufferers, marks the beginning of the 'bulimic' phase of the illness. The following account describes this point clearly.

> I had resisted for so long and now in the space of about half an hour I had eaten more than I had ever eaten at one time in my life – with no consciousness of what was happening to me. I was just a pig. I hated myself. My stomach was enormous. I got up very painfully and made my way to the toilet. I locked the door and leant over the sink. I wasn't concerned with getting rid of the calories, I just wanted to get rid of the bulk, the swelling and the terrible choking feeling in my throat. I stood over the sink and as quietly as possible made myself vomit. The horror of being out of control faded . . . I didn't realize then that I was forging the first link in an endless chain of starving, bingeing, vomiting and purging. It was the beginning of a new horror.[7]

The shift in the above account was preceded by a distinct low-weight episode during which this sufferer was refed in hospital and subsequently persisted in restricting her food intake and maintaining low weight. In some cases the phase of self-starvation and/or relentless exercising can be quite short. Again such is the acceptability of food restricting and the value placed on exercise and fitness, it can go quite unnoticed by relatives and friends. Whether it has been recognized or not, a substantial majority of those who are seen or see themselves as bulimic have been through an initial period in Square 1 and/or Square 2. It is possible to inhabit both long enough to become trapped, but without attracting a great deal of attention.

> I had anorexia when I was in my teens. It wasn't for very long, but I did lose quite a bit of weight and they put me in hospital to get my weight up. Afterwards I never used to eat anything during the day. That was when I was still in control. I had to hang on to that. But I'd save everything up for the night time, when my parents had gone to bed. Enormous boxes of chocolate, sweets – I'd save everything for then. I'd hide it in the wardrobe, under lock and key. I'd get excited beforehand, and very irritated if my parents hung around and didn't go to bed. Then all the control would go. I would – well, I behaved just like an animal. Then I had to get rid of it. I'd hate myself. All the excitement would change to fear. I'd have to make myself sick. Really sick. On and on till I'd got rid of it all. I'd be terrified there was still a bit left in me.

'Advantages' of a bulimic pattern of control

Invariably bulimics would like to return to Square 1, but this move is not easy, and for good reasons. Once it has been discovered or learned that, after slipping into Square 4, it is possible to regain a sense of control by vomiting and/or using laxatives, the likelihood is that the sufferer will be unable to resist taking such immediate and visibly effective action again after further episodes of uncontrolled eating. Elimination by whatever means tends to provide swifter reassurance than can be gained by attempting to re-establish a starvation regime.

> I was relieved that the unbearable full feeling was lessened (by vomiting) and that I had undone some of the damage of the last hour. If I could get rid of the food as easily as this . . . I had discovered the answer to all my problems. I could eat what I wanted to without gaining weight and there was a means of easy relief should I ever overeat again.[8]

Controlling food intake by underfeeding or self-starving can take weeks, or even months of sustained effort. It requires continued surveillance to gain a sense of achievement, with the horizon ever retreating as the effects of starvation themselves increase the imperative for absolutely sure success. But by inducing vomiting, or using increasing quantities of laxatives, or both, the loss of control that is so damaging to the sufferer's self-esteem can be 'put right' in the space of about twenty minutes, or at most a few hours, and this in itself can provide a sense of satisfaction and achievement, as this male sufferer describes:

I'm not going back to that control. I did it. I'm clever [stated with pride and assurance]. I can do that. I lost three stone five (21.4 kg) by dieting. I feel proud of that. But this way I can have the food. I can eat something really good for me like wholemeal bread with tomatoes and lettuce and salad cream, and then I can get rid of it. That's what I do. And it's quicker. [This speaker's current weight is 74 per cent of his AEBW.]

There are further aspects of food elimination that tend to make it a useful alternative for sufferers who are desperate to regain the certainty of being in control. They may learn very swiftly that self-starving and becoming emaciated earns the unwelcome attention of parents, partners and doctors, whereas the effects of vomiting and laxative abuse are generally invisible. They may discover they can fool even such knowledgeable people as doctors, dieticians, nurses or other professionals. Although the dentist may be aware of the loss of tooth enamel as an indication of persistent vomiting, the condition becomes virtually invisible at this stage, even to those who are medically trained. All a general practitioner may come across is perhaps a biochemical imbalance, revealed only if laboratory tests happen to be carried out, and which even then may appear inexplicable if the doctor is unsuspecting.

Sufferers who vomit their food generally maintain a lower body weight than those who are primarily laxative users,[9] and neither strategy brings about the weight loss that is achieved by systematic restriction of food. So while vomiting and/or purging may not enable them to remain as thin as they would like, at least they have the comfort of knowing they can get rid of the food they have eaten.

These forms of control also enable sufferers to keep up appearances of normal eating, and so to 'manage' on social occasions. It can enable them to join colleagues or workmates for mealbreaks without attracting comment. It means they can eat in front of parents or partner, join family mealtimes, eat in the company of friends. This keeps everyone happy, which is an important consideration for the sufferer. Thus, once the transition has been made from straightforward starving to controlling food by attempting to regulate its absorption, the condition can persist completely undetected for many years, or, indeed, for a lifetime.

My weight went down to six and a half stone (41.3 kg) (71 per cent AEBW) which was low for me because I was quite tall, even at 15. But I started eating because they said they wouldn't let me go to Italy for the summer with my cousin if I didn't put on weight. I put on a bit, and I got my cousin to persuade them I was all right. They let me go, but I wasn't all right. I'd try and keep control, then it would snap and I'd eat and eat and eat. Then I started making myself sick. I wasn't thin, so they carried on thinking I was better. I couldn't tell them. I didn't want to disappoint them. I managed to keep it to myself for nearly seven years.

Though self-starvers may remain in Square 1 for some time, they are sooner or later forced out, or hunger takes over. No position on the 'four square' board is stable. The limited range of options that exists for maintaining control, and the tendency there is for there to be a natural progression between them, together show up the hazards of authoritarian approaches to weight gain. Coercion may be exercised indirectly, for instance by playing on the sufferer's sensitivity to others' needs (see Chapter 6), so she or he may gain weight to reduce others' anxiety. Or it may be exercised directly, for instance by insisting upon refeeding taking place in hospital. Either way sufferers who are low weight may be brought up to a healthy weight, but, as we have said, this alone does not switch off their concern with control. They may be physically heavier, but *their anorexic attitude will remain unaltered.*

All too often authoritarian or coercive intervention accelerates the change in the pattern of control. Weight gain and exercise restriction that sufferers feel they have been forced into may result in their simply moving around the board. Such intervention will also subsequently make creating or sustaining a therapeutic relationship the more difficult. Anorexia nervosa/bulimia sufferers do not easily forgive those they see as having crushed their control.

Completing the board game

Sufferers who gain weight or who have their weight restored, but whose feelings and attitudes in relation to food and body control remain unchanged, are emotionally in a highly unstable or chaotic state which itself causes enormous and constant distress. The turmoil they feel is reflected in their chaotic behaviour in relation to food and eating. To reassert control is their one reliable source of reassurance; the one satisfying action. It is the only way they have of redeeming themselves. They may succeed in restricting food intake and return to a low-weight state. But the greater likelihood is that, as they swing from one extreme to the other, they will move around the board, landing in a disorganized fashion on any square that offers the hope of feeling at least in some measure in control. The nearer their weight is to their AEBW, the more continuously aware they will be of how uncomfortable they are with themselves. As awareness is no longer so narrowed, so closed down by the anaesthetizing effects of being underweight and underfed, the more conscious will they be of their total ineffectiveness. They will be more aware of their inability to make even the most minor decisions, except the decision to regain food/body control, by whatever means. So a sufferer's entire experience is deeply degrading and humiliating and highly destructive of self-esteem. Feelings of failure and hopelessness can become so intense that those trapped in this cycle can be desperate to escape and oblivion can seem to be the only way out.

Thus sufferers may resort to using alcohol, legal drugs (either prescribed or obtained over the counter), illegal drugs and in some cases solvents. Any substance, or substances, in any combination is fair means in the attempt to obtain relief from feelings of panic, confusion, extreme self-hatred and despair.

It transpired that my patient, a mother with three children, all primary-school age, would, as a normal routine in a seven-day week, have been attending nine one-and-a-half hour aerobics classes and have run twenty-six road miles if she hadn't broken her pelvis. She was in near total panic at not being able to do any exercise at all. That was why she had begun coming to the surgery in tears asking for more and more tranquillizers. Her weight at the time was quite normal (103 per cent AEBW). But it had previously been much lower.

Overdoses are not unusual at the stage when weight is normal or near normal. They may be suicide bids, but they are not necessarily so. An over-dose to many a sufferer is merely a reasonably guaranteed way of obtaining oblivion; as one woman said, 'a way of dealing with a mind that won't shut up'. Even so, actual suicide is always a real possibility.

There are sufferers who contrive to deaden or blot out their feelings by physically harming themselves, stubbing lighted cigarettes on their arms, legs and hands, and/or cutting themselves with razor blades, or with fragments of china or glass, often broken for the purpose. Acute physical pain centres awareness. Nothing else but the pain thus created can be thought about while it is being induced, and this is a relief.

To complete the board game, then, there are two further squares that need to be added to allow for the possibility of self-harm of all kinds and to admit the possibility of attempted suicide (see Figure 3). Between a quarter and a third of sufferers resort at least once to this latter solution, and almost always after a bout of eating they have been unable to control. Deaths do happen, although as the anorexic mindset produces wide variations in behaviour that carries risk, precise figures tend to be difficult to ascertain. Mortality has increased over the years, however. Estimates put at about 2 per cent in the mid-1980s ranged, in 2001 for instance, between 5 and 20 per cent. Not all deaths are a consequence of starvation. Suicide attempts that succeed – or overdoses that go wrong – have been estimated to account for approximately two-thirds of the deaths that occur.

Of all the deaths that result from anorexia nervosa/bulimia the majority occur when weight has increased, or when whatever has been eaten has felt totally out of control; that is when a swing has taken place from the 'good' to the unacceptable, or 'bad', category. This is illustrated in the case of the college student who jumped to her death from a multi-storey car park. Her anorexia nervosa was new. She had lost 15.9 kg (2 st. 7 lbs) in the previous four months, a sharp drop in weight that typically marks the 'onset' of the illness in the weight charts of anorexics. In the local newspaper article that referred to her death, and to the fact that she was anorexic, her family was reported as saying that she had not eaten a meal for months. But a few days

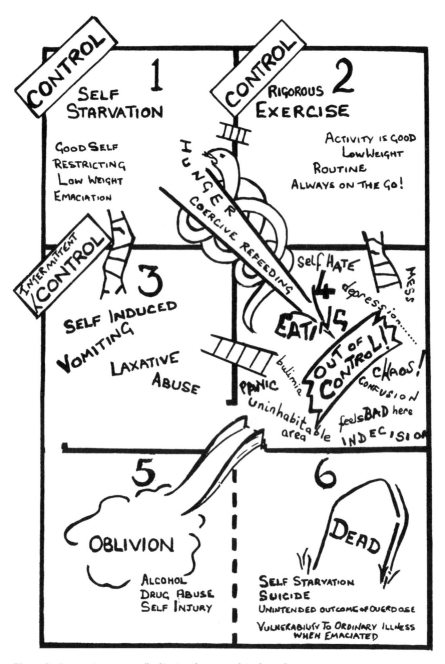

Figure 3: Anorexia nervosa/bulimia: the complete board

later, following the post mortem, the same newspaper gave an account of the pathologist's report. The pathologist had found that the girl had eaten a large amount of food shortly before she died.

Those who continue to starve successfully and maintain themselves at a low weight will feel more consistently 'good'. While they are managing this they will be less at risk of hurting themselves in other ways. But because the pattern of 'successful' control of food intake involves compensating strategies such as 'undercutting what I let myself eat just to make sure of not eating too much', and 'keeping a few calories in hand in case I can't get out of being made to eat', the starver runs the risk of spiralling downwards through low weight into a state of dangerous emaciation. When, on the other hand, control slips, sufferers may find themselves unaccountably accused of shop-lifting – from foodstores usually, but not exclusively. On the rollercoaster that is bulimia they may become explicitly reckless and generally careless of themselves, drinking, drugging, becoming promiscuous in sexual relationships, being 'totally spendthrift'. Binges can involve vast quantities of food. As many sufferers and their families are aware, a bulimic's addiction can be as disastrous financially as that of any alcohol or drug addict: 'My marriage broke up. That was because of bulimia. And everything I got, like my share of the house, it all went on food that I vomited. Thousands of pounds literally straight down the drain.' As another sufferer explained:

I just bought stuff. Not just food. Everything. Even health club memberships, gym memberships . . . four, or five . . . They thought I had a problem with credit cards. It wasn't that. All I thought about was losing weight. The first time I managed it. After that . . . I only ever made myself sick.

Expressing anorexia nervosa/bulimia as a game that has a limited number of moves also indicates clearly the way 'players' are trapped within the boundaries of the board. This is the more tragic because those who become anorexia nervosa/bulimia sufferers are typically intelligent and highly sensitive people who have the potential to live and respond in complex and varied ways. As one voluntary worker said of the anorexics she had met in the hospitals she visited, 'It seems so sad. They're such nice girls, all of them. So sensitive and thoughtful, and *very* intelligent.' Yet paradoxically, if they had not been intelligent and sensitive, and put every effort into being 'nice', they would not have become anorexic in the first place.

It must be emphasized too that this is a game that hardly any of them meant to play. Being on some of the squares on the board will provide sufferers with a sense of achievement and security, but it also hides from them the potential dangers, and can do so to the extent that they have no idea that they are ill, or trapped, or 'playing' this board game. It takes them a long time to perceive there is a problem; to see how they are living with the unanticipated consequences of their actions. The eventual realization of how trapped they are is one of the things that can drive them to despair. Coming to terms with this is often the step that brings them face to face with the hopelessness of ever being able to get out of the trap, of ever being able to feel confident, effective, self-directed and real.

It is important to be aware of how deep is the despair that is felt, how complete the lack of hope and how instantaneous the relief brought by self-injury and oblivion. But the helper need not, indeed must not, share this hopelessness. There are sufferers who recover completely. Many improve enough to resume the course of their life, and it is possible to accelerate the process of recovery.

The helper's dilemma

In recognizing the potential hazards of the simple authoritarian response to anorexic food restriction, helpers themselves come face to face with the dilemma that seems to lie at the heart of any attempt to assist or care for a sufferer who is low weight.

On the one hand the physical and psychological constraints of starvation have to be reckoned with. This necessarily involves acknowledging that much of this person's intellectual potential is temporarily unavailable, and is so in proportion to the amount of weight that has been lost. It also involves being aware that emotional development has slowed down, or stopped. Familiar to those involved in recovery from alcoholism, 'development ends where addiction begins' is no less true for those who have become dependent on food restricting or exercising. The helper needs to be sensitive to the fact that not only in terms of weight but in every respect the food restricter/over-exerciser is someone who is very much less than she or he could be; someone not only in the process of losing the years of youth, but years of life.

On the other hand there is an equal and opposite need to be aware that this is also someone who, in being controlled, has discovered a way of feeling 'positive' that is profoundly relieving. It replaces a deep sense of failure and confusion (see Chapters 6 and 8). Food/body control has not only become central to self, but is all this person has to maintain any sense of self. If this control goes, he or she no longer has a self to be.

So the dilemma is that while the helper would like to lift the constraints and the dangers of the effects of undernutrition by simple refeeding, to do this without attending to the way the sufferer feels is to risk annihilating a sense of self which is already very fragile. On the other hand, while the helper would like to respect the sufferer as a person, since this person's sense of who she or he is resides in successful food/body control, to adopt this course can lead to the helper's allowing, or colluding with, the sufferer's persistence in a lifestyle that can eventually lead to a degree of emaciation that is lethal. Parents, friends, inexperienced helpers unaware of the nature of the anorexic's 'self' not infrequently find themselves confronted with the consequences of their having taken this latter option. Thus occasionally sufferers can die in the bosom of a caring family.[10]

To look at the dilemma in another way, forcing weight up risks moving the moderately low-weight anorexic (i.e. the sufferer whose weight is *not* below 65 per cent AEBW – see Chapter 5) to a position where – because biological complications created by bingeing and vomiting or laxative using can medically be more hazardous, and because the nature of these strategies is such that the experience, when using them, is that 'more is always needed' – the chances of dying are doubled. Allowing a sufferer to continue in being the 'controlling self' is safer temporarily. Yet, because of the momentum self-starvation generates, because of the whirlpool's force, the natural progression is more extreme emaciation.

All too often the cost of solving one problem is to make the other worse. Hence those looking on from the outside can feel as trapped by the condition as the sufferer is on the inside.

There is no reason, however, why those concerned to help should respond solely to the problem of weight and exclude any consideration of the sufferer's sense of self, or why they should respond solely to the anorexic 'self' and exclude any consideration of weight. There is no reason to become stuck with the dilemma. It is possible, as we will show in Part III, to nurture a new sense of self whilst at the same time enabling the slow relaxation of dependence on food/body control. It is possible, in other words, for a sympathetic and informed helper to encourage gradual weight gain in a way that is not a total assault on the person the sufferer currently is.

References

1 Gull, W. (1874) Anorexia Nervosa, *Transactions of the Clinical Society*, London, 7: 22–8.
2 Shabi, R. (2001) Muscle mania, *Guardian* Weekend, 21 July: 19.
3 Ibid., 20.
4 Ibid., 24.
5 Ibid., 19.
6 McLeod, S. (1981) *The Art of Starvation*. London: Virago, 74.
7 Roche, L. (1984) *Glutton for Punishment*. London: Pan Books, 71–2.
8 Ibid., 72.
9 Lacey, J.H. and Gibson, E. (1985) Controlling weight by purgation and vomiting; a comparative study of bulimics, *Journal of Psychiatric Research*, 19(2/3): 337–41.
10 Dunbar, M. (1986) *Catherine*. London: Viking Books.

four

Bad medicine

When weight continues to fall, and relatives realize all their efforts to encourage the sufferer to eat are coming to nothing, they generally seek out
medical help.

Doctors have a range of sophisticated techniques at their disposal. They
may also be able to command greater authority than many a parent or
spouse. Yet faced with a person's adamant refusal to eat, they are constrained
in much the same way as everyone else. There are very few additional
responses they can make just because they are medically trained, for there is
no cure for anorexia nervosa that is, strictly speaking, medical.

False leads: appetite and mood

Sufferers at this stage typically present a healthy body that is adapting or has
adapted to undernutrition as a result of their overriding need to restrict food
intake. Direct manipulation of appetite is of little use because they are not
suffering from a loss of appetite. Where others have not yet realized this, or
have realized but overlooked the point, the self-starver's response to the idea
is characteristic and often vehement: 'Of course I'm hungry. I think about
food all the time. I can't stop it. I hate it. It's like my enemy. I've got to fight
it. I won't let myself give in. I've got to control it.'

In the hope of stimulating appetite, family and friends too are already likely to have tried tempting the sufferer with especially interesting food, or food that used to be liked, but with little success. The problem from the anorexic point of view is to control hunger. Hence sufferers' anger and fear when they are plied with food, and the tension and violent scenes that arise at mealtimes.

There is no reason therefore to prescribe appetite stimulants, yet some practitioners may still do this. If appetite stimulants are effective, they merely increase the frightened struggle against food. Typically, low-weight restricters will allow theselves something like a carton of plain yogurt, an apple or tomato, a slice of chicken and a lettuce leaf in one day. But more than this they dare not eat because they are terrified that the desire for food will run away with them and they will lose their precious control. This is a terror that can escalate to the point where eating stops altogether.

The use of appetite suppressants might be considered a logical approach, in view of the overwhelming fear of weight gain. The hope might be to enable a shift from total starvation to a point where moderate amounts are eaten, or to avert an eventual low-weight crisis. Substance abuse is frequent in the later stages of the condition, however, so any drug treatment that carries the risk of addiction poses a particular danger for the anorexic or bulimic.[1] In appearing to hold out the promise of control, particularly to sufferers whose restricting has come to demand that 'food must be fat-free', the need to encourage eating might tempt the use of drugs designed to reduce the absorption of dietary fat by altering enzymatic activity. These drugs are not chemically addictive but, as they interfere with the ordinary process of digestion, they are, to anyone with an anorexic or body controlling mindset, akin to laxative use.

Using any chemical assistance they can obtain, including nicotine, some sufferers attempt to regain their ability to achieve their self-starvation goals themselves. A determined sufferer making out a good case to an unwary general practitioner may obtain 'help to start slimming'. To quote: 'I can get anything from my GP. He's so fanatic about the dangers of obesity. That's why I stay with his practice. It's worth the journey, and he never asks too many questions.'

Little can be achieved by prescribing psychotropic – that is, mood-changing – drugs, for the condition is not essentially a mood state. There are some sufferers who, as well as being entrapped in food/body regulating, may be clinically depressed and some may also be anxious. Drugs may profitably be used to alleviate secondary states of anxiety and depression. Considerable store has been set by the use of the group of drugs known as selective serotonin reuptake inhibitors (SSRIs) which act by blocking reabsorption of serotonin by the nerve endings in the brain, so increasing the levels of this neurotransmitter. Serotonin is believed to have an important influence on mood. A sufferer's fundamental belief in the need for food/body control will not be altered by psychotropic drugs, however – a point that continues to be borne out by the experience of those who have been prescribed them as part of hospital treatment programmes.

The distinction between anorexia nervosa and affective disorders such as depression has, in the past, been a contentious issue. But now it is more widely recognized that the condition is distinguished by the central dynamic that revolves around the idea of control – the dynamic that, in conjunction with self-starvation, creates the whirlpool described in Chapter 2. Feelings of depression and anxiety in the early stages of anorexia nervosa are directly related to whether or not there is a feeling of being in control. The more control sufferers have over food, eating and exercising, the fewer anxious episodes they will have, and they will feel unhappy far less often. This pattern is distinctly different from the pattern that occurs in anxiety states, or with depression that has become an illness in its own right, where the persistent, disabling and unrelenting mood of hopelessness is the main problem.

Where people become emaciated as a result of a depressive illness, an increase in their weight will be accompanied by a lessening of their depression. On the other hand, and importantly, anorexics/bulimics become significantly more depressed with *any* gain in weight, however minimal. For this indicates that they are out of control. For them it is clear evidence of their *total* failure as a person, and a feeling of failure of this order is depressing.

The central role attitudes and values have, both in the genesis of anorexia nervosa and in its perpetuation, clearly indicates the limitations of medicine here. Beliefs, attitudes, values by their nature are not amenable to change by simple drug therapy.

Treatment objectives

Given physical medicine offers no cure for anorexia nervosa, and doctors like anyone else are constrained by the sufferer's rigid refusal to eat, there are, broadly speaking, two possibilities. Doctors can either set out to overcome an anorexic's 'wilful' food avoidance and use whatever medical techniques are necessary to do this, or they can set about gaining sufferers' cooperation, however minimal, in taking part in organizing their own nutritional first aid and eventual recovery.

The situation a doctor faces with each individual case is more detailed, of course, than this dichotomy suggests. However, short-term treatment objectives have a very important influence on outcome. Everyone wants the sufferer to 'get better'. The more immediate question is how a particular intervention is supposed to bring this about. The question of control is crucial. For it is upon developing a sense of personal autonomy that eventual recovery depends. Even doctors who realize that, beyond the minimum necessary to maintain life, weight gain alone is not a cure may still be tempted to use in the short term methods that will actually frustrate their aim to produce recovery in the long term. The manner in which intervention is taken is often more important than what is actually done. The question always to be considered is whether the proposed intervention is designed to overcome the food/body control, or whether it is a step towards helping a sufferer gain real autonomy. Some interventions, which we will describe, can only be used for one of these purposes, which is to overcome the control. With others, particularly drug therapies, the distinction is not so clear.

In addition to the issue of control, the amount of weight gain the doctor is aiming for a patient to achieve is also important. Methods which may be justifiable as a life-saving measure are psychologically destructive when used to return the sufferer to normal weight. Some basic assumptions about the nature of the condition are involved in this objective, and we will return to these later in this chapter.

Confusingly, both the cooperative and coercive approaches are likely to be called 'medical help'. So it is important for sufferers, and their relatives, to differentiate between the two ways medicine may be used when weight is low.

There is a limited number of ways in which any patients who are emaciated can be given the nourishment they need. Intravenous feeding is one of these. Tube feeding into the stomach is another. But a liquid diet of regular, bland nutritional drinks, widely used in geriatric wards and for post-operative cases, is the mainstay of such help. Sufferers who feel they are being stripped of their food control will not cooperate in this. They may be dying of starvation, but they will actively resist by removing the nasogastric tube, or switching off the drip that is supplying their essential nutrition. Chapters 10 and 11 will be devoted to describing how sufficient cooperation may be achieved in enabling the patient to accept the minimum necessary intervention. This chapter will look at the situation where doctors willingly or unwillingly become drawn into using medical techniques to overcome the low-weight sufferer's 'wilful' refusal to eat.

While it can be acknowledged that genuine, or unambivalent agreement to being refed is unlikely to be forthcoming, the very authority conferred by medical knowledge, together with the expectations families have of those with medical training, tend to push doctors in the direction of coercive intervention before they have elicited even minimal consent. Faced with a stubborn anorexic who is steadfastly refusing to eat, and desperate relatives looking to them for help, their recourse may still be to institute a refeeding programme and overcome a sufferer's resistance rather than undertake the lengthy, time-consuming process of encouraging a gradual change in attitude.

Additional medical interventions and their limitations

A wide variety of medical techniques have been used in the hospital setting to overcome the low-weight anorexic's refusal to eat and increase weight. Sufferers generally have found these very alarming. Nor have they necessarily been alone in this. The techniques described below are being or have been used with the aim of lessening resistance.

Insulin therapy

Insulin therapy has been used to solve the problem of making the anorexic eat by creating an uncontrollable hunger for sugar and carbohydrate that the sufferer would relieve – along with the other unpleasant side effects of sweating, dizziness and increased anxiety that this treatment brings about – by taking in food containing these substances.

In an emaciated body, however, there are no reserves of glycogen, and insulin levels may already be very high. So there is considerable risk in using this form of intervention. All anorexics' reactions to insulin are not standard, and it has been found that even a very small, apparently safe dose can prove to be dangerous in some particularly sensitive patients, and deaths have been reported. An instance has been recorded where the high-carbohydrate breakfast, which is the essential second half of this medical treatment, was forgotten. The insulin injection that had been given caused the girl to go into irreversible coma and suffer lasting brain damage. For these reasons insulin therapy is generally no longer used, though it is not inappropriate for families to be aware of its dangers and the need to decline it as treatment.

Electroconvulsive therapy

Another approach is electroconvulsive therapy (ECT) which has been routinely used by some doctors as a measure of last resort in patients who persist in not eating. It is one psychiatric treatment for conditions that display fixed patterns of thinking and acting that do not change in response to new information or changes in situation.

A small amount of anaesthetic is injected into the vein on the back of the patients' hand or into their arm which quickly puts them to sleep for a few minutes. Whilst they are asleep a psychiatrist places two electrodes on their head and a small electric current is passed. This causes them to have a very mild fit. The procedure is painless and patients will not be able to remember the experience of the fit.

It is believed this treatment temporarily disrupts the neurological basis on which patients' behaviour depends so that, for a while, they are unable to return to their usual ways. It is used in the hope that during this interval a more productive style of thinking will develop. ECT is most commonly used for people who are severely depressed.

Although in clinging desperately to food control anorexics may appear to be similarly rigid and immovable, their fixed pattern of behaviour is not the result of a mood state. It has a different basis.

Surgery

A rather drastic approach is surgery. Leucotomies have occasionally been performed in cases of anorexia nervosa.

A leucotomy is a brain operation in which a portion of nerve fibres (white matter) connecting the two cerebral hemispheres is separated by an incision. Older methods of performing leucotomies produced widely variable physical results in the areas of brain actually cut by the surgeon's knife. Newer stereotactic operative techniques can allow a more precise target to be established and limited cuts to be made. While such an operation lessens the power of the person's beliefs to shape his or her behaviour, the beliefs themselves remain unchanged. The subsequent psychological results have been generally unhelpful and even disastrous. There has been an instance of a sufferer committing suicide because, following this treatment, her eating changed and she put on weight, but her overwhelming desire was still to be thin. The procedure had created no change to her anorexic attitude. So it seems doubtful whether such a drastic measure is either appropriate or justified.

Drug therapy

Ways of giving nourishment to a patient are limited. Medication may be used in this process, but when, why and how it is used can differ profoundly. It can be used as assistance in a cooperative exercise between a doctor and the anorexic patient who wants to damp down the terrors of the refeeding process (see Chapter 11), or it can be used to coerce.

Among the variety of psychotropic drugs that has been used in the treatment of difficult and resistant anorexia nervosa patients in hospital, chlorpromazine, an antipsychotic, was early on given a prominent place in the medical literature, being described there by one authority as 'the drug of choice', and as 'remarkably free of dangers'.[2] Though creating fewer problems than other drugs of this kind (e.g. thioridazine and trifluoperazine), chlorpromazine nevertheless is epileptogenic. It also depresses bone marrow and stops the production of new blood cells (aplastic anaemia), and it can cause jaundice.

Its main value as a treatment is in helping a patient to start eating. Unlike the minor tranquillizers that may alternatively be used, it does not disinhibit the patient, so does not create problems with 'management'. (Minor tranquillizers – i.e. benzodiazepines – carry the danger of releasing more feelings and impulses than sufferers and those who care for them can cope with. Benzodiazepines, which include diazepam (Valium), lorazepam (Ativan), chlordiazipoxide (Librium), are again known to carry the risk of addiction.) But chlopromazine does not bear on core attitude. 'One year after admission there is no difference, either physically, emotionally or in attitude towards eating, between those given and those not given the drug.'[3]

Taking control of the anorexic patient

Chlorpromazine does not cure anorexia nervosa/bulimia, and its effects preclude any alternative therapy that depends on talking to the sufferer. Thus the purpose of its use lies in the control it gives the doctor. This is a treatment aim that survives. It was advocated in the 1870s that the physician should take 'firm moral control'.[4] The main advocate of the use of chlorpromazine, nearly a hundred years later, provides a conspicuous example of the doctor taking control of the patient as a treatment objective, and illuminates how the need for the doctor to be in control can take other direct forms, and involve actions that make few acknowledgements in the direction of sophisticated medicine.

> We rely mainly on response-prevention for vomiters, but have occasionally employed the technique of telling the patient that she will have to eat anything she vomits. One practical demonstration is usually enough to break the pattern.[5]

It is not unknown for vomiters to take such recourse themselves, however. They are no strangers to devising rigours of their own, including going to this kind of extreme.

Rather than rely on medical interventions to overcome sufferers' resistance many centres involved in treating the condition prefer instead the organized and systematic use of the pressures the hospital as an institution can exert. It is well known that total institutions can change behaviour. Monasteries, prisons, boarding schools and army barracks, as well as hospitals, are total institutions, because they regulate all aspects of an individual's life twenty-four hours a day. Those who run them generally have little difficulty in gaining the compliance of members or inmates.

This sort of pressure may be seen by some people as less drastic and therefore more appropriate than some of the medical approaches outlined above. Nevertheless it is important to be aware of the extreme degree of environmental control that can be used in hospitals in the attempt to change anorexic behaviour.

Sufferers who undergo this kind of treatment may find themselves separated at least temporarily from home, family and friends, with their possessions and clothes taken from them, this being a well-known strategy for preventing a person from leaving hospital. They may be confined to bed, and may be denied pillows, television, reading materials, visitors and 'privileges' such as letters and phone calls, or these may be rationed according to the extent of their compliance over eating. Here they will certainly be under continual pressure and surveillance.

> I wasn't allowed to go to the lavatory. They told me I'd got to use a commode. They said it would be brought in after meals and that was when I had to use it. I wasn't allowed to have a bath. I said I usually had a bath every day but that made no difference. I would have to make do with a strip-wash, and that meant a bowl and water being brought because the sink in the room had been blocked. That was just in case I had any ideas about getting rid of food down the sink, or being sick down it. The windows were bolted closed for the same reason. It wasn't a hospital. It was a prison.

While undergoing such restrictions and privations anorexics have been required to eat very large quantities of food (see Chapter 5).

Behaviourism: a theoretical rationale for taking control

Behavioural psychology is often used as a theoretical rationale for the above approach in the treatment of low-weight sufferers, although it is doubtful whether it does in fact provide one. There is no doubt that coercive hospital regimes can and do result in anorexics eating and increasing their weight. But whether this outcome is really explained within the concepts of behaviourism is also debatable.

This psychological theory asserts that almost all behaviour is learned and ultimately controlled by the environment within which the organism acts. A person's behaviour is assumed to be a response to stimuli impinging from the environment, or a response to the consequences to a person for having behaved in a particular way. By investigating the relationship between external events and the organism's responses, the psychologist hopes to arrive at laws of behaviour broadly analogous to the laws of natural science. To the extent that anything that can be learned can also, given the appropriate techniques, be unlearned, behaviourism may be seen as a liberating theory and has been the source of many useful therapeutic techniques.

Academically, behaviourism is at its weakest when it attempts to explain the development of morality and higher intellectual functions in human beings. Yet it is precisely these qualities that are so distinctively a part of anorexia nervosa/bulimia, a point that will be elaborated in Part II. It is not surprising, therefore, that those approaching the task of help from within this theory make a fundamental mistake about the nature of the condition. The sufferers' food and body control is not an isolated item of learned behaviour. It is their sense of who they are. The problem at heart is not about food or exercise but about personhood, and about autonomy, which is also why the manifestations of a sufferer's need for control can take a variety of forms.

From its philosophical roots, and in the research tradition, behaviourism deals with behaviour in small segments. It is held that links are reinforced between the stimulus properties of particular situations and specific responses by the individual. In therapy undesirable links may be extinguished. Consequently treatment programmes designed on the basis of this approach are characteristically very detailed, systematic and structured.

Used correctly, behaviour modification techniques have often proved an effective way of dealing with troublesome symptoms, but symptoms that are limited in their extent. Helping people to stop smoking or to overcome irrational fears are just some of the areas in which they have been successfully used. These problems may make a general mess of a person's life, but the trouble flows from a relatively isolated item of learned behaviour. In these

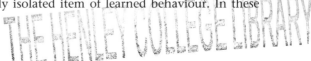

THE HENLEY COLLEGE LIBRARY

cases individuals feel their symptoms inhibit their capacity to get on with and enjoy life and, since behavioural approaches can have an ameliorating effect, their use seems appropriate here. The behaviour therapist is carrying out these patients' wishes by showing them one way to do what they want to do. In the case of anorexia nervosa, however, it would seem that there are moral and possibly legal objections that might be levelled at the use of the kind of procedures illustrated above, because the patient does not *want* the aim the therapist has in mind.

Although anorexic refusal to eat may be construed as a symptom, it is not a limited symptom in the sense that it interferes with their enjoying life. It *is* their way of living. They are people who have come to understand and experience their enjoyments, their effectiveness, their whole being, in terms of their ability to restrict and control food intake. For this reason, and unlike those who have a fear of open spaces or who want to stop smoking, those who restrict food and/or exercise, who have been made to eat, rest, gain weight, do not feel they have been liberated from a tiresome symptom. Rather they feel they have been destroyed, their will crushed by a superior force.

Legitimating coercion

It is hard to avoid the impression that behaviourism is primarily a convenient language to justify taking control by institutional coercion. What has tended to happen in wards or units where behaviour modification has been used as a policy seems to support this. Behaviour modification does not properly operate by lecturing people about what they should or ought to be doing, but by changing the reinforcements attendant on what they actually do. In practice, however, the responses of hospital and other staff can be very moralistic. Comments such as the following are not uncommon.

> You told me you'd eaten those sandwiches, and then we discovered you'd hidden them down behind the radiator. You're really deceitful, aren't you! It wasn't a very nice mess for the cleaning staff to find. I'm surprised an intelligent girl like you would do such a thing. You know you've got to eat.

Staff may be instructed not to be moralistic or judgemental. Yet such feelings nevertheless run deep, and so sensitive are sufferers, they will tune acutely to the real attitude that those around them may attempt to hide (see also Chapter 9).

Furthermore, behavioural techniques, as they are ordinarily employed in psychotherapy, do not usually involve environmental control of the order described above. Indeed it would seem to be questionable whether the behaviour-modification regimes that low-weight anorexics may be subjected to in a hospital context are compatible with behaviour theory at all. When other people take direct and total control over the minutiae of an individual's life – when they take control over their ingesting food, their access to lavatory facilities, their reading material, their contact with the outside world, and so on – it seems doubtful whether a learning theory is needed at all to explain the individual's resulting actions. Much of the original research in behaviour modification was done on the pecking responses of pigeons; but the procedure as it is used in cases of low-weight anorexia nervosa is rather more akin to taking the pigeon by the neck and shoving its beak on to the green button. It is a situation in which the recipient's personal psychology becomes irrelevant.

The apparent success of such programmes in organizing weight gain may have nothing to do with the theory of behaviourism. Looked at from a different perspective, these methods can be seen as creating very stark situations in which communication takes place in a very simple way, with the result that anorexic patients, quickly receiving the message that is being put across, manoeuvre effectively to extract themselves from that situation. This is their experience as typically reported.

> They told me I was going to have to eat 3500 calories a day. They sat there till I'd finished everything. If it wasn't food it was thick milky drinks they made me force down. Once I'd put on half a stone (3.2 kg) they let me walk to the lavatory which was down the corridor, but a nurse always had to come with me to make sure I didn't bring all the food back up. It was so humiliating. Disgusting. And I hated it. Then it began to dawn on me. The way to get out was to go along with what they wanted, and after that it wasn't too bad. I ate to get out. They were all very pleased and said how well I'd done. But as soon as I got out I got back to my routine. I lost all the weight they'd made me put on – and more.

When black-and-white thinkers meet head on

Communications of the above kind may be unambiguous, but they are not necessarily productive. In whatever context it occurs, this is a situation in which the rigid polarized thinking of the starving anorexic is being met, quite simply, with a response that is equally and oppositely rigid and polarized. It is a situation that can be parodied thus:

> *Anorexic*: Whatever you say, I *won't* eat, because that's the most important thing for me.
> *Others*: Whatever you say, you *will* eat, because that's the most important thing for us.

Except in the purely physical sense that it will avert a medical crisis, organizing the sufferers' surrender to external control is not the progress it appears. For it represents to them the shift between the absolute alternatives they face anyway – 'total control' or 'total loss of control' – extremes that are the more marked the lower their weight and the more polarized their thinking.

The use of behaviour-modification techniques or any other confrontational approach that sets up a situation in which two wills meet in opposition can effectively allow, and even enable, sufferers to hide from their problem. For it is a situation in which they can direct all their efforts into maintaining or re-establishing food/body control in the face of opposition. It provides them with an opportunity to be a success in their own terms; an opportunity to set out once again to win – and win they will. For the anorexic, or bulimic, or hardened exerciser, as for many other people, it is easier to be against something or somebody than to confront their own feelings. So they will cling all the more to their own views in opposition to 'these stupid doctors'.

> I was five and a half stone (34.9 kg) when they made me go into hospital. That was a moment of weakness. But they weren't going to make me eat. That was the one thing I was certain about. They weren't going to make me put on an ounce. They threatened and wheedled, but I knew I was right, and I was going to win . . . and it wasn't till later, a few years later I realized how frightened I was.

Not only is no change created in their situation by establishing external control. As the board game shows, sufferers will do all they can to revert to their preferred position when these controls are removed.

Anyone who thinks in terms of rigid polarities and who has a poor sense of self typically responds to coercion or persuasion with an attitude of 'no change' or 'total change'. This is a phenomenon that has been well investigated, and is acknowledged as one of the likely processes that underlies the change in attitude that takes place when people undergo dramatic religious conversions and abrupt switches in political allegiance.

Where anorexic/bulimic illness is concerned, it would seem that this pattern is reflected in the large numbers of sufferers who, having had their weight restored in hospital, are readmitted after they have successfully starved themselves yet again to the point of being severely emaciated. It would also seem to be reflected in the further numbers who, though they appear to have benefited from such treatment in that they have sustained a more viable weight and have not needed to be readmitted, have in fact slipped into using the other less visible forms of control. These are the so-called 'recovered anorexics', or 'false positives', who may or may not eventually reveal themselves as still suffering. Janet's story is by no means unusual.

> I had anorexia when I was sixteen. I know I lost a lot of weight, but it didn't last long. The doctor was very brusque and I was sent into hospital where I was drugged out of my head and fed till I weighed ten stone four (65.3 kg), which is what they said I ought to be. Then they let me out. I think I tried to get back into a routine, but I don't think I managed very well. It was easiest while I was at university. The harder I worked the more I could push it all out of the way. But after that – going without food when I could. Making myself sick. I did that till about two

years ago. I just seem to lurch from one mess to another. I thought it was because I couldn't cope, I was so inadequate I couldn't manage like everyone else. I still feel better when I'm thinner. I get nearly suicidal if I put on – well, even just a pound. It's taken me a long time to realize . . . to face the fact that . . . (pausing for some time) the anorexia's still there. I don't want to accept it. But . . . well, it is.

The use of legal powers to detain and treat the anorexic

Most of the procedures described in the present chapter can be backed by legal powers. The criteria and procedures for compulsory admission to hospital and treatment are set out in Part II of the Mental Health Act, 1983.[6]

Although this may be judged to be necessary in the interests of his/her safety, the decision for a patient to be thus detained cannot be made on the judgement of doctors alone. A patient may be detained under section 4 in the case of 'urgent necessity' for admission; under section 2 'for assessment (or for assessment followed by medical treatment)'; under section 3 where it is appropriate for the patient to receive such treatment as is likely to 'alleviate or prevent a deterioration of his condition' and this is necessary for the health and safety of the patient. But in addition to a recommendation by one medical practitioner under section 4, and recommendations by two medical practitioners under sections 2 or 3, there must also be an application by an approved social worker (ASW) or the patient's nearest relative (section 11 (1)). Either the social worker or the nearest relative has to agree that, in his or her view too, it is reasonable, given the patient's behaviour and/or circumstances, that he/she should be compulsorily detained.

Usually, where the question arises of admitting someone to hospital against their will, that person would rely on the understanding and support of parents, family and people such as a social worker or community nurse to provide a balance of opinion and defend the person's right not to be legally detained. Where anorexic nervosa/bulimia is concerned, however, this issue raises all the difficulties about the nature of the sufferer's behaviour that were set out in Chapter 1. That is, the difficulties over whether, and to what extent, their food/body control is to be considered rational, self-directed and the action of a well-functioning human being; or whether, and to what extent, it is to be considered irrational and actually out of control. As a result of the confusion that can still arise over these issues, the agreement of all parties that is required under any of the relevant sections of the Mental Health Act to admit and/or treat sufferers against their will is not in practice always forthcoming.

Meanwhile sufferers are often left to drift on with their anorexic lifestyle innocent of the possibility that they may find themselves in the position where they or their family have to defend their behaviour as rational if they are not to be legally detained in hospital against their will, and such is the nature of the condition that, by the time this situation arises, a sufferer may have alienated family members to the extent that they will be unwilling to help to defend this right. Nor do sufferers usually know that, if the Act is invoked and they are at the same time classically emaciated and have failed to keep a previous undertaking to eat and gain weight, in these circumstances they and their family are unlikely to win an appeal against the decision that has been made.

The anorexic's alienation from the medical profession

Intervention procedures such as those described above readily poison the relationship between the sufferer and members of the medical profession. This can effectively hinder their obtaining medical help, even for minor ailments or injuries.

> I'm afraid Sally won't go near a doctor for anything. She had a very bad gash on her chin when she came off her bike last summer. It really needed a couple of stitches. I suggested she saw our GP, but she got into panic about doctors dragging her into hospital. She ought to have had the right treatment. But I was worried . . . I know she didn't eat at all for several days. I kept finding food in the bin. So she's got a nasty scar, and it needn't have been so bad.

Sometimes their experience of previous 'treatment' can have been so distressing that, combined with the extreme thinking that underfeeding and weight loss bring about anyway, they can come to the point where they would rather die than succumb again to medical help. The close friend of one male anorexic gave the following account of such a situation.

> He looks dreadful. His bones are quite clearly visible and his skin is sort of hanging on them. His eyes are sunken too, and of course he's very weak. He can't get out of bed except by rolling on to the floor. He'll crawl across to his chair too, unless he thinks I'm looking, and if he thinks I am then he'll make an enormous effort to stand up first, before sitting in the chair. He absolutely refuses to entertain any idea of going into hospital. I've tried to talk to him about it, and to his mother, but she really doesn't know what to do. You see, he had a terribly bad time when he went in there before. He was sectioned, so he had to stay there. But it was a question of being strapped to a bed in a darkened room, which he found quite . . . horrific. I can understand he doesn't want to go through that again. But what's so worrying is that he's saying he'd rather die than be taken in there again.

Sufferers may not always reach this extreme. This man's weight had fallen to 52 per cent AEBW, at which level he was indeed dying. It is by no means unusual to meet more viable-weight sufferers who are not only unwilling but absolutely determined to have nothing further to do with the medical profession; as was the middle-aged woman who shuddered visibly at a counsellor's suggestion that it might be wise if her doctor checked whether her physical health had been impaired by her vomiting. Having said very little before this point, she remained entirely mute for the rest of the meeting.

In self-help groups it has been found that sufferers tend not to see medical practitioners as a source of support, comfort and caring. There is a persistent and universal undercurrent of fear associated with 'medical help', with talk about 'being locked away and fattened up'. The experience of being processed rather than understood by doctors has emerged strongly in many accounts. One study has documented the alienation of sufferers from the profession as a whole. Of members of self-help groups in one health region it was found that only one in five of group members were known to medical practitioners as being anorexia nervosa/bulimia sufferers.[7]

The doctor's point of view

Whilst it is possible to appreciate anorexic fears and anxieties, doctors have found themselves in a difficult position *vis-à-vis* such patients. Medical practitioners are not usually allowed the luxury of inaction. They are conventionally the people who 'do something' about obvious physical symptoms. Therapy that involves a gradual approach to change tends to lack the appearance of doing something. Hence doctors may feel pushed towards the more confrontational methods of dealing with the sufferer who is low weight. Instituting a refeeding programme is at least to be seen to act.

Given the unrelenting nature of this illness, and the reputation sufferers have gained for being unrewarding patients, many doctors would rather not get involved. The problem provides no opportunities for using high-technology medicine to achieve a patient's rapid cure, nor for gaining kudos this way. Hospital physicians can be more than ready to hand over any anorexic patient whose condition is not yet life-threatening; 'She needs someone to talk to' can be a dismissive phrase in such a situation. Meanwhile social workers or community psychiatric nurses who might be expected to respond are unlikely in the ordinary way to be knowledgeable enough about the illness.

Even informed and interested members of the medical profession can still find themselves in a difficult position from which to develop a cooperative approach. Not only are sufferers likely to be brought or referred for help when their weight loss is quite severe. They can also come with their resistance to change greatly increased as a consequence of the doctor having been set up as adversary. 'Seeing the doctor' is a threat that parents or a partner often use. Unless the sufferer has been his/her patient previously, the doctor is also at a disadvantage in that he/she does not begin with any kind of relationship with the sufferer – and the lower weight is, and the more polarized the thinking, the more difficult the communication that might achieve this.

Doctors can become understandably irritated at having an extremely emaciated anorexic handed on to them only after the best opportunities to build a therapeutic relationship have been allowed to slip by a counsellor who has not been aware of the need to confront the problem of falling weight. It is important for helpers of any persuasion not to have wide-ranging discussions with a sufferer whilst ignoring the fact that this person's weight is drifting downwards. We would stress that weight is not the only thing a helper will need to talk about; but there is no point in talking exclusively about other things if weight is falling rapidly to a physically dangerous level. Generally there seems little point in criticizing doctors for using draconian measures to restore sufferers' weight if they are only called upon to help at the point where urgent life-saving intervention has become necessary. A combination of late referral and high resistance to intervention of any kind can leave a doctor ultimately with no option but to adopt a purely physiological solution to the presented problem.

How much weight gain?

It is not generally realized how much of the conflict between the anorexia nervosa/bulimia sufferer and the doctor arises, not so much over the necessity of some weight gain, but over the question of the *amount* of weight gain to be achieved. Those aware of the real nature of the condition accept that a sufferer's weight has, in the end, to reach a stable, near-normal level in relation to height, age and gender (that is, a minimum of 90 per cent AEBW). This, they are aware, is intrinsic to recovery. Below this point it is weight level itself which indicates that a person cannot be counted as recovered. While there are those who feel this amount of weight restoration has to be the *first* step, others, including ourselves, believe the more modest goal of restoring weight to a level that is merely medically safe is the better first option in the long term. This is a level (75 per cent AEBW) that is considerably lower (see Chapter 11).

Children who become anorexic and emaciated present a particular problem, both because of the protracted nature of the illness and because of the permanent change to their bodies that will occur if the bones in their limbs cap before reaching their full length. So the speed of weight restoration will need to be considered in the light of possible stunting. Advisable as it is in terms of physical development, rapid refeeding will cause the same mental and emotional confusion in an anorexic child as it does in older sufferers.

Simple, yet skilled, and above all accurate explanation provided to the child will be helpful. Young people often gain the impression from doctors that they will feel better when they are refed, and are devastated when they find this is untrue. As older sufferers who have more experience of the illness know, the anorexic mindset persists beyond mere refeeding. So the attitudes and beliefs that take children into this spiral can be expected to persist, in their case too, beyond the period of weight restoration.

As the confusion which occurs during this process is an experience that is in itself a particular kind of upheaval for a child whose emotional development is halted, the possiblity of his/her feeling disturbed at a later date cannot be ruled out. At any such later point, however, a young person who is the more aware of the likely history of this unease may not only identify its source more swiftly, but connect in a way that enables any help needed then to be the more effective. To this end it may be useful if the trauma of refeeding together with the preceding time during which weight fell is conveyed to the child in terms of being a particular segment of experience.

Sufferers meanwhile who have reached adult height, who are in a starved state and whose thinking and perceptions are altered because of this, will see the demand that they should tolerate being refed in a short period of time, e.g. ten to twelve weeks, to a normal or near-normal weight as extreme and unreasonable. It is a demand that virtually guarantees non-cooperation. For they will understand it categorically as 'having to be made fat'. Although they will often resort to a strategy of compliance to escape from a situation that is so utterly intolerable, typically, outright conflict over refeeding is any sufferer's first response. It can by contrast sometimes be easier to negotiate or bargain a cooperative agreement with the person in question if the aim is only to raise weight to a medically safe level.

The problem of coping with the danger of a medical emergency at very low weight is quite different from the idea that it is therapeutically necessary to achieve a rapid restoration of weight to a normal, or near-normal level. That both may take place in hospital tends to obscure this fact.

Where weight has become dangerously low, the immediate and very practical problem will be to prevent death from starvation, and there is no doubt that medical skills can be essential in achieving this. But again doctors may believe that, for their efforts to have any lasting effect, weight must be increased to a level near normal for the sufferer's height, age and gender. It is this assumption that has tended to result in their becoming embroiled in lengthy battles with anorexic patients, and adopting methods that may be questionable.

There is a direct connection between the theory a doctor has in mind and the amount of conflict he or she experiences with such a patient. The use of the procedures we have described in this chapter is not usually motivated by the desire to be cruel or retributive towards a particularly resistant patient. Rather it is a calculated response to the problem of anorexia nervosa as doctors are led to see it.

Relatively few doctors with any experience of dealing with anorexic/bulimic patients believe weight gain alone is a cure, and those with experience are more likely to be aware of patients' feelings about its enforcement, but they may continue to insist upon it because they believe effective psychotherapy is not possible unless weight is at a near-normal level. They may believe that, despite the unpleasant experience it entails, it is the best approach they have. As it is the cause of so much trouble, it is important to consider where this conviction comes from.

The tyranny of assumptions

There seems little doubt that the assumed desirability of rapid and substantial weight restoration has been one of the consequences of an over-emphasis on sexuality. The most explicit source of this was the 'psychobiological regression' theory outlined in Chapter 2 which saw the root problem of the illness as avoidance of sexual maturity and the responsibilities of adulthood. Weight was held to be important to the sufferer because it made this avoidance possible, for sexual feelings are effectively switched off by the biological and emotional changes brought about by self-starving and weight reduction.

This focus followed from the theory of personality development that was being used. As pointed out, it was in the Freudian tradition, so placed great emphasis upon the role of sexuality in the development of a person's sense of self, particularly during the adolescent stage of development when its resurgence, together with changing social expectations, can create an identity crisis.

Sex roles

Given these two assumptions, enforced weight gain can seem logical. If weight loss enables a sufferer to avoid issues of sexuality, and if these issues are at the core of selfhood, then it would seem to follow that weight gain must be necessary before the 'real' problem can be addressed.[8] This reasoning would not have seemed so persuasive, however, nor been so widely acceptable had it not derived strong support from the female sex role stereotype, and had the majority of identified cases both in the closing decades of the nineteenth century and in the latter half of the twentieth century not been female.

The assumption that women are primarily nurturers and child rearers generally leads to their experiencing great difficulty in being taken seriously in any other way, and to their having to continue to struggle to develop their full potential as human beings. Research has shown these assumptions at work in, for instance, the quite different responses that can be observed when the behaviour of males and females becomes a matter of public concern. It has, for example, been found that, when boys and girls are arrested for similar public order offences, the investigations centre on strength and violence where boys are the offenders, and on sexual behaviour and promiscuity where the offenders are girls. As the majority of identified sufferers were underweight girls and younger women, those who made the ready assumption that anorexia nervosa was rooted in sexuality trod a familiar path. Likewise the impression that gender-role expectations lie behind the emphasis on sexuality has not been lessened by references to the physical attractiveness of anorexic patients that occur in otherwise clinical texts on the subject,[9] or by such comments as 'She's a pretty little thing' made by both male and female members of medical teams during ward rounds.

Thresholds

In terms of influence exerted over treatment programmes, there is another assumption as important as the idea that being underweight provides a way to avoid growing up and sexual maturity. This is that there is a clear weight threshold at which this effect takes place. For anyone working with such preconceptions, and focusing on the idea that there is a weight level below which sexual feelings are not experienced, the logical step was to restore a sufferer's weight to a level where these would return. Likewise, given the belief that no 'issues of significance' would emerge until this point was reached, the view was that near-normal weight might as well be achieved rapidly. This weight to be attained effectively became the target, and introduced the idea of 'the target weight'.

Those who endorsed this theory were not inclined to accept that others who provided psychotherapy while a sufferer was still below a threhold where menstruation would return were using a valid alternative approach, and an approach which had the advantage that it need not be coercive. Arguing that, if they could, underweight sufferers would always stop gaining weight as this threshold approached, these theorists believed such helpers would find themselves unwittingly collaborating with sufferers and perpetuating the illness by giving significance to their low-weight or still underweight condition and supporting them in it while they had no awareness of the 'real issues'. This illustrates the important connection there is at the level of ideas between the selection of one significant consequence of starvation and the treatment strategy of engineering very substantial increases in weight in an in-patient context.

To place such a focus on sexuality is to draw attention to the one effect of starvation about which it is plausible to think both in terms of on/off switches, and in terms of one single, clear threshold. It is also to draw attention to the one effect that also, conveniently, has an obvious physiological marker in the cessation of menstruation. At the same time it is to ignore the way blind eyes are generally turned to the endocrinological status of muscular, non-menstruating female athletes who, in spite of their amenorrhoea and rigidly controlled lifestyles, do not appear to be in receipt of accusations of avoiding maturity, sexual or otherwise.

Such selective emphasis contrasts with the whirlpool concept in the way that it sidelines or ignores the many other changes that are gradual, where steps are progressive, even though to do so creates further theoretical problems. The most obvious of these problems is that the effects of starvation on sexuality are not particularly immediate, so extra arguments are needed if this theory is to explain why anorexic food control actually begins.

Where there is self-starving and weight is falling, loss of menstruation does not occur until a weight loss of approximately 15 per cent has taken place. Yet, as indicated in Chapter 2, it is only a matter of hours before self-starving creates experiences that can be perceived as 'good', and 'virtuous'. It is only hours before 'clarity of thought' and feelings of direction and increased well-being are achieved. Rather than their being rewarding indirectly, or solely in terms of removing sexual feelings, self-starvation and over-exercising are rewarding in many direct and immediate ways. There would therefore seem to be little that justified the selective emphasis this theory placed on sexuality except the preconceptions of those who adhered to it.

The assumption was not shared by the two earliest female medical authorities on the subject, both of whom, notably, had a much wider perspective on the nature of the problem.[10] Both developed theories in which sexuality was one issue amongst many relevant to explaining the illness. Both in practice also found Freudian ideas unhelpful in the case of anorexia nervosa.

With the recognition of sexual abuse as a more widespread problem than previously had been understood, it became evident that, as in other sectors of the population, there is a proportion of those suffering anorexia nervosa/bulimia that has a history of being abused in this way. It became clear that here was specific disturbance that could precede the illness. Consequently a certain wariness developed about asserting low weight and endocrine shut-down as avoidance of sexual maturity, and its twin assumption about sufferers' sexual inexperience, which had originally accompanied this view, was forgotten.

Amidst a welter of other assumptions about the condition, these ideas concerning avoidance of adulthood persist, and exert their influence, but in a more covert manner. Hence it is possible that some now working in the field are unaware of the origins of the commitment to rapid weight gain. As they talk freely about target weight, they may not realize the antecedents of this treatment aim.

Overlooking male sufferers

The focus on teenage female sexuality, together with feminist theories, has also had direct consequences in terms of the under-recognition of anorexia nervosa/bulimia in males, and delay therefore in diagnosing the condition.

> I took my son to the doctor several times. I thought it was anorexia, but the doctor said he'd never heard of a boy with anorexia. He wouldn't listen to me. He just dismissed my worries. To him I was just an over-anxious mother. But Giles was getting thinner and thinner, assuring me he was eating when I knew he wasn't, and I didn't know what to do, or where to go.

Doctors do not readily anticipate that they will come across the illness in young men, or indeed males of any age. Nor may parents and friends necessarily appreciate that this is possible. This bias is not helpful, for greater care is often required to detect the condition in males. Menstruation is of course not a guide, and often neither is body weight. As indicated in the previous chapter, this is because males are more likely to fall into the subgroup that exercises excessively, and some physical training regimes maintain a high level of muscle bulk, even though adequacy of food intake remains marginal. As the effects of food intake that is only marginally adequate for the amount of energy being expended combine with the stress of excessive exercise, and as preoccupation with 'being good' grows, either thinness or muscle can be set in opposition to the 'badness' that is fat. Whichever 'the bad' may happen to be, there is no end, either way, to the striving against it for proof of success.

Neither the situation they are in nor the prospects for recovery of male sufferers is helped by sex-role stereotyping. Nor does it encourage helpers to concentrate on the particular needs of men. The assumption that anorexia nervosa/bulimia is a female illness is humiliating. For those males who acknowledge, if only to themselves, that they have a problem with food, weight and/or exercise, it increases feelings of worthlessness and inadequacy. It deepens the sense of shame in boys and men who are already in severe difficulty in terms of being able to value themselves.

References

1 Neuman, P. and Halvorson, P. (1983) *Anorexia Nervosa and Bulimia – A Handbook for Counselors and Therapists*. New York, NY: Van Nostrand Reinhold.
2 Dally, P. and Gomez, J. (1969) *Anorexia Nervosa*. London: Heinemann Medical Books, 115.
3 Ibid.
4 Gull, W. (1874) Anorexia Nervosa, *Transactions of the Clinical Society*, London, 7: 22–8.
5 Dally, P. and Gomez, J. (1969) op. cit., 113.
6 Gostin, L. (1983) *A Practical Guide to Mental Health Law*. London: Mind, 10–12.
7 Society for the Advancement of Research into Anorexia (Sara), Billingsthorpe, Sussex, Newsletter no. 12, April 1986.
8 Crisp, A., Norton, K.R.S., Jurczak, S., Bowyer, C. and Duncan, S. (1985) A treatment approach to anorexia nervosa – 25 years on, *Journal of Psychiatric Research*, Oxford, 19(2/3): 393–404.
9 Dally, P. and Gomez, J. (1969) op. cit., 93.
10 Bruch, H. (1974) *Eating Disorders*, London: Routledge and Kegan Paul; Palazzoli, M.S. (1974) *Self-starvation: From the Intrapsychic to the Transpersonal Approach to Anorexia Nervosa*. London: Human Context Books, Chaucer Publishing Co.

Part II

five

The picture at low weight and foundations for help

Theories of anorexia nervosa that recognize the way a person can be trapped by the effects of starvation share common ground in that they lead to the view that the condition has different stages and, more importantly, that each stage requires different responses from the helper. There is no single counselling or therapeutic approach that is appropriate or sufficient throughout. A helper must employ different skills at different times. The view is also that something very important changes when a person's weight is reduced to approximately 80 per cent AEBW.

Those led by the assumptions they make to consider anorexia nervosa as concerned essentially with sexuality see the alteration in the secretion of reproductive hormones and the falling off of sexual interest as the important change at this weight level. Returning to the whirlpool process, however, we suggest the change that is important when a person's weight has reduced to the level that is around 80 per cent AEBW is the change that is more widely relevant in that it applies to moment-by-moment living, that is the change to thinking. For every moment is affected by style of thinking, and as starvation influences thinking, it influences experience as a whole.

The move to low weight

Intellectual shut-down and food preoccupation proceed by such gradual steps, an uninformed observer may not at first appreciate that a person is shifting across a narrow band – 82–83 per cent AEBW – into a different psychological position. However, the change in thinking in *all* people that takes place as they move down into the threshold where weight is between 81–78 per cent AEBW, or 'around 80 per cent', is as noticeable to those alert to their altered state of mind as the cessation of menstruation in female sufferers is to those who focus on physical change.

Conversely, when weight is rising, the opening up of intellectual functioning can seem quite dramatic, particularly to a helper who has been working for many months or years with a sufferer whose weight has been consistently below this level.

The sufferer who is within the 81–78 per cent AEBW threshold is likely to appear distant and unreachable. Those meeting such a person, who are unaware of the reasons for his or her inaccessibility, can get drawn into seeking 'the truth' about this elusive and unfathomable, or otherwise 'interesting', individual without realizing there is less to find than there might once have been.

> I was intrigued with Bel when I first met her. We were in a first-year tutor group (at university). She was very bright, and always looked pretty good. But she was kind of mysterious. So it was somehow never possible to get through. That wasn't just my experience. I remember Tim and Candy saying that too. It was a bit of a shock when she got so thin. None of us realized till then there was anything wrong.

Nor is it only potential friends who encounter this problem, as one long-term sufferer revealed when she happened to say the Jungian psychotherapist she had been seeing had told her he found her 'a difficult client'. She was so 'inscrutable and unforthcoming'. Her weight at the time was 73 per cent AEBW. When she had begun psychoanalysis she had been about 95 per cent of her AEBW, but her weight level was already sliding downwards. The significance of the weight loss was missed by this psychotherapist.

For sufferers the 81–78 per cent AEBW threshold is important for its relevance to their understanding of self and for their understanding of the world. It is also important therefore in terms of the kind of communication that can take place with them. For this threshold includes the range of weights from the top point of which, as weight falls further, it becomes progressively more difficult to communicate in an ordinary way. It is by no means impossible to work with sufferers whose weight is within this communication threshold, or below it, but the possibility does depend upon a helper's capacity to make certain necessary efforts of imagination to 'move' to the relevant weight range, and communicate with them in terms of their particular low-weight experience of self, and world.

The task is analogous to talking to someone whose thinking is altered by the effects of alcohol or drugs. How someone sounds when body weight has reached these levels of restriction is less familiar to most people than how someone sounds when they are drunk or 'stoned'. Familiarity, however, enables the same kind of swift recognition. With some guidance, and practice, there is no reason why a helper cannot become skilled, not only in recognizing the person who is food/body controlling, but in communicating with that person when he or she is at a lower weight (see Chapter 10). It is skill in communicating that provides the way out of the dilemma described in Chapter 3, where the choices facing the helper seem to be between restoring weight in a way that is psychologically destructive or allowing sufferers to persist with a lifestyle that has the potential to destroy them physically.

Different approaches and how weight gain is implicated

To acknowledge that the experience of starvation itself makes food restriction increasingly compulsive is, in practice, compatible with two approaches to the question of weight gain in those who are less than approximately 80 per cent of their AEBW. These two approaches produce radically different experiences for the sufferer undergoing therapy. They also lead to very different ideas about who is capable of providing help.

Weight gain as a prerequisite to psychotherapy

Whatever the reason for its being favoured, in practical terms rapid weight gain usually involves bed rest to reduce the amount of energy expended, and an increased diet which is built up, within, say, three or four weeks, certainly to 3000 calories and often to as much as 4000–5000 calories a day, this latter being about twice the average calorie intake for an active adult female, calorie increases for males being commensurately greater. Sufferers' unwillingness to consume this amount of food, or to contemplate so great a weight gain at one stretch, means this treatment usually entails a considerable amount of coercion.

Because such rapid refeeding, with or without the use of medication, can cause marked physiological reactions such as oedema, gastric dilatation and, if chlorpromazine is used, epileptic fits, this is an approach that necessitates in-patient treatment. Nor would the necessary control of the patient be possible other than as an in-patient. For these reasons rapid refeeding is an approach that is beyond the capabilities of both the general practitioner and the helper without medical training. Hence to concentrate on such an approach is to put severe limits on the amount of help available.

It cannot be denied that enforcing weight gain does provide the helper with a window of opportunity as the constraints of starvation ebb, but it is an opportunity that in practice is very difficult to use to good effect. Those whose weight has been forced up by rapid refeeding usually become very unwilling to take advantage of psychotherapy where it is subsequently offered. This process of refeeding is so much a violation of their person, so great a destruction of all of their important principles, they will not tolerate further contact with those who have done this to them. In the words of one sufferer: 'You manage to get yourself out of hospital and you feel disgusting and abused, destroyed and really in a mess, and you just think, "Sod the lot of them!" '

Gradual weight gain and psychotherapy in parallel

The alternative approach is to encourage a gradual weight gain and enable sufferers to have some charge over what is happening to them. Where this approach is adopted there is the possibility of confining the use of in-patient refeeding to those whose emaciation is endangering their life, and continuing only until a medically safe weight is reached (see Chapter 11). This is usually 70 per cent or more of the average expected body weight of the person in question. For instance, a girl whose AEBW is 50.0 kg (8 st.) who has become a skeletal 28.0 kg (4 st. 7 lbs) will be restored to somewhere between 35.0 kg (5 st. 7 lbs) and 38.0 kg (6 st.) – that is, between 70 and 75 per cent AEBW – before her treatment as an outpatient will be resumed. In other cases, where weight is not so dangerously low, its increase need only take place as fast as each sufferer will allow, as the necessary therapeutic support is given.

Enabling sufferers to regulate their own weight gain means proceeding relatively slowly over a substantial period of time. It involves their first learning to hold their weight stable and then gradually gaining weight. Individual sufferers can differ in the rates at which they will allow their weight to increase, but it is not often any faster than 0.5 kg (1 lb.) a week, and is commonly much slower than this.

The aim in enabling sufferers to initiate, sustain and regulate their own weight gain is to help them to maintain some sense at least of personal autonomy. At lower weight and with non-eating central to their existence, this will necessarily involve, above all else, their own careful control of food intake. This approach, described in Part III, is in distinct contrast to approaches that contrive to overcome anorexic food restricting.

Where a gradual approach is used, help can be given on a hospital out-patient basis, or as regular individual therapy. There is no reason why, where they are adequately informed, a general practitioner or non-medical helper should not play a major role in providing support and assistance to a sufferer through the process of change. Since this draws on human skills rather than on technical ones, it is an approach that allows help potentially to be plentiful rather than rendered scarce by the need for expensive hospital units.

Different meanings of the same words

There is a difficulty in comparing these different approaches to helping a sufferer who is clearly underweight and refusing food in that the same words are used by the adherents of each, but used to convey very different meanings. The result is a conceptual confusion that can leave proponents of each school of thought unaware that they are not actually discussing the same thing, however much it may look as though they are. This is a situation that can generate more heat than light.

The use of two ideas in particular needs to be clarified. It needs to be made clear what is meant by 'opposing food control', and secondly, what is meant by 'weight gain'.

'Opposing food control'

Any therapy that recognizes starvation effects has, from the start, the eventual aim that sufferers will achieve a weight that is at least at the lower end of the range of weights that are normal for their height, age and gender. For as we have said, it is not possible to recover from anorexic/bulimic illness while remaining substantially underweight. This aim is in opposition to the desperate commitment sufferers have to maintaining control, to the moment-by-moment struggle to shore up the dyke that holds back both the need for food and the pressures to eat. But there is a great difference between approaches that use vast machinery to bulldoze the dyke and approaches that help each sufferer individually to dismantle the dyke whilst acknowledging the push of the surge tide that is hunger.

Enabling sufferers to regulate their own weight gain, and create some sense of autonomy, requires a helper to adopt a position alongside them, and to work with their anorexic values and beliefs. By sharing their perspectives a helper will find these values and beliefs are more ambivalent, even when sufferers are quite low weight, than would appear from their consistent refusal to eat.

There are, for example, some consequences of continued weight loss that anorexics/low-weight bulimics do not want, if and when, to their mind, these do become real prospects. Usually they would prefer not to fail their exams, nor lose their job. They can be very unhappy about the way their are upsetting their family, and the idea of being taken into hospital and being made to eat fills them with terror. Any sufferer would usually like to avoid some or all of these eventualities. Yet, constrained as their thinking has become as a consequence of their starved state, they can see only the alternatives of total control and thinness on one hand, and total surrender to the impulse to eat and resultant 'instant obesity' on the other. Losing control is their greatest fear. So it is that, if the price of holding on to food control happens to be losing the job, or upsetting parents or a partner then, left to themselves, this is the price they see themselves as being compelled to pay. They see no alternative to being totally in control over food and body.

In working with or alongside, rather than against, lower weight sufferers to achieve gradual change, the helper will have to make adjustments, or efforts of imagination to see the situation as they see it, and let them know clearly that their feeling of having no alternative but control is understood and appreciated. The task is then to begin to bring into focus some of the intermediate positions the anorexic mindset consistently eliminates. This is the strategy that makes the gradual dismantling of the dyke possible (see Chapter 12).

In bringing repeatedly into focus some of the consequences of continued starvation or underfeeding that are unwanted but which follow from the extreme position such restriction generates, and in assisting the sufferer in making such small changes as enable these consequences to be avoided, the helper is still opposing that sufferer. In this instance, however, the 'opposition' arises from clarifying conflicting ideas that already exist there within the sufferer. Doubtless, even in being approached this way, the sufferer can still feel opposed. For the helper will still be cueing into the supreme fear of being out of control, and awakening a great deal of anxiety and panic. This happens on the mere suggestion of the slightest move to an 'intermediate position' which, in terms of the anorexic mindset, is 'the opposite extreme'. Yet by focusing on the conflict there is in this person's own values and beliefs, and at the same time providing support in making minute changes in the direction of resolving these conflicts (see Chapter 14), the helper is offering a way out that leaves the anorexic sense of control *intact enough* for the sufferer to cope gradually with further change, and avoiding the blatant and destructive clash of wills that is usually the outcome of the approaches described in Chapter 4.

The fact is, very modest increases in the amount of food consumed at lower weights can begin to alter the situation and make possible some of the other things a sufferer would also like. They may enable the family to feel less anxious and upset. If family tension can be reduced, the relatives involved may find it easier to learn about the nature of anorexia nervosa as the problem that has beset them. Small but gradual changes may likewise enable the sufferer to keep a job, or hold on to it until it feels like the time to leave, rather than being given the sack because progressive emaciation and mental shut-down has reduced his or her competence.

'Weight' and 'weight gain'

Between the alternative approaches to therapy there are important differences as to what is meant by the term 'weight', and in the way this meaning relates to the idea of 'gaining weight'. Those adhering to the principle of rapid weight gain tend to use these words purely in terms of changes in measured body weight. If they are using them with any subtlety beyond this in the initial stages of therapy, then they fail to communicate this to the sufferer. It is this use of 'weight' that provokes such characteristic comments such as: 'They treated me just like a piece of meat. All they wanted to know was how much this piece of meat weighed, how quickly they could fatten up this carcass.'

In using a gradual approach to weight gain on the other hand we are explicitly concerned with the fact that, as a result of the way preoccupation with food is intensified by the effects of starvation, by the time a person is in the threshold band – that is 81–78 per cent AEBW – he or she will have developed a 'food control self': a self for whom weight has become crucial as one of the clearest measures of existence. This is not simply a physical measurement. It is this person's identity. 'You can't not weigh yourself. You've got to know. If you don't, you disintegrate. You just go to pieces. Terror and panic. Spinning off into terrified panic, like becoming nothing . . . nothing at all.'

It is the lack of a sense of self other than the self which is centred on the regulation and control of food, weight and eating that underlies the problem of anorexia nervosa in all its forms. Because food/body regulation and control *is* 'self', all interventions must acknowledge this and be calculated to maintain this sufficiently for a sufferer to continue to function, and interventions at lower weights are no exception. The food/body-control self needs to be nurtured until it becomes possible for the sufferer gradually to begin to be able to let that self go as it becomes replaced with a self that is more certain, that is not so absolutely dependent on control. This in our view is the task of therapy. Weight gain that is purely physical, that is not accompanied by experience that develops self in this wider sense, is no progress at all except where it is necessary to keep a person alive.

Important though it is to separate out weight as meaning 'who I am' and weight as a scale measurement, it is essential in this that the helper does not discard either meaning of the word. It is important to appreciating their position to be able to think in exactly the way sufferers think. But it is also vital not to lose sight of changes in weight. This must be kept in perspective for the sake of a sufferer's safety. So the helper must learn to process in parallel information about sufferers' experience and information about their physical state.

Low weight and non-medical help

It is not always realized that even when they are at lower weights sufferers can be helped by others who do not have medical qualifications; though an irreducible minimum of ordinary biological information will be needed about the physical aspects of the condition.[1]

The bodily signs of underfeeding in anorexia nervosa, which include emaciation and endocrinological changes (signalled in women by loss of periods – amenorrhoea), low blood pressure (hypotension), slow pulse rate (bradycardia), mauveness or blueness of hands, feet and other extremities (acrocyanosis) and an increased hair growth (lanugo) on the face and body, are all the normal adjustments of a healthy body reacting to increasingly inadequate nutrition. They are not strictly medical problems in their own right.

Monitoring physical safety

There is no need for the non-medical helper to withdraw as soon as, or just because, such physical effects develop. The process of gradual weight gain and personal change is one that is helped, overall, by human rather than technical skills. However, it is that point at which emaciation becomes physically dangerous which sets the limit for helping a low-weight anorexic without medical advice or assistance. At and below this level, where a helper is not medically trained, care of the anorexia nervosa/bulimia sufferer must be shared.

The threshold where emaciation becomes physically dangerous is reached when a person's weight falls to between 65–60 per cent of his or her AEBW or to 50 per cent of an obese original weight, whichever comes first. So the person who originally weighed 100 kg (approximately 16 st.) whose AEBW is 63.5 kg (10 st.) will already have reached a critical point when his or her weight is 50 kg (8 st.), which is the 50 per cent level. It is *this* that is the significant calculation, *not* the 41 kg (6 st. 7 lbs) that would be 65 per cent of the 63.5 kg (10 st.) AEBW.

Whatever a person's original weight, the grounds for medical concern will be much greater if this critical threshold has been reached by rapid weight loss than if weight has been low but relatively stable for some months. For when weight is lost rapidly, there is less time for the body to adapt. For instance, a drop in weight from 63.5 kg to 44.5 kg (10 st. to 7 st.) in eight months is more worrying than the loss of the same 19 kg (3 st.) over two years, followed by a stable 44.5 kg (7 st.) for a further year.

The kinds of control a sufferer has been and is currently using are also relevant to the question of physical safety. Where a helper has reason to believe body chemistry may be disturbed as a result of persistent vomiting or the use of laxatives and/or diuretics, a biochemical check on serum electrolytes is essential. A sufferer can request this from his or her general practitioner.

While appreciating anxieties about food and about weight gain, and supporting the sufferer in overcoming these, any helper, medically trained or otherwise, must be clear about his or her own anxieties concerning the sufferer's physical safety. Helpers must not only acknowledge their own fears. They must do something appropriate about them. This advice also applies to the wider circle of professionals who have marked anxieties about being able to cope with any severely underweight client at all. It will still be a useful experience to a sufferer if the professional, who for this reason is declining to take them on, makes it clear that it is his or her own worries about the illness and about low weight that has led to this decision. The straightforward statement to be made is: 'You need more help than I can or know how to give.'

It is appropriate to pass anorexics/bulimics to another source of help if the other source is seen as more likely to be able to be effective. Though a series of rejections is best avoided, it is not damaging to let sufferers know their condition has the power to cause grave anxiety. Rather, it is constructive in the long run. Solidarity in the expression of anxiety can help in getting the message through to self-starvers/exercisers who are currently certain they are perfectly well that perhaps all is not as well as they think it is (see Chapter 9).

Counsellors or therapists who do decide to help may find it essential, in order to keep a check on their own fears, to decide in advance upon the weight level below which they will not be prepared to continue without organizing medical support. This may be a level above the threshold where the person's emaciation would actually be physically dangerous, but which would be important nevertheless to ensure the helper's peace of mind. Meanwhile sufferers will need to be told about this arrangement well in advance of their reaching the stipulated level, and told repeatedly. They will need this, not as a threat or as a warning but simply as *constant, reliable* information that their position is not as sound or as well-managed and organized as they believe it is.

It goes without saying, if weight does still drop to the stated low level, then the arrangement to contact the nominated doctor must be carried out without any postponement, no matter what the sufferer says. The helper must be reliable, even if it is painful for both parties.

A stepladder for recovery

The gradual approach to weight gain follows from our view that any two-stage division into non-functioning low weight on the one side and, on the other, a more viable-looking weight where the sufferer can 'pass for normal' is a division that is too simple. It fails to acknowledge the variety of changes in experience that persistent or intermittent starvation/underfeeding bring about, and the very gradual way these changes actually take place.

Not only is there a whole variety of experiences related to restricting food. They are placed like rungs on a stepladder throughout the entire process of starvation and weight change from the initial, rapidly induced sense of euphoria to the severe breakdown of rational functioning and ability to relate to the world that occurs at very low weight. Their effects are subtle, particularly in the way they mesh with a person's values and beliefs and blend into their understanding of who he or she is. Yet unless a helper develops a facility for moving mentally into the 81–78 per cent threshold – i.e. into 'low-weight thinking' – the many subtle distinctions that there are in their behaviour and experience when sufferers are in that threshold band – and then again, below 78 per cent AEBW and well into the starvation whirlpool – will be lost to the helper's awareness. Certainly anyone who makes a basically twofold distinction in the stages of the illness, who assumes that little or nothing of any therapeutic significance can take place below a level around 80 per cent where 'all important' feelings concerning sexuality are switched off, misses a great deal that is important to the sufferer, and in consequence loses precious therapeutic opportunities.

Seeing the process of recovery as moving on the rungs of a stepladder, and a stepladder that reaches down to other threshold bands, beyond this 81–78 per cent band where thinking is first noticeably changed and the person removed into an altered psychological state, is to provide a much closer fit with the subtleties of the sufferer's experience through every stage of the condition. Nor have we found that, where weight increase is gradual, progress in gaining weight will stop as sufferers specifically approach an immediately pre-pubescent, 'phobic' level, or that there is one level only where they will 'stick', or which they will avoid reaching. There are many levels, and a wide variety of reasons too for their inability to gain further weight at these points.

For many their resistance is related to the imminent need to change to a larger size of jeans. Others have their own personal 'magic number' weight levels. These are expressed by such typical statements as: 'I can't be seven stone anything! I've *got* to stay under six stone thirteen', and 'I mustn't be 43 kilograms. I'm not going there. That's too frightening.'

It is often the case that the 0.5 kg (1 lb.) that will move the sufferer from 43.5 kg (6 st. 12 lbs) to 44 kg (6 st. 13 lbs) is the particular 0.5 kg that is most difficult to gain. These sticking points are entirely unrelated to possible menstrual thresholds. The first of the above statements, for example, was made by a sufferer who at 44 kg (6 st. 13 lbs) was only 72 per cent AEBW, and far from menstruating. The second was made by a girl who eventually revealed that the 42 kg (6 st. 9 lbs) sticking point was the highest level she had reached being refed in hospital. The reluctance of another very tall, older and normally menstruating bulimic was just as great when it came to her weight moving the 0.5 kg from 69.5 kg (10 st. 13 lbs) to 70 kg (11 st.). Her desperate comment was: 'It feels like failure to be 11 stone.' But this weight would have been 94 per cent of this young woman's AEBW – below the average weight for her height and age, but within her normal weight range.

Those sufferers who were previously overweight are usually more frightened of weight gain and will stall as a result of this particular fear. Some stick because they are comparing themselves with slender friends or sisters, or see other sufferers whose weight is low which leaves them convinced they are 'not good enough'. A mere glimpse across the street of another sufferer who looks thinner will be enough to stir this response. The low-weight sufferer who is allowing weight to increase even very gradually is someone with many fears and many anxieties, and who feels many pressures. At any time, and whatever weight has been reached, all of these can become too threatening, too over-whelming and sufficient to stop all progress in terms of further gain. It is not that sexual issues never play a part where resistance to weight gain occurs. They may. There are many ordinary anxieties and uncertainties concerning sexuality, and these may need addressing. The trauma of actual abuse is one of numbers of possible disturbances.

At any point there will be plateaux in the process of therapy, just as there are plateaux in any other process that is about learning and change. As a reflection of this a sufferer's weight can remain stable for a while, or may fall slightly. These plateaux can be temporary. There is no need to assume that they signify 'The End of Progress', but here the sufferer will need continuing help. Where sufferers learn that they can live through adjustments and changes while they are still low weight, they are more likely to manage each later adjustment with a little more confidence as weight gradually increases. This includes any adjustments at the later stage where sexual feelings will return.

Following the analogy of the stepladder it is possible to see the therapy that allows slow weight gain, and provides understanding and emotional support at each stage when weight is low, as securing the ladder's foundations, making the lowest rungs safe first, before encouraging a sufferer to climb higher. Where weight is gained gradually and sufferers also have time to encompass changes in their attitudes and beliefs about themselves, the progress they make will be their own.

Where on the other hand they feel they have been coerced into gaining weight they will see themselves as having 'weakened', or as having been taken over by a superior force. The experience will either strengthen their resistance to change as they cling more tightly to their conviction that their control is the *right* thing, or the failure they feel will plunge them into deeper despair – and the likelihood is that they will swing between these extremes.

Mapping low weight

The way an underfed person's style of thinking becomes polarized and predictable after a measurable loss of body weight makes it possible to map the area low-weight or emaciated sufferers inhabit. This not only helps others to begin to understand their world and appreciate the way they are constrained within it; it also provides a background for making the mental adjustments necessary for effective communication and care.

The single most significant piece of information a helper can have is a sufferer's current weight in relation to his or her height and age. For this gives an immediate 'map reference'. It provides the skilled helper with enough information to have a shrewd idea of how this particular sufferer is likely to be thinking and experiencing self and the world. Finally therefore we will outline a number of identifiable low-weight stages, looking at each from the point of view of physical emaciation, and patterns of thinking and experiencing.

100–85 per cent, and viable weight

Rather like the bands, or standing-waves, that show levels in a whirlpool's downward course, there are similarly distinguishable bands which mark levels in the process of emaciation (see Figure 4).

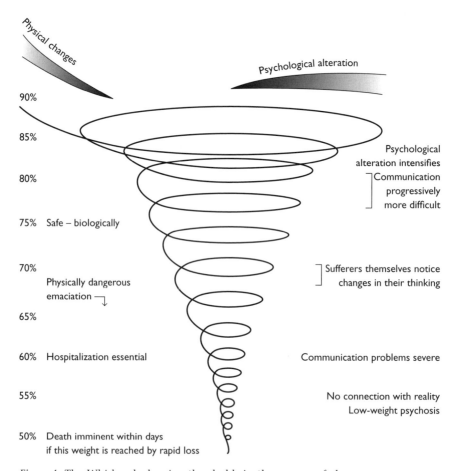

Figure 4: The Whirlpool, showing thresholds in the process of change

Sufferers may have circled, often for some time, within the pull of the whirlpool, at levels above 85 per cent AEBW, intermittently or repeatedly achieving high or euphoric states through underfeeding or food avoiding, or through exercise. During this time weight may have fluctuated, or fallen as more sustained change was obtained. Thinking will have been altered intermittently, or more permanently, depending on food intake and on the duration and intensity of exercising. From 85 per cent AEBW downwards, sufferers are within a broad 85–75 per cent AEBW 'transition' stage.

The 83–82 per cent AEBW band: alteration

Within this transition, at approximately 83–82 per cent AEBW, there is a quite narrow but significant band of weights where there is a tightening or intensifying of the whirlpool effect and sufferers shift into a permanently altered state. In terms of their altered thinking they have psychologically moved into the low-weight stage, and towards the important communication threshold which ranges from 81 to 78 per cent AEBW.

The communication threshold: 81–78 per cent AEBW

Weights between approximately 81 and 78 per cent AEBW mark the communication threshold. This is for a person whose weight has originally been about average for his or her age and height. For example, if X has an AEBW that is 60.3 kg (9 st. 7 lbs), X's thinking will be altered by the time his or her weight has fallen to 48 kg (7 st. 8 lbs), i.e. 80 per cent of X's AEBW.

From a small sample it would appear that, for obese people, if weight loss has been swift, communication difficulties occur around 80 per cent of their original obese weight. So if for the last eight years Y has been an overweight 100 kg (nearly 16 st.), and in five months this falls to 80 kg (12 st. 8 lbs), this 80 kg point is the level at which Y's thinking will be altered, even though at this level Y is still nearly 20 kg *above* his or her 60.3 kg AEBW. Both X and Y, at 80 per cent of their significant original weight, have the same altered thinking, even though at this point X is below, and Y is still considerably above, their respective AEBWs.

For those who have developed significant muscle bulk too, altered thinking can occur within their average weight range, or at levels higher than this. Meanwhile, in those who are underweight before weight loss, altered thinking occurs commensurately sooner.

Hence 'losing a stone, or a stone and a half' may be a coveted aim, but in terms of changes in attitude, behaviour and ability to communicate, the 14 to 21 lbs (6.4 to 9.5 kg) that this implies are, clearly, a crucial percentage of a person's weight. For when weight has fallen to this level, i.e. to within the 78–81 per cent communication threshold, a person is already in the low-weight stage of the illness.

Problems in communicating are already likely to have arisen by the time weight has fallen to this level. Yet as long as weight remains at or around 78–81 per cent AEBW, a sufferer's appearance is unlikely to cause adverse comment. This degree of low weight does not produce striking physical features, though menstruation in female sufferers will be slighter and/or intermittent, or may even have ceased if this amount of weight loss has been extended over some time.

Those who are close to someone who is newly anorexic may have a sense of uneasiness about the person, particularly if they are aware that a significant amount of weight has been lost, or if they know food has been cut down and they see no sign of a return to a less restricted pattern of eating despite the person in question having achieved a 'better figure' or being 'more fit'. They may have noticed changes in behaviour, such as an increasing preference for spending time alone. They may be beginning to suspect that weight is still falling, but generally the anorexic brightness, the wide-eyed appearance, alertness, enormous energy and increased activity deflect anxiety at this stage. When sufferers are with people who have not known them at a higher weight, the fashion for extreme thinness ensures that this symptom passes unnoticed, often for a long time.

It is as weight falls below the 81–78 per cent AEBW communication threshold that sufferers move into the world of extreme black-and-white thinking. Here food and not eating is their total preoccupation. They feel clear, directed and in control (see also Chapter 2).

> At last I had life organized. Things were different. I was in my own world. Controlling what I ate was everything. I weighed every bit of food; knew the exact contents of every packet; how many calories there were in half a peanut. My clothes went on in the same order. Every moment of every day was absolutely routine. (80 per cent AEBW)

Enveloped as they are in their altered state, sufferers do not know they are ill; hooked on starvation. In the early stages, far from feeling anything is amiss, they will feel better about themselves than they have done for a long time.

> I was happy all that summer. I'd lost some weight. I didn't eat much, and worked long hours at the stables. No one interfered with what I did. I just got on with it on my own. It was always easier if I didn't eat. I was happier than I'd ever been.

During the summer in question this particular girl's weight moved from 83 to 79 per cent of her AEBW.

Moving towards the classic picture: 75–69 per cent AEBW

By the time weight has fallen to 75 per cent AEBW the helper will begin to see the classic physical picture of anorexia nervosa, and this will certainly be noticeable by the time weight has dropped to 69 per cent. Sufferers at this stage will look clearly frail. Limbs will have become more stick-like. Shoulder blades, spine, cheek bones, collar bones and hip bones will be more clearly prominent and the bone structure of their hands will be quite marked. They will no longer have a healthy, or pinkish, glow, but will appear pale and sometimes rather blue. Hands, nose and other extremities will take on a bluish-mauve colour (indicating acrocyanosis) as their body attempts to conserve heat by closing down the supply of blood to its peripheries. Their skin will be dry, their nails brittle and cracked, and they will usually be cold to the touch. Their hair will be dry and brittle too, and they may by this time have a covering of downy hair, or lanugo, on other parts of the body, such as the cheeks and back, which would not normally have hair growing on them.

In any context where thinness has not only become unremarkable but is also a desirable state, even at a weight as low as 75 per cent AEBW a sufferer may be seen merely as 'rather thin'. Where it is fashionable, an over-thin girl or woman may still be seen by others as having a 'model' figure. An anorexic male may still be seen as being wiry, lithe, 'a thin, creative, arty type' or lean, and, if exercising, as working on building up muscle which is 'healthy'. Parents and friends who see a severely underweight sufferer day in and day out can become visually accustomed to this emaciation and dulled to its hazards.[2] Subjective judgements of those looking on are important in many respects, and certainly create experiences for the person who is low weight that cast doubt on the idea that help should be sought. This is a recurring problem in relation to providing help, as the following contrasting cases show.

One 18-year-old, at a weight of 75 per cent AEBW, was told by her friends, who knew she was anorexic, that she looked like a famine victim, and that she reminded them of ET (the alien from outer space in Spielberg's film of that name). This upset her. She wanted to look attractive. The experience pointed up the conflict between this desire and her wanting to stay in control, and in the event it led to her making a small step in the direction of eating just a little more. This girl had already increased her own weight slowly over approximately eight months from a low point of 68 per cent. Another 18-year-old meanwhile, at the same 75 per cent level, became confused and doubtful about whether there really was anything 'wrong' with her totally constrained anorexic lifestyle after a workmate, ignorant of the girl's difficulty with eating, assured her during a conversation at the dress shop where they both worked that she 'really had a nice figure and wasn't too fat'. The confusion this experience created was unhelpful for the girl who was at this time finding it hard to increase her food intake from 700 to 800 calories per day and was thus set to continue to lose more weight.

Should others see a sufferer's body undisguised by clothes, its thinness can arouse discomfort and disgust at this stage. But the real extent of a person's emaciation may still remain hidden by many layers of clothing. This may be a way of contriving to hide thinness, particularly where sufferers fear their control will be threatened if others find out how thin they really are; or extra clothing may be to keep them warm. For by this time the discomforts of low weight will also have intensified. They will feel continually cold and tired and the protruding bones in their buttocks will make it uncomfortable for them to sit on hard surfaces, especially in the bath. They will also become noticeably more accident prone and more irritable.

As the starvation whirlpool draws them in, the greater and more desperate their need is to sustain their control, and the more intense their fear of losing it. Against this need every other aspect of life loses significance. Work, career, education fade into the background. The ability to relate to others diminishes.

> I wanted to keep my job, or I thought I did until my boss said he couldn't keep me on any longer, then I realized I didn't care. The only thing that matters is that you don't eat. That comes before everything else. I was six stone five (40.5 kg) – i.e. 67 per cent AEBW – I had to get down to six stone (38.2 kg). It's the most important thing in your life.

On any matter concerning food, weight or eating, sufferers at this stage are absolutely rigid, stubborn, apparently self-willed and totally inflexible. Where they maintain their control they will remain unruffled, satisfied, calm, happy. When food control slips they will become very panicky, irritated, frightened, angry, filled with self-recrimination. Others receive the backlash from these mood swings, and however they might try, they are less and less able to get through to the anorexic. When control is lost, 'negative' emotions take over. At such times frustration, violent anger, fear and despair can result in more widespread destruction.

> Her behaviour is absolutely appalling and completely irrational. I don't know any other father whose 22-year-old daughter gouges the kitchen table with the bread knife, just because she has to eat. Or sits in her room banging her head against the wall.

Few appreciate the extent to which the illness can wreck family life, either by the way it erupts into physical violence to people or property, or by the suffocating tension it creates.

> The skinnier he got the more absolutely precise everything had to be. Any disruption, and he got mad. You couldn't work around him. It was all plans, organization, lists, routines. Everything predictable. Clockwork man. We tried to talk. He wouldn't have it that there was anything wrong. In the end the family just kept out of the way.

It can make any sharing difficult.

> We shared a flat with Del in the second year. We knew about her anorexia, but it was really difficult. We'd come home and find things like she'd squirted washing-up liquid over the pizza to stop herself eating it. Or else she'd eaten every single thing so you'd get back from lectures and there'd be nothing to make a meal with.

The lower weight is, the clearer it becomes that there is no engagement with what is happening. Sufferers forgetfulness will become increasingly obvious, even to themselves. The anorexic nurse on night duty for instance, who was able to remember the telephone messages she had to pass on to the day staff when her weight was 70 per cent AEBW, found, when it dropped to 66 per cent AEBW, that she could remember having a call, but could not remember what it was about. Another sufferer described herself as 'having holes in my memory'. Sufferers will become increasingly and obviously clumsy. One girl, at 71 per cent AEBW, remarked that she kept bumping into doors. Another noticed herself constantly tripping up, and 'making mistakes like pouring the boiling water over my hand instead of into the cup'.

Emaciation and danger: 68–50 per cent AEBW

From this point on, as weight continues to fall, appearance will become more skeletal. Sufferers will be physically weak and clearly accident prone. Between 68 and 63 per cent AEBW, road using becomes distinctly hazardous. At this stage a red traffic light may be seen by the anorexic driver, but it will not carry meaning.

Increasingly there will be a danger of physical collapse. The point where the condition becomes life-threatening will depend on the rate at which weight is being lost. Changes in attitude and patterns of control are important indicators of the whirlpool's gathering momentum and should not be ignored (see also Chapters 11 and 12). A weight level of 50 per cent constitutes a medical emergency. Without food at this weight the sufferer will die very soon.

By the time weight has fallen to 65 per cent AEBW the extent of emaciation will no longer be hidden easily by clothing, which will look as though it is covering a wire coat hanger rather than a body. Nevertheless, because sufferers are likely to be well covered up, it is important for a helper to be aware of the physical changes that can be seen in those parts of the body that are visible, such as hands and face, and to note the significance that increasingly prominent bone structures and the extension of bluish-mauve colouring beyond the hands to the wrists and forearms have for continuing weight loss. Shock and repulsion is the usual response of non-sufferers catching sight of such a body uncovered. For accurate information about their position, there is no substitute for weighing sufferers in minimum indoor clothing and without shoes. This stage of low weight is no exception.

Polarized thinking and the sufferer's lack of connection with the world will be quite apparent. At this weight level it will sound like 'madness'.

Anorexic: I can't stay here. I've got to go home now.
Nurse: You're dangerously thin (i.e. 59 per cent AEBW). You have to put some weight on before you can go home.
Anorexic: You're going to keep me here for ever.
Nurse: No, we don't want to keep you here for ever.
Anorexic: So I can go home now.
Nurse: No, you've got to put some weight on. You're not safe as you are. When you've put on enough to be safe, then doctor says you can go.
Anorexic: So you are keeping me here for ever.
Nurse: No, just until you've put on the weight doctor said.
Anorexic: But I'm fine, and you're keeping me in here for *nothing*!
Nurse: You look much too thin to me.
Anorexic: I'm not too thin. There's nothing wrong with me. I don't see why you should keep me here for ever. [Pause] Can I have some more of that stuff for these bedsores? [These have developed in spite of the rubber cushion she is using to protect her buttocks where her bones are sharply protruding.]

Interest in anything other than maintaining non-eating will have entirely diminished by this time.

He's terribly strong-willed about refusing to eat. But otherwise he's not interested in anything at all. He has two dogs, very beautiful red setters. He loved those dogs, even until a short while ago. I think he loved them more than anything in the world. But now there's nothing he cares about. Not even the dogs. I find that terribly alarming.

Alarm of course is entirely appropriate. This man's weight had fallen to a dangerous 55 per cent AEBW at the point when the above account was given.

Sometimes, when a person is extremely low weight, the psychological changes this produces are so bizarre it is difficult to know what psychiatric condition she or he is suffering from. Appearances may suggest the onset of an acute psychosis (a sudden break with reality). Nor is it possible to make an accurate diagnosis of such states until a certain amount of weight has been regained. This very extreme or bizarre behaviour tends to occur when the less complex brain functions begin to disappear. These are the functions, as we have said, that are concerned with memory, with controlling the movements of the body, and with being able to know where one is, or locating oneself in relation to the rest of the world. Sufferers may experience themselves at this stage as being controlled by their surroundings. They may, for example, hear physical objects demanding that they behave in a particular way, or hear voices that are continually criticizing them.

> There's no respite from these voices. It's the books on the bookshelf. They're nagging and nagging. They want to be arranged in the right order. I've got to do it. They say so. They keep on at me, criticizing all the time. Then when I've done it, they start again. Telling me I ought to have lined them up exactly with the edge of the shelf, it's not good enough otherwise.

This person is not a schizophrenic hearing voices but an example of the effect of acute starvation on top of chronic low weight. This girl had, for two days, stopped eating the small amount of stewed apple and yogurt she had previously been taking each day.

Once a diagnosis of anorexia nervosa has been made, even though such bizarre, extreme behaviour has occurred, it is still no longer necessary to consider other psychiatric diagnoses such as schizophrenia. Nor does such a psychotic episode indicate a more depressing prognosis for the anorexic illness. Sufferers who have experienced psychological change of this kind are no less likely to achieve recovery than those who have been less evidently disturbed throughout their illness.

Such experiences can be very frightening for sufferers themselves, who feel on the verge of going mad. Sometimes long-term anorexics become aware of their own individual weight levels below which they are likely to become this disturbed; when further weight loss of as little as a kilogram (one or two pounds) or an event such as the weather turning cold can bring about effects which terrify them because they feel distinctly unreal. So they may choose to eat slightly more at this point in order to avoid experiences of this kind.

The sufferer's response to the experience of starvation

Anorexia nervosa/bulimia sufferers are not always recognizable by their extreme thinness. No square but the last (i.e. death) on the games board described in Chapter 3 is stable, and as sufferers move among the other squares their weight can fluctuate dramatically. Some begin their food/body controlling career imperceptibly, maintaining themselves on the cusp of low weight (just above 83 per cent AEBW) for many months before a further drop in weight or other change in behaviour alerts others to the fact that all is not well.

Long-term or experienced sufferers who have endured many fluctuations in weight – from quite low levels to levels where weight is viable, and even to an obese weight and back again – may become aware that their thinking alters as their weight levels change, but this is unusual. Generally they will have no awareness of the way in which cognitively they become constrained. Nor when they are low weight are they able to imagine what it would be like to exist in anything other than the low-weight state they are in at that time. But the one thing they will certainly know when they have lived through any significant weight fluctuations is how very much better, and safer, they feel at low weight, and how this emotionally more comfortable state compensates for the physical discomforts of being very thin. Like the emptiness and feeling physically lighter, the perpetual feeling of coldness and tiredness are positive experiences. They spell success. They tell the sufferer she or he is in control.

> Yesterday I felt quite good. Well, not good . . . because I was feeling really cold, and sort of weak. But that was all right because that meant I hadn't given in and eaten anything. So yes, I did feel good. You know when you feel like that you can manage to get through the morning. (72 per cent AEBW)

Those who are experienced within the illness carefully manage their intake to maintain this kind of optimum 'good' feeling, but the panic and desperation that grips them at the prospect of their control being threatened is overwhelming. It is analogous to the panic of the drug addict faced with going without a fix.

> As long as you can keep the emptiness, the feeling you can float along on that 'high', then you're all right. But if you get forced to eat you're terrified. So you don't get into that situation. You avoid being anywhere you might have to eat. Then you can cope. It's your fix – you're a starvation junkie.

There may be some who would reject the idea that thinking and experiencing at low weight can be mapped because it seems depersonalizing, stripping people of their individuality. Yet the sad truth is, though it may take those who are caught up in the illness some time to realize it, as they have restricted their eating and weight has fallen, this has already happened, and very effectively. Consistent food restriction does not produce uniformity solely in terms of physical emaciation or 'slimness'. It produces psychological uniformity too. The more constrained the anorexic or indeed any other starving person is, the less variation there is in that person's actions and responses. At low weight sufferers are all much the same in the way they think, feel, relate to others and experience day-to-day events. The lower their weight, the more 'standard' they become.

Simply to thrust this information at any individual sufferer is not helpful, though. It may destroy too quickly the lifestyle that is still needed. If help can be given so sufferers can slowly learn the truth of this for themselves, the benefit in the long term will be greater and more lasting.

It is only when the stage beyond 80–83 per cent is reached, where thinking changes and awareness opens up once more, that a greater variety of ideas can begin to emerge. Difficulties will still remain, and how these come about and why they persist will be discussed in the following chapters. But the quality of communication between sufferer and helper will be different, and the possibilities for learning, both in the context of therapy and elsewhere, will be greater.

References

1 See Slade, R. (1984) *The Anorexia Nervosa Reference Book*. London: Harper and Row, 32–67.
2 Ibid., 45.

six

Viable weight and the picture that is hidden

As weight, on increasing, approaches the lower end of the 78–81 per cent AEBW communication threshold, sufferers change physically and psychologically. There is a change too in the way others respond to them.

Physically, where previously they were pallid and drawn, there will begin to be a glow in their cheeks and lips. Earlobes and fingertips will have a healthier pink colour. Although as they move towards this threshold band they may still be on the skinny side of a normal weight, the 'famine victim look' will no longer be there. Where they are seen to be eating more, relatives and friends will be reassured. Psychological changes will be noticeable, mainly in the way that communication seems more possible. For this is the level – from 75 per cent AEBW upwards – where there is change as sufferers move from the very distant, 'self-contained' state maintained below 75 per cent AEBW and begin to be more aware of, and responsive to, people and situations. They may resume school, college work or a career. So it will seem they are getting on with life.

It is at this point therefore that the people around them begin to relax and turn their attention to other matters, believing everything must now be all right. As far as the world is concerned, when a sufferer who has been below 75 per cent AEBW reaches the 78–81 per cent AEBW threshold, anorexia nervosa disappears. From the sufferer's point of view, however, this is not being better. It is being worse.

...but ever more came out by the same door as in I went

Compared with the sense of well-being achieved while weight was lower and food more restricted, their own experience, as they regain weight and move into this 'communication threshold', is disturbing. As the effects of starvation lift, feelings become stronger. Intellectually they become more alive to all the subtleties and complexities of the situations they find themselves in. They feel thrown into an overwhelming turmoil, inadequate, and utterly confused.

> When you put weight on everyone thinks you're better. My family didn't think there was any need for me to keep on seeing the therapist, so I stopped. I was still scared of putting on an ounce. I started dieting again, without letting on. It was useless, I couldn't even keep to that. It got really desperate. I was just going round in circles . . . felt suicidal. Like there's no other way out. But everyone thought I was OK . . . You can't explain the hell. You just can't explain what hell it is.

It is during this process of weight gain that sufferers relive the combinations of experiences that created their anorexic illness in the first place; so bringing to mind the quotation from the Rubayat of Omar Khayam: 'Myself when young did eagerly frequent doctor and saint, and heard great argument, about it and about: but evermore came out by the same door as in I went.'

As a consequence of there being two different sets of criteria at work over the question of 'being better', well-meant comments turn out to be destructive. Remarks about a healthier appearance that seem pleasantly accurate and conversational to the onlooker who makes them, sufferers receive in a negative way. 'You're looking better' provokes the instant thought: 'That means I'm fat.' To hear someone say they are 'looking healthy' induces immediate panic. Any comment of this kind confirms their worst fears. 'Someone's only got to say you look well, and that's it. You know you're fat. You don't eat for the rest of the week.'

This can still be the reaction after one or two, or even more years of 'improved' near-normal eating. Just a single comment to this effect, however innocent, may be all the prompting needed for someone emerging from a lower weight into this threshold to reduce food intake and spiral downwards again.

Being told they are looking well underlines the difference between other people's assumptions and sufferers' own experience. It emphasizes their separateness. Feeling more apart can reinforce the conviction that in their food control they possess something unique, something special, which in turn can vindicate their withdrawing. The greater isolation thus achieved makes it easier to re-establish or continue restricting without others criticizing or interfering. Yet, as they illustrate just how wrong *are* others' assumptions about them, remarks about their looking better also increase sufferers' despair of ever being understood.

A helper who has been suggesting that the way forward requires some weight gain may find the sufferer responding at this stage with statements such as 'You said it would be better, but nothing's changed. I've just got fat, and disgusting, and lost control.' It takes a great deal of skill on a helper's part to encourage the maintainance of this just viable weight long enough for some of the confusions to be resolved (see Chapters 13 and 14). A therapist who has a track record of having assisted in creating small increments in a sufferer's feelings of autonomy while weight was lower will have more credibility in his or her eyes at this stage, and will certainly need that credibility.

While it may be felt that there is more to life than avoiding the issue of the feelings that well-meaning comments arouse, it can nevertheless reduce the pressure on a sufferer if others refrain from remarking on increased weight, looking healthier and so on. Meanwhile a helper who knows that, as weight rises, sufferers will predictably have to cope with others' expressions of pleasure at their more healthy appearance can usefully warn them that they are likely to react with panic. The helper cannot protect them from this, but there will usually be some comfort in knowing there is someone who understands the terror, which may help stall the instant anorexic responses: 'Don't eat for the rest of the day, don't eat – ever'; 'Get rid of it'; in other words rush to vomit, rush for the laxatives, or rush to the gym.

Being invisible

Just how great the psychological discomfort is for sufferers in maintaining a weight through this threshold band – around 80 per cent AEBW – is not generally appreciated. While it is known that anorexics do not want to be 'fat' or 'heavy', what this actually means to them tends to be dismissed as 'distorted' and 'out of touch with reality'. Few know how they feel.

Helpers they meet may be professionally committed to giving much less significance to the way sufferers feel than to symptoms that are observable, and quantifiable. Yet neither professional bias nor any lack of encouragement there might be in hospitals or other institutions to giving expression to actual emotions is sufficient to explain the general lack of awareness there is about the feelings sufferers endure when weight reaches this physically more viable level. This is because, in so far as they are able to do so, sufferers themselves deliberately and systematically tidy their feelings away. By preventing them from reaching the public domain, they themselves contribute to the ignorance there is about the way they feel, and to the mystery that surrounds the illness.

They are not to blame for this, for as they endure the day-to-day experience they cannot easily stand outside it and explain it – a difficulty that will be elaborated in Chapter 8. However, the result is that when weight is low and feelings suppressed by the effects of starvation, theoreticians of all kinds rush in to fill the gap created by their inability to provide a coherent explanation for their determined food restriction. But as weight reaches this physically more viable level, and as the the mask or false front is put on, it seems there is no gap to fill. As long as weight and behaviour appear to be normal, ordinary (and working hard and going to the gym are clearly part of normality), no explanation is considered necessary. Indeed, there seems to be nothing to explain.

So well in fact do sufferers hide how they are, and how they feel, even from themselves, the way later difficulties connect with their 'former' anorexic illness becomes hidden too. More evidently problematic activities like vomiting, 'compulsive eating' or self-harming through cutting and other skin damage, increasing drug or alcohol use, or endless purchasing can seem to appear completely unrelated, entirely separate from the previous 'bit of anorexia' they had 'some time back'.

It is unfortunate too that so much becomes hidden, because invisible though they may be behind the competent, efficient, hard-working and acceptable exterior, the feelings sufferers endure when weight begins to be viable are sufficient in themselves to explain the condition. In these lies the information that makes the supreme need for food/body control intelligible.

The key to the self-starvation whirlpool

There are three underlying characteristics that are particularly marked in any sufferer. These are an intense morality, an extreme sensitivity, particularly to the needs and feelings of others, and a profound sense of worthlessness. Though descriptions may be cast in different theoretical terms, there is a large measure of agreement amongst authorities on anorexia nervosa that these are key characteristics. While they can be separately identified, however, they do not create discrete experiences. Rather they weave seamlessly together to produce an anorexic style of thinking that protects and defends against ineffectiveness, failure and overwhelming confusion, so creating the person who becomes drawn into the whirlpool of self-starvation.

It is as sufferers emerge from lower weight levels into the 78–81 per cent threshold that their morality, sensitivity and extreme sense of worthlessness can be seen more clearly.

Morality

It is out of their intense moral awareness that sufferers' strong convictions arise about what they should or should not do, how they ought or ought not to behave, even how they should or should not feel. As one girl observed: 'I'm just full of shoulds and oughts.' It is characteristic of those who become entrapped in the illness that they are completely rule-bound.

At a normal or near normal weight, when food intake is consistent and thinking no longer so directed by the polarizing effects of starvation, the 'shoulds' and 'oughts' emerge as thoroughly conflicting. Hence the complete and paralysing confusion sufferers feel about what they ought to do and how they ought to be, and their overwhelming sense of ineffectiveness.

They apply their moral rules to food, to eating, to exercising as to everything else in their life. Yet significantly, it is only where they apply them to the regimentation of food and their body that they find themselves able to be decisive. It is in the clear single-mindedness and the *lack* of conflict regarding controlling food and being active that the potential lies for the degree of control they achieve in these areas. This is how their rules also obtain an alien quality, as expressed by one sufferer who referred to the moral prescriptions she applied to herself as 'The System', and talked about what 'The System' required of her. Another observed his life was 'all down to a formula'. On this issue he was very 'decided'. 'Everything's formulaic. There's no other way.'

The extreme self-restraint and denial in relation to food and exercise is a standard that a sufferer is actively striving to maintain. This is why the behaviour does not have the passive connotation usually associated with the word 'symptom' (see Chapter 1). Although those who concentrate on physical symptoms and on the compulsive quality of behaviour can miss the moral quality there is in food/body control, for sufferers this control is an absolute, an undisputed virtuous action. It is this phenomenon that confronts the helper.

Public rules and personal rules

In moral rules there is a duality. At one and the same time they exist as important features of an individual's psychology and as public rules in the culture to which that individual belongs. In the one form they have an important function in integrating the many divergent processes in a human being and in producing coherent actions. In the other form they are one of the ways in which the group exercises control over its members.

Broadly speaking, therefore, when people subject themselves to a particular kind of rule, common sense provides two sorts of explanation. It may be sufficient to point out that many people in a certain group behave in a particular way because in the culture of that group this way of behaving is important. Sometimes, on the other hand, something about the fervour and extremity of a person's commitment to a rule, or precept, suggests it is doing some personal psychological work for them.

In the case of anorexic food and exercise rules it is probably true to say that most theorists have chosen to delve into the individual's psychology in search of an explanation. For at first sight it seems implausible that life-threatening emaciation could be compatible with the moral ideas of the sufferer's social group. Some fairly complicated theories have gained a certain credibility in this way, usually leaning on a particular view of psychological development. One of these, considered earlier, was that an ascetic lifestyle created by moral rules defends people, particularly in adolescence, from their

THE HENLEY COLLEGE LIBRARY

sexual feelings. Another was that anorexic control is typical of the kind of morality found in an early stage of cognitive development, and it is at this stage that development has been arrested. Yet, as we have shown, the extremity of their behaviour is in large part the result of starvation itself. As the whirlpool sucks a person in, it hides the extent to which public rules organize the individual's behaviour.

Initially food and body controlling is only a part of a potential sufferer's system of rules, but as calorie intake decreases and weight proceeds to fall, their moral code becomes increasingly and ultimately totally centred on restricting food. Conversely, when starvation is reversed, the pattern of beliefs and moral attitudes emerges that is characteristic of that person's background. The condition has its roots in, and draws support from, the everyday ideas of those around the sufferer. It is persistent undernutrition that pushes these familiar values to almost unrecognizable extremes.

This is not to suggest that those who are a part of the sufferer's usually middle-class and generally rather conforming social group believe those who are anorexic ought to be denying themselves food to the extent that their actions endanger their life. Rather it is to bring into focus the fact that, for reasons that will be considered in the following chapter, sufferers typically adhere very strongly to a cluster of values that centre on hard work, self-control, personal responsibility, high standards of achievement, deferred gratification, not receiving rewards that have not been *earned*, not receiving where this is not *deserved*. It is to point out too that these values and aspirations can be applied to food and body regulation as effectively as they can be applied to work, educational achievement, career success, personal relationships and of course sport, where encouragement for these values to be extended to body regulation is explicit.

It is important to appreciate the continuity there is between a sufferer's personal rules and those of his or her social group, for many problems that arise in attempting to help stem from this (see Chapter 9). Anorexics, bulimics, all those striving to get their body 'into shape' or aspiring to obtain a particular kind of shape are people who place very high value on control. So as long as they are behaving in a controlling and controlled manner, they know they have moral right on their side. It is the continuity between the sufferers' moral attitude and that of their social group or culture that again explains why the condition can be lethal.

Public rules from two sources

There are in fact two sets of rules to which the sufferer adheres. One bears the clear imprint of the female role, often in quite an extreme form. The other, following the sterner theme outlined above, comprises the values of the Protestant or 'work' ethic. These are the two sets of rules that combine and conflict to produce the sufferer's value confusion (see Chapter 8). But the imperative that feelings and emotions should be hidden belongs to both.

Worthlessness

Improbable though it might seem from the way they appear to the world and from all their apparent successes, sufferers have a deep sense of personal worthlessness. They do not value their achievements, their skills, their experiences, their feelings. They do not value themselves. Where others see them as intelligent, they see themselves merely as someone who works hard, or who has fooled the examiners. Hence comments like: 'They marked it wrong, because I know I did a rotten essay, and they gave it A minus.' Where others see them as bright, cheerful and capable, they see themselves as frauds. 'I hate it when they say how good I am. *I* know I spend all the time working in the library because if I didn't I would eat. So of course I got high grades, but it's just a lie. It's all phoney.'

Where others see them as helpful and considerate, they see themselves as someone who lets other people down. Where others see them as successful, they see themselves as total failures.

> Jay was bright, very outgoing, seemed confident. She put a tremendous amount into everything she did. She was captain of the first hockey team at school, and it was a good team. She walked into university. I think she'd have got a first if it hadn't been for this anorexia. And you say she feels a failure. I can't see that.

On standardized psychological tests designed to quantify low self-esteem, sufferers generally score as low as it is possible for these tests to measure. Statements that may be part of such tests, such as 'All in all, I am inclined to think that I am a failure', and 'I feel I do not have much to be proud of'[1] receive their strong agreement. Furthermore they will typically endorse their agreement with comments such as 'I'm not just *inclined* to think I'm a failure, I'm a total failure', and 'It's not that I don't have much to be proud of. There's *nothing* about myself I can find to be proud of.'

Helpers will not only need to be aware of, and accept, their belief that they are worthless. It also has to be understood that in the ordinary course of events this belief is unassailable. They do not just think they are bad. They know it with every fibre of their being. It is an assumption they bring to all their transactions, that permeates all relationships. Furthermore it is self-sustaining. Any view that is not consonant with the experience of self as bad, ineffectual, undeserving, is a view that is rejected. There is always some way in which any response or opinion that does not confirm or conform to this fundamental belief is nullified. Thus all praise, compliments, appreciations, love, affection is filtered out and low self-esteem remains intact. In the words of one anorexic's boyfriend:

> I can honestly tell her I think she's intelligent and attractive. I can tell her I like the way she paints, she's a good cook, loads of things I like about her. But it gets to be a kind of meaningless game. Anything I say like that just bounces off her like a brick off a dustbin. Say anything critical though, and that goes *straight* in.

While sufferers accept criticisms as fundamental truths about themselves, praise and compliments stand either as evidence that the person giving them lacks any understanding of how useless and unworthy they really are, or as transparent attempts to manipulate. The person who is saying pleasant things about the sufferer is plainly stupid, or devious and out to get something. If a helper is to have any degree of competence in their eyes, he or she will need to acknowledge how badly sufferers feel about themselves. For anyone tempted to employ easy reassurances will be dismissed as either a knave, or a fool.

The sense of extreme worthlessness is a feeling sufferers have had for a long time, well before the illness became explicit. The condition sometimes does occur after a particular, clearly unpleasant or traumatic event or episode in a person's life. Events in the closing decades of the last century revealed a far higher incidence of sexual abuse in the backgrounds of anorexia nervosa/bulimia sufferers than had previously been recognized, for instance. A similar finding emerged in relation to the backgrounds of those in counselling for their alcohol and drug addiction. Though the incidence is not without significance, it is also the case that neither among alcoholics and drug addicts nor among anorexia nervosa/bulimia sufferers is this a universal experience. There is a danger, where anorexia nervosa/bulimia is concerned, that evidence of instances of this kind of abuse can work too easily as an available 'explanation' for a condition that many find opaque. There is the further danger too, then, that it becomes another assumption that can itself be an abuse.

Often feelings of worthlessness seem to coalesce around an event that to anyone else can appear to be relatively trivial but which, to the potential sufferer, is the straw that breaks the camel's back. It is because they experience themselves as so ineffectual in every other respect that success at food/body regulation becomes so important at this point. Where it seems that everything else is going wrong, food control is the one thing that *can* be got right, the one area in which it is possible to feel effective and relatively confident. Hence the enormous relief that it is. It becomes *the* way of clawing together some sense of self-worth, of attaining some self-respect. To this extent food and body control resolve the feelings of low self-esteem.

Throwing self away

Sufferers do not value their own feelings. If they do allow them, then their rules dictate that they have to be the 'right' feelings. Since they cannot guarantee they will have the 'right' feelings, they treat feelings and emotions generally as irritating intrusions, better obliterated. 'I oughtn't to be so unhappy. I shouldn't feel like that, and I don't want to. If I can't feel positive, it's better if I don't feel anything.' This is, of course, exactly what sufferers achieve at low weight, and/or through persistent exercise or activity.

If any real feeling intrudes it will be pushed aside. If emotions are too clearly evident to be denied, they will be derided. Frustration is unnecessary, anger is wrong and unjustified, jealousy unpleasant. They have no right to feel upset. Their happiness is unwarranted, their need for comfort too demanding, their caring for others inadequate; they ought to do more. Their sense of confusion is illegitimate, just proof that they are useless and 'mentally flabby'. Whatever they sense of their self, invariably they judge it in harsh and negative terms. Because their feelings and emotions are so unacceptable, they consistently and determinedly attempt to suppress, denigrate or deny them. So they end up with a sense of being separate from them, and consequently separate from self.

Distanced though they may be from their feelings, there is little evidence to suggest that they are actively prevented from generally gaining access to them by unconscious defences. Often they are too well aware of them. Their systems of rules and their sense of worthlessness combine to create a moral resistance to acknowledging the feelings they have.

Generally it is easier to live effectively, in a self-directed and autonomous way, if feelings are treated as facts that provide basic information about oneself. Anorexia nervosa/bulimia sufferers, however, morally prohibit themselves from accepting the information that would indicate to them what they want, need, or indeed who they are. In this respect their position is analogous to that of a student who does not like a particular subject, who is convinced it is completely worthless, and so makes determined and concerted effort to pay as little attention as possible to it. As any teacher will know, such students are unlikely to have the kind of knowledge which will enable them to have the confidence to work with that subject in an effective and creative way.

Humiliation in the guise of help

The helper's task often lies not so much in enabling sufferers to become aware of their feelings as in enabling them to begin to change the way they value those feelings. How to enable such change is problematic. Simply pressing any person to express emotion, or to notice how they are feeling, is not necessarily a helpful or liberating experience for them. Convinced they do not have the 'right' feelings, it can merely bring sufferers face to face with so much of themselves that they cannot bear. They will experience the forced exposure of any feeling as humiliating and degrading, as confirming their wrongness and their inadequacy.

Hence any self-awareness technique requires careful use, particularly in the early stages of a helping relationship. Provoking more emotion than they can cope with or bringing to the surface issues they are not ready to confront will generally result in their clinging all the more desperately to food/body regulating in response to feeling out of control. In effect such techniques can produce a similar experience to the reawakening of feeling that is brought about by rapid refeeding, and reinforce the belief in the virtue of their control. As control is their haven, they will return there whenever they feel frightened, threatened, angry, desperate or otherwise unable to cope. Where they are already only intermittently in control, where the pattern is bulimic, the swinging between control and chaos will become more violent and more chaotic. These events can be prompted by very minute incidents, as their biographies bear out.

Sensitivity

The person who becomes anorexic or bulimic is highly sensitive to the feelings of others. To those who live with them, who daily come up against their intransigence over food, who endure the continual tension and disturbance this brings, this may seem implausible. Anyone who feels their family life is being, or has been, wrecked by a relative locked into food/body control, who is 'so selfish, and so completely inflexible', might be forgiven for finding the idea that this person is sensitive to other people hard to believe. Altered thinking, preoccupation with food and non-eating and desperate fear of losing control have much to do with this, of course, at low weight. Below that 83–82 per cent AEBW band where the force of the whirlpool intensifies and thinking clearly alters, sufferers are not so much selfish as entirely immersed in a 'non-food' self which they see as having to be maintained at all costs.

As they move upwards in weight, through the communication threshold, the nearer they are in approaching the 83–82 per cent band, the greater their awareness and their sensitivity will be. This, as we have said, has unbearable consequences for their feeling of being able to cope. For they pick up on the slightest atmosphere. They are alert to every resonance in the web of interaction there is in any group. They perceive individual needs, feelings and preferences with remarkable acuity. At the same time they are equally aware of and responsive to all the obligations, prohibitions, expectations and demands generated by others' needs.

Responding and responsibility

There are two aspects to sensitivity. One lies in being perceptive and aware. The other lies in responsibility. Sufferers do not distinguish between them. This is not because, at a level of ideas, they are unable to differentiate the two aspects. Their difficulty is that their moral rules will not allow them to make a distinction between being responsive and being responsible. Their belief is that they ought to be sensitively aware of others' needs and preferences and, in being aware, that they ought to respond. Low self-esteem supports and sustains this obligation: other people are more important, their needs more pressing, their preferences more significant. Hence sufferers must be sensitive to others. Their conviction is: 'My parents [partner, children, friends, colleagues, workmates, teachers] have a right to be happy. I shouldn't upset them. I should make them happy. I want to please them. I ought not to let them down.'

So convinced they are in this belief that, typically, they will see the helper – or indeed anyone – who is 'insensitive' enough to suggest otherwise as lacking standards, as being morally deficient, and therefore only to be despised.

This is a style of thinking that, as we will show in Chapter 9, serves to enable sufferers to keep their rules and beliefs intact, and to resist change. However, because they cannot allow themselves, in being aware of others' needs, not to try at least to respond, they are defenceless against others' wishes and wants and obligations, clearly stated or otherwise. They ought to comply, their feeling is they have no right to refuse. If they do refuse, or withdraw to avoid the situation, they feel deeply guilty. So they are vulnerable not only in relation to their family and friends, but potentially in relation to anyone they meet, including the would-be helper. Compliance is something they must do. Responding is the sufferer's responsibility. Characteristically they feel responsible for the whole world.

How sensitivity becomes a burden

Even if they could allow themselves the choice point that there is between being aware and actively responding, even if they were to allow themselves the possibility of not taking on a perceived need or obligation without feeling guilty and wrong, they would still have the problem of knowing whether responding was something they themselves wanted or not. For constantly dismissing their wants, needs and feelings as worthless leaves them with no clear idea of their own personal preferences.

The sense of obligation is not entirely of their own creation. There is evidence that the structure of their family is such that the sufferer has come to be the recipient of whatever obligations and expectations there may be. One authority has observed a tendency for female anorexics to come from families where there were no sons to fulfil the family's aspirations.[2] Another observation has been that the sons in families where a daughter has become anorexic have tended to be 'failures' in some way by their family's standards, which appears to have created the greater obligation for the potential anorexic to succeed.[3] Nor does there seem to be any lack of sensitivity in male sufferers to equal and opposite pressures.

So acute is their sensitivity, sufferers respond to emotional needs in others that those others fail to recognize, or are unwilling to accept, in themselves.[4]

> I ought to try for Oxford. My father would be really pleased if I went to his old university. He says he'd be happy if I got a place anywhere, but I know he'd be disappointed really about Oxford, and I don't want to disappoint him. The trouble is that Oxford doesn't combine modern languages with business studies, which is what my French teacher says would be more useful.

It is quite commonplace for people to be unaware of their real feelings, or to deny feelings they have no wish to own. But the problem for anyone who responds to emotional needs in others who are unwilling or unable to acknowledge that they have them is that, by the nature of this situation, it is not possible to check or clarify that the response is appropriate. So it is easy for the person thus responding still to feel uncertain. It is also impossible to meet everyone's needs, meet everyone's preferences and take up every obligation, implicit or explicit. Either way sensitivity becomes a burden, and one that sufferers cannot easily alleviate by exercising their own personal preferences because they are not in the habit of allowing these.

> It's a good job. I ought to feel pleased. But I don't. I only applied for it because they thought it'd be good for me. My mother's pleased. It would be selfish to spoil that for her. But I somehow resent it. But if I gave it up I'd feel guilty. The careers teacher went to a lot of trouble getting me the interview. And there were loads of other applicants who'd have been glad to have got it. Anyway, I ought to have a job. And I don't know what I'd do if I left.

External control

Though intelligent and capable of highly complex thought processes, their harsh and unrelenting moral judgements and condemnations of themselves, their deep sense of worthlessness and their extreme sensitivity leave sufferers entirely vulnerable to external control. Their experience is of being pressured, regulated, organized by the whole world. So diminished is their sense of self, other people automatically intrude; others' needs, feelings, expectations automatically become obligations. Devoid of any way of resolving the inevitable conflict these create, they feel confused and trapped, the more so the nearer they are to normal weight, because, simply, here they are the more open and the more aware.

From the point of view of psychological theories of anorexia nervosa, the sufferer's sense of being externally controlled can be misleading, for it is far more usual for external control to be associated with limited intellectual potential. There has been some debate therefore as to whether the sufferer's sensitivity to the emotional needs of others is a skill or a handicap. Since external regulation occurs quite normally in the early stages of a child's development, it has been proposed that its continued presence in people who are chronologically older is evidence that they are suffering from a conceptual handicap enduring since childhood; that their conceptual development has been arrested at this earlier stage.[5]

There is no doubt that sufferers have great difficulty in making certain distinctions which other people make more or less successfully as a matter of course in their everyday lives; as when they do not distinguish between perceiving another's need and the obligation to meet that need. The question is, however, whether their failure to make such distinctions indicates that sufferers are deficient in ideas, or whether their moral beliefs, sense of worthlessness and extreme sensitivity combine and conflict in such a way as to deny them the possibility in practice of using distinctions that, in a purely intellectual sense, they are perfectly capable of grasping.

In our view it would seem to be unnecessary to postulate conceptual deficiency in anorexia nervosa/bulimia when these three clear characteristics, that are evident as sufferers emerge from low weight, constantly combine to produce the same effect. The problem would seem to be not so much that these are people who prior to experiencing the psychological changes wrought by underfeeding had a limited conceptual capacity, but rather that they are people in whom high intelligence and extreme sensitivity create an abundance of ideas that open up innumerable possibilities for action, but action they cannot realize because their rules lead to them being unable to choose or order their priorities in terms of their own personal preferences. Thus their potential for highly complex and flexible responding is paralysed.

Hidden feelings

When weight reaches a level above the 78–81 per cent AEBW threshold, feelings are no longer so attenuated, no longer so predictably 'good', and awareness is no longer so shut down. Not only are there more feelings to hide; sufferers have to create the cover themselves, because they are no longer obliterated by effects of starvation. At low weight they were able to say truthfully that they felt fine, certainly if no more food had been eaten than the intended minute amounts.

At a viable weight, though they may feel a great deal, not only will they strive to hide their real feelings, they will strive equally to express only what they sense, or assume, will keep everyone else happy. Yet in this, as we have said, they set themselves a task at which, conscientious as they are, they can only fail, because by its nature the task is impossible.

Feeling inadequate at their failure, and totally unconfident, they hide both feelings and self. For the more hidden and private they are, the less possibility there is of anyone discovering their uselessness, and the less chance there is of disappointing and hurting others because of it. Even so, whichever way they move they are caught. If they express what they really think and feel, they might cause upset, and feel guilty, hateful and blameworthy for making others' lives a misery. If they hide their real feelings and do their best to please, they feel ungenuine, inauthentic. They see themselves as fraudulent and as liars. With no way of feeling the least bit good about themselves, remaining hidden becomes all the more imperative.

Where the imperative is thus to stay closed, to be private, then performance is all. A great deal has been made of sufferers' educational performance. They are known to be high achievers, and certainly they qualify as lawyers, doctors, teachers, architects, accountants. Nor is their ability to perform limited to these spheres. Characteristically they excel at sport, at dance, in the various arts. Theatre can supply a more than adequate mask for hiding real feelings. There are so many ways of working hard and keeping everybody happy. There are many who, as media figures, stage their successful acts and continue to do so for as long as they are physically able. The commitment that the anorexic or bulimic who is a professional performer has to pleasing his or her audience is no less great than that of the sufferer whose father asked the nurse on the ward where the girl was being refed:

> Has Dee given you one of her performances yet? She's a wonderful mimic. She's had us in stitches for hours with her impersonations. They're spot on. She can be really amusing – although she hasn't been recently . . .

People generally remain unaware of the extent of the effort sustained by sufferers to present a convincingly pleasing exterior, or how it is the nature of the condition for them to strive to make everyone happy. Others have little idea either of the extent to which they are themselves being sensitively protected from their own anxiety, pain and other uneasy realities in their lives by the anorexia nervosa/bulimia sufferer in their midst, or how much guilt and self-loathing that same sufferer feels when, 'not being sensitive enough', or 'not careful enough of others' feelings', she or he feels those efforts fail. Thus sufferers will take care of a helper's needs too, in ways so subtle the helper is never likely to know.

> They made me see a psychiatrist. He was very patient and kind. I went several times. But it didn't really get me anywhere. I pretended I felt better so's not to disappoint him. He was very nice. He didn't deserve such an awful patient as me.

While hiding feelings when weight is viable is certainly symptomatic of the problem that is still present, again the struggle to do so is entirely consistent with social and cultural values. Sufferers, male and female, are doing only what they have learned as a consequence of their having been brought up in a part of society where feelings are difficult, unacceptable, 'unnecessary trouble'. Feelings have no place. To put them aside is the proper and required thing to do, and is likely to have been so for generations.

References

1 Rosenberg, M. (1965) *Society and Adolescent Self-image*. Princeton, NJ: Princeton University Press.
2 Bruch, H. (1978) *The Golden Cage*. London: Open Books, 24–5.
3 Slade, R. (1984) *The Anorexia Nervosa Reference Book*. London: Harper and Row, 177–8.
4 Ibid., 182.
5 Bruch, H. (1974) *Eating Disorders*. London: Routledge and Kegan Paul, 51; Slade, R. (1984) op. cit., 105–9.

seven

The culture of control

To most women, at least to some extent, the feelings discussed in the previous chapter, the personal worthlessness, the feeling of moral obligation and sensitivity to the needs of others, will be familiar. Many too would be quick to point out that it is not just an anorexic's feelings that are hidden. In a context where the work women do is taken for granted, many feel they are as good as invisible.

In part, anorexia nervosa is a rather extreme example of such experiences. Many of the things sufferers say have an almost Victorian ring about them. A magazine article written at the end of the 1800s expresses sentiments that are typically those expressed by today's female anorexics and bulimics:

> The term 'lady' describes one with a gentle heart, who considers others before herself, and is, in plain words, the servant of all.
>
> The housewife who comes down to breakfast with a scowl on her brow and finds fault with everything, contriving to make husband, children, and servants thoroughly uncomfortable, and setting their teeth on edge for the day before the meal is over, is not behaving as a lady, and half the time she is aware of it. She may have received a disagreeable letter; she may have found her skirt unbrushed; she may have a headache. Why should others be made miserable on these accounts? What use have her education and comforts been to her if they have not taught her

to put small annoyances on one side and make things pleasant for all round her?[1]

The form of personal psychology that makes this one-way caring possible is also very familiar. For as we have seen, the systematic devaluation of the individual's own needs, combined with a high degree of sensitivity and awareness of others, virtually guarantees that life will be lived for other people rather than for the individual herself, or, indeed, himself. For either, it is a personal psychology that is pivotal upon low self-esteem.

The female role: only part of the explanation

It is clear, even from the earliest medical accounts appearing in England in the seventeenth and eighteenth centuries, that anorexia nervosa is not exclusively a female illness. The similarity, however, between some aspects of anorexia nervosa and the female role, together with the fact that more recently, of those recognized as sufferers, the majority have been women, has been sufficient to convince many that the female role alone explains the condition. As women in particular have been consistently subjected to the quite explicit demand to conform to changing fashions in body shape, it has been argued that the anorexic's extreme slimming is both an overconforming to the female role, and a rejection of it; as an emaciated body ceases to be a sex object.[2]

Yet anorexia nervosa is not so simple. It has not generally been found that girls or women who have become anorexia nervosa/bulimia sufferers have been restricted to the nurturant activities of the female role. Typically they have been given every encouragement to make the best of their education and to pursue a successful career. Historically, in terms of the resources made available for the development of their skills and talents, they have been found to be a markedly privileged group.

Yet with such encouragement comes another, and in many ways conflict-ing, set of values and beliefs which play just as significant a part in creating 'anorexic symptoms' as those described in the previous chapter. These are the values of the Protestant, or 'work' ethic. The connection between these and 'anorexic symptoms' can often be missed, because they are values sufferers share with many professional people, including those involved in attempting to help. Yet these are precisely the values that provide an effective training ground for the extreme self-control that marks the condition, whilst at the same time making easy conformity to the female role impossible.

The Protestant or 'work' ethic

The rules or values of the Protestant ethic – so called because it has its origins in Calvinist theology – stress the moral worth of sustained effort and productivity, of individual strength and of taking personal responsibility. The belief is that rewards must be deserved and pleasures deferred in favour of more worthwhile pursuits, and certainly deferred until they have been earned.

Judged in terms of Protestant or work ethic values, worthwhile people are those who take full responsibility for what they are, who accept the obligation to make something of themselves and believe their success and failure is largely of their own creation. Evidence of goodness and worthiness is to be seen in what a person does. Because it is an ethic of 'doing' rather than 'being', time and resources have to be used well; not frivolously wasted. Nor can goodness be a once-and-for-all achievement. There is no virtue in those who rest on their laurels. There is no level of achievement that justifies no longer trying to do still more. Those who follow these precepts are precluded from saying to themselves 'I don't have to keep on proving myself. I don't have to strive any more. I am all right just as I am.' They must always aspire further, strive for greater success. Goodness must be continually reaffirmed. The sense is: 'I know I've been busy, but I can't just give up. That's wrong. I would feel guilty. I ought to be doing something more.' So the horizon is forever retreating. There is always something else to be attained. This is the cultural theme that gives sense to the remark made by Mrs Simpson, late Duchess of Windsor and wife to the abdicated Edward VIII, that 'You can never be too rich, or too thin.'

These ideas gain much of their importance from the way they are used to justify and maintain the distribution of resources in the inherited social order. They have become the dominant ideology of industrial capitalism, an ideology which was vigorously reasserted in the closing decades of the twentieth century, during which time the number of cases of anorexia nervosa/bulimia also notably increased. For those who adhere strongly to these beliefs, life is a serious business. It is necessary to be good, to be deserving. A person must be worthy, and the certainty of this has continually to be organized. Hence spontaneity is distrusted. There is little, if any, place for fun.

Inherent in the Protestant ethic is a profound mistrust of feelings and emotions, a mistrust that goes back to its Calvinist roots. It was of the utmost importance to the early Calvinists that they 'felt God's will working within them', because this provided the only evidence that they were among the saved. To this end they believed it was essential to regulate every detail of behaviour. For it was through the minutiae of personal conduct that 'the enemy of mankind finds his way to the soul'.[3] Awareness of feelings was far from being a source of information essential to the development of selfhood. It was dangerous. To give in to emotion signified weakness, a loosening of resolve that could constitute evidence of eternal damnation. The unguarded moment was not just a lapse. It was evidence of a lost soul. Amusement and frivolity were out of the question. The devil would find work for idle hands.

Though it may be stripped of its original religious significance, the belief still persists quite strongly that giving way to feelings and emotions is a sign of personal weakness, and that such 'weakness' hinders the process of 'getting on'. It puts a brake on productivity, progress and success. In a word, emotions are an impediment to everything that is deemed essential to prove individual worthiness. Whether sufferers are female or male, their characteristic unwillingness to pay attention to these aspects of self receives strong support from beliefs that are deeply ingrained in this culture. It receives support from the legacy of Puritanism bequeathed from generation to generation. It is the Puritan attitude too that underpins the expectation, illustrated by a young girl in the following comment, that as a female her own feelings should be covered up, that her priority is to defer to the needs of others – particularly to their need for productivity, progress and success.

> You shouldn't go burdening people with the way you feel. It's so self-centred. In any case they've got more important things to do than listen to me. I used to talk to my brother till he went to college, and my parents used to get at me for that. They didn't want me upsetting him with my problems. He had exams to pass. I was stuffing all this food and vomiting and crying all over the place. It was disgusting and I hated myself. But, if I was making a mess of my life, they didn't want me wasting his time and spoiling his success. And I agree with them. It was *utterly* self-centred.

Typically, as this also demonstrates, where sufferers are accused they will side with their accusers.

The belief, characteristic of sufferers, that if they cannot have the right feelings then it is better to have none at all is strikingly reminiscent of the beliefs of the early Calvinists.

> You ought to be useful and efficient, and be really positive about things. That's what you're told, and I think that's right. So what's the point of this? What's the use of sitting here (with the helper) talking about me in this stupid, self-indulgent way? I ought to be able to do something about myself, manage on my own. It's not doing any good, feeling negative and irritable. Better to feel nothing than feel like this.

Though they do not know this in any real way at the outset when food restriction or relentless physical exertion is first bringing about feelings of euphoria, being 'free of all but good feelings' is the state that physical and psychological emaciation create. In this light, their unwillingness to 'recover' becomes the more understandable. For what they recover, when they regain weight or fail to sustain the levels of physical exertion they have attained, are the undesirable and untrustworthy feelings they *ought* not to have. They recover the feelings that they *ought* to be able to subdue, or banish.

It is the Protestant or work ethic that is largely the source of the deliberate, active, striving quality that is fundamental to the anorexic attitude, or mindset, discussed in Chapter 1 – the attitude that is a defining characteristic of the condition and crucial to its diagnosis.

The 'therapy culture' in conflict with the sufferer's culture

The idea that feelings and emotions are the core information an individual needs to be effective, and that they are integral to a sense of 'knowing who I am' is fundamental to many therapeutic approaches (see Chapter 14) but it is an idea that will seem implausible to anorexia nervosa/bulimia sufferers convinced that experience of this kind is untrustworthy, unnecessary and dangerous. Thus helpers who approach them with the simple belief that focusing upon, and expressing, feeling and emotion are positive activities and a source of existential strength will find there is a crucial difference of understanding between sufferers and themselves.

A helper who attempts to encourage sufferers to focus upon themselves, to accept their emotional experience as valuable, will not be preaching to the converted in the sense of working with people who already believe in this aspect of the therapeutic process, or who are already generally familiar with this, as a way of life anyway. The helper will be attempting rather to communicate a way of being to people who, particularly if they are successful self-starvers or effective in their dedication to a sport, will believe they ought not to be converted. He or she will be attempting to convey a notion that will be construed not as a way forward but as subversive, or sinful. Any helper who remains unaware of this particular pitfall runs the risk of being swiftly dismissed as misguided, someone who does not have the right ideas and beliefs, and sufferers have cultural right on their side on this.

Since helper and controlling anorexic are making opposing metaphysical statements, conversations between them reach unreconcilable end-game moves very rapidly. This is particularly important at the stage of the initial meeting between the sufferer and a potential helper. The very nature of the sufferer's moral attitude is likely to create a clash of cultures rather than a cooperative venture. It is sufficient to prevent therapy getting started. Rather than becoming moral advocate, someone whose suggestions the sufferer should try to obey, whose needs and demands the sufferer ought to try to fulfil, the helper becomes devil's disciple, the person the sufferer should not allow to break her, or his, will.

Their own characteristic solution to their problem, if they allow that they have a problem, is to work harder, produce more, be more organized, more independent, more in control and to stop wasting time, which often also means 'stop wasting time over help'. They will believe there is nothing wrong with them that 'a good slapping' or 'a really good telling off' would not put right. Alternatively, all they see as wrong is that they have not demonstrated enough willpower, or exercised enough self-discipline, to achieve the necessary 'goodness'. Thus, typically, they will maintain: 'I doubt there really is an illness called anorexia nervosa. I don't believe it exists. There's nothing wrong with me that enough hard work wouldn't put right.'

If, on the other hand, they have reached the stage where they can acknowledge that they have a problem, this often translates into the belief that they have not tried hard enough to be 'normal'. Being normal – or better, or cured – is thus the particular goal they now feel they *ought* to have achieved, but do not know how. However, since their view in any case is that 'help is for weak people', they also ought to be able to manage, be responsible, independent. They should be able to 'get on' and get better on their own.

Social standing

Though they permeate the culture, Protestant or work ethic values are particularly congenial to those who are relatively privileged, especially if they feel their higher incomes and social standing are the just reward of their effort, industriousness and commitment. One of the most consistent socio-logical findings has been that anorexic/bulimic illness occurs predominantly in relatively privileged sections of the community. Where upper- or middle-class status is not conferred explicitly by wealth or 'father's occupation', families have been found typically to be aspirant, either working to achieve higher social standing, or struggling to regain status that has been lost.[4] They may also aspire in terms of being principled in living the way life ought to be lived, and so committed to an 'alternative' lifestyle, striving within a 'new' ethic.

It might, of course, be argued that these values and attitudes, rooted in Calvinist theology as they may be, are so widespread in this social group that they could not possibly play such a significant role in creating and maintaining such an illness. It might be argued that compared with the very many people who adhere to them, cases of anorexia nervosa at least in its classic form where emaciation is fully developed are still, relatively speaking, few. But while the ethos is important, it is not so much from its existence that the condition develops as from the intense commitment to these specific values that is found in sufferers' families. Moreover, the pattern of circumstances that creates this commitment is present so often in their backgrounds that it is possible to make certain generalizations about them with a degree of confidence.

Circumstances that intensify commitment to the work ethic

Characteristically sufferers come from families that are strongly committed to the work ethic, families where there is the often quite intense attitude that, whatever is undertaken, it must be done from the highest possible motives; there must be purity in the cause. Everything that is done must be solid in this way; or '*sound*'. Their adherence to these beliefs is apparent in the way that many of their members have lived their lives, not only in the present generation but in previous generations too.

Social mobility

Sufferers' families are typically those in which major change in social position has been experienced. Their background or history is one in which social mobility – upwards or downwards – has played, or is playing, a significant part. Amongst the biographies of their parents, grandparents and great-grandparents there are lives that read like classic tales of rags to riches. But the riches, in terms of enhanced social and economic status, will have been achieved as a result of thrift, diligence, frugality, sobriety and individual striving. These are the stories of the miners' sons who became university professors, and the labourers' sons who became doctors and preachers. Equally there are stories where forebears went from riches to rags: biographies that indicate that the struggle is, or has been, to regain lost status and lost respectability. These are the stories of the shame of fortunes lost through gambling, through drink, or through family upheaval of an otherwise 'unacceptable' kind, as, for instance, through bankruptcy, or the 'unwise' marriage of the middle- or upper-class girl to the lower-class boy, or of the middle- or upper-class boy to the lower-class girl.

Movement from one social class or position to another is known to be a source of stress. It is a change that involves making adjustments for differences in conventions of behaviour, for altered expectations and new patterns of consumption. Those who are upwardly mobile tend to find themselves estranged from the people they grew up with, but they will tend to feel anxious and ill at ease in the social class they have attained. Downward mobility, meanwhile, brings disappointed expectations and the need for adjustments that are often painful. Those who find themselves unable to keep up their social status attempt to do so by clinging to the 'old rules', but without the resources to do so easily.

> We never had any money. That's what we were always told. And it was a real struggle. But we were all sent to expensive private schools. All four of us. We had to be properly educated. That was essential, no matter what we went without. Of course, it showed at school. We were never like the others.

Those whose improved social status is recently attained have the task of properly fitting to new and unfamiliar rules and expectations of what is right, what is the accepted, or 'done' thing. Migration from one part of the country to another creates the same kind of task, as it does from one country to another. Both kinds of geographical move are often to be found in sufferers' backgrounds.

Social mobility of whatever kind increases sensitivity to outside opinion. Sufferers' families will often have led very private lives. Children's friends are likely to have been vetted. There will have been the preference for outsiders to arrange to call beforehand. Social occasions are likely to have been controlled, and managed, rather than permitting of any casual or spontaneous 'dropping in'.

The status that has been achieved, or clung on to, in these families is usually reflected in the present generation in the careers and occupations of the sufferer's own parents. One or both parents are likely to occupy professional positions, or be employed at a high scientific or managerial level, or run their own businesses. Significantly they will be working as lecturers, ministers of religion, doctors, consultants, teachers, judges, social workers, policemen, lawyers and so on, and thus are engaged in occupations which explicitly require the application of Protestant or work ethic values as a workaday task.

'Missing' people

A close look at a sufferer's family history usually reveals that in previous generations there has also been a striking number of people missing, either because they died or were divorced, or because, for some reason or other, they disappeared and deserted the family. In other words, there is a high probability that one or both of a sufferer's parents – and if not parents, grandparents – were thus deprived of a parent, or in some cases both parents, often before the age of 14.[5] This loss will characteristically have been endured, like every other adversity, in an ethos of emotional control, where the rule is that feelings ought not to exist. Whatever the event, grief or anger, confusion, dismay, it must not show.

Apart from people actually missing, sufferers' family trees also characteristically reveal a high incidence of people who were handicapped, either through physical illness or injury, or as a result of their being alcoholic – so absent in this sense. It appears twice as likely that these members will have been male. The corollary to this is the 'strong' grandmother, or great-grandmother, who recurs in the family folklore, the woman, that is, who might otherwise be understood as emotionally undernourished and seeing herself as having no choice but to take control, to be independent and successful and by sheer hard work and determination improve her lot for herself and for her children. Thus success or survival has very often been achieved against great odds. It is also clear that whatever the adversity, and in whatever generation, the response has been for this family to have drawn itself in more tightly and demanded that its members exercise even greater virtue, greater loyalty and commitment, greater self-control.

The transmission of values

While sufferers grow up in an ethos of strong Protestant ethic values, the way these are transmitted by each parent is complicated by gender roles and their parents' own experience of these roles. Their mothers are likely to have been ambivalent about encouraging a daughter to adopt the straightforward, traditionally nurturant female role, since their own experience, and the experience of their mothers and grandmothers before them, is likely to have shown them that to survive, a woman needs to be more independent than this. Within the context of 'death, desertion and disablement' in the family's history[6] there tends to be a feeling amongst sufferers' mothers that other people, and men in particular, are not to be trusted. Self-reliance is essential. Their daughters certainly should be able to 'stand on their own two feet'. These mothers are likely to have alternated between encouraging independence in their daughters, and so expecting high standards of performance at school and work, and encouraging them to be nurturant to other family members, and so expecting extreme loyalty, caring and sensitivity within the family, while being cautious of their contacts with the outside world.

The vulnerability of their children will generally have evoked painful memories of their own unmet emotional needs. Their sense of being unable to cope with their own feelings will not only have led to their rejecting emotional neediness in their child, but will also have vindicated their belief in the desirability of self-control. The stiff upper lip, carefully maintained by the emotionally controlled parent, will scarcely give permission for the child's expression of feeling, for this threatens to disrupt rational order and arouse fears of yielding to primitive chaos.

It has been argued that this alternation between encouragement of nurturance and rejection of feelings is the crucial experience of all female children in a society in which it is women's role to nurture others without themselves being nurtured.[7] While this may or may not be true for women in general, there is certainly every reason to believe from what is known about the backgrounds of girls and women who are anorexia nervosa/bulimia sufferers that this is their particular experience.

Their fathers meanwhile are equally likely to have been ambivalent about expecting their daughters to adopt the conventional female role. Sufferers' fathers are often absent from the day-to-day life of the family, both physically absent, as a result of working abroad or many miles away, and emotionally distant. Typically they are austere, demanding, engrossed in their work, judgemental, stern in their criticism: 'I came home from school and said I'd got 95 per cent in a physics exam, and all I got from him was, "Hm, and what happened to the other 5 per cent?"'

They want competence, achievement and success from their children. They will usually have given their daughters no encouragement to be frivolous or feminine. Intellectual prowess is acceptable. Stupidity is not. Physical exercise and sport are also important avenues for achievement and prowess in these families. Not infrequently sufferers' have felt that it is only through academic achievement or skill at sport that they can relate to their fathers.

> Try as I might I couldn't get through to my father. He was so distant and unemotional, and the only thing he was interested in was sport. I wanted him to approve of me. I was brilliant at sport. I thought if I was good at that he might like me, or at least take some notice of me – you know? Give me some recognition and approval.

Sufferers' families are also likely to be facing stress in the present time. Where an economy is in relative decline there are generally greater odds against achievement and success than where it is expanding. Where the nature of production changes, or there is alteration to established methods or other previous certainties in the workplace, the demand is for adjustment. A parent may suffer redundancy, or have to cope with the change created by early retirement. A family business may be verging on bankruptcy. Given the family's marginal status that follows from its recent social mobility, experiences such as these will tend to re-echo the insecurity of earlier generations. Yet committed as they are to their belief in the value of hard work, consistent striving, personal responsibility, its members have the greatest difficulty in adjusting their expectations to economic situations in which the chances of 'appropriate' and 'just' rewards are less certain, or are actually ebbing away. They still respond to adversity by striving harder, holding fast to their aspirations. Thus there is the feeling about the sufferer's family that in some way its members are clinging to their status or their position in life by their fingernails. Hence the importance of education and career success.

Creating the symptoms

It is in the ethos the work ethic creates that the sufferer learns many of the forms of self-control that one day will be called symptoms of anorexia nervosa. This ethos is one that influences not only body regulation, but also the extremity to which the regulation is carried.

The moralization of body regulation

The imperatives of this ethic are quite routinely applied to the areas of food and body regulation. An anthropologist looking at our society from the outside might well conclude from clear evidence that we believe that by controlling our bodies we can make ourselves morally good. This is explicit in public policy on deviant behaviour. The penal innovation of the 'short, sharp shock' rested on the belief that harsh and persistent routines of physical exercise would bring about moral improvement. A sense of moral rectitude has never been far away from ideas of muscular fitness. It is not difficult to obtain a sense of being bad, or sinful, for not 'working' our bodies. There is moral failure in not going to the gym as there is in not going to church. There are probably few who do not respond, at least sometimes, to a moral lapse or degrading experience by reasserting or establishing some kind of body regulation to make themselves 'better'.

It is important for any helper to note the extent to which body regulation is offered either as preparation for a career or as a career in itself, at all levels of education. Many schools, colleges and other high-status institutions place great and increasing emphasis on the value of sport, where the connection between self-regulation and moral goodness is quite explicit. With the stress that is placed on playing hard, and developing ultimate physical control, sport appears to have become a secular vehicle for beliefs that originally had religious significance within the Protestant ethic. Performance in sport is held up as the epitome of excellence, with enthusiasm and commitment culminating in festivals like the Olympic Games where its values are ritually celebrated, and without reservation. It is the more influential too because of the unthinking support it obtains from those who hold powerful positions in education, industry and government.

The great majority of those who become anorexic/bulimic have not only been very good at some form of sport before their emaciation became noticeable. They have also been very committed. In the initial stages of the illness there is often little to differentiate the person who is on the way to becoming anorexic or bulimic from the person who will one day run or swim for his or her country. Because of this many sufferers pass through the early stages of the illness with the full cooperation of their parents and their schools. It is no accident that the highest incidence of anorexia nervosa/bulimia occurs not only in dance schools and schools of drama and modelling but in sports colleges, and in university and college departments that offer sport as part of their higher education curriculum.

How moral imperatives fit extreme actions

We saw in Chapter 2 how continued underfeeding results in extreme or polarized thinking. Yet, while undernutrition pushes a person's values to absolute positions, it becomes clear that, rather than protecting against extremes, the moral imperatives that derive from the Protestant or work ethic can be entirely compatible with them as ever more diligence, ever fiercer striving is required to reach new and higher goals. This goes a long way towards hiding the anorexic nature of the body regulation that is taking place, particularly when the illness is in its very initial stage.

There are individuals whose moral codes are moderate, flexible, and tentative; but when values are used to create or to restore social order – as work-ethic values notably are used – they seldom have these qualities. Hence it is quite usual for moral views to be expressed in extreme black-and-white, all-or-nothing terms. It is not considered enough for children to be encouraged to be 'moderately good', or 'good enough'. The demand is generally that they should be 'good', or 'very good'. The message all too often is: 'Your best isn't good enough. Try harder!' – a message epitomized by the official motto of one private school: 'Beyond the best there is a better.'

If there is any adversity it must be the sufferer's own fault, and to avoid blame, it must be met by a redoubling of effort. It is wrong to give in. No achievements, however great, are as valuable or worthwhile as those which we have had to strive for, and feeling the pain of it is proof of striving. It is knowledge that goodness has been achieved. Hence there is no gain without pain. These are the ideas, reiterated in countless pep talks, that find their echo in what is sometimes referred to as the psychopathology of anorexia nervosa. Nor is it any wonder that bulimic or 'out of control' aspects of the problem become overlooked, separated, cast aside – an uncomfortable counterpart to the major theme.

The competitiveness that is engendered in this ethos meshes with polarized anorexic thinking. It is essential to be 'absolute best'. Sufferers must be outright winners. Without winning they are nothing. If they do not win, they totally fail. Characteristically they are highly competitive. They compete against each other, and against themselves.

> I got down to six and a half stone (41.3 kg) last time, and I've got this thing in my head now: I've been six and a half stone before, so I've got to get it lower this time. Otherwise I might as well be second man on the moon, and that's not good enough. If I'm not first, I'm nowhere.

Hence the sufferer is the person who has the determination and the will-power to go on long after others have fallen by the wayside. Yet in striving to win, it is the very self that is at stake. Even as she was being helped to her hospital bed, one skeletal young woman said desperately: 'They're not going to make me eat. They can't. I won't let them. I haven't given in so far. They're not going to make me give in now. I'm not giving in for anyone. I've got to beat my personal best.' The same aspiration drives the muscle-bound, food-controlling, male cyclist who each day goes out on the road for increasing lengths of time.

The assumption that moral principles work in opposition to basic and unrestrained impulses leads to their being expressed in extreme terms. Otherwise the fear is that these principles will not be strong enough to hold such impulses in check. But people who are vulnerable to anorexic illness, who do not have a firm sense of self, are in danger of taking these precepts literally. They can come to construe moral principles not as a restraint on what they are, but as a prescription for what they might become.

> The feeling of guilt and intense self-loathing just grew and grew. I had this private vision of being wrong in every way – physically, emotionally and intellectually – as a whole person I was wrong in every situation. I never got over the sense that, although I'd got an A for the work I'd done today, I might not get an A tomorrow. So I had to do the same tomorrow – and there was no security that I could do the same. Then there came this enlightenment. It gradually became apparent that control was the answer: control that self to make it appear as it *ought* to be, by working hard, being useful, being kind and helpful. The only way forward seemed to be to *do* things to change what I was. But I only got temporary relief by succeeding. There were some rewards, but never enough to make it more than temporary. And controlling what I ate was just the last manifestation of what I had been doing all along.

Rather like the requirements for becoming a lawyer or a doctor, an accountant or an international athlete, being anorexic/bulimic demands a great investment of time and effort, and considerable discipline. Driven though their choice is by the deep sense of being unable to achieve in any other way, it is not unusual to hear sufferers, particularly those who are 'successful' as food restricters, speak of their preoccupation with food and body control as a chosen career. 'When I left school, I only had two ambitions. One was to write, and the other was to be thin. I became thin – but I never managed to write.'

Such striving does not necessarily guarantee the good behaviour, or the academic excellence, that has been suggested as marking out the anorexia nervosa sufferer. Though she may be female, a sufferer is not always identifiable as 'the best little girl in the world', as illustrated here.

> I got into a load of trouble at school. If I was with one lot it wasn't too bad. They never went too far, so I'd go that much further, and I could do that without getting clobbered. But when I was with the others, they always had to go over the top. I still had to go one further. I had to be the best at being worst.

The outcome of this girl's anorexic striving would also seem to indicate a link to behaviour patterns in young males.

Moving the spotlight away from women

In discussions of anorexia nervosa it is commonplace to point to the pressures exerted by the fashion industry upon women, and there is no doubt that the female image as projected by the media does have influence. With the connotations it carries of cheap, commercial exploitation, the fashion industry is also an easy target for blame. As such it tends to draw attention away from the part played by moral pressures exerted by the work ethic. There are, in our society, underlying assumptions about femininity, about the female role and about the basic irrelevance of women where 'matters of consequence' are concerned. These are highlighted by the fact that it is easier to advance an explanation of this illness entirely in terms of the frivolities of fashion, cosmetics and manipulation by the media than to indicate the relevance of the stress created for serious-minded young women by, for instance, any significant ebbing away of opportunities for success in middle-class occupations that there might be during periods of economic change. The playing down of moral pressures in relation to women also diminishes the perceived role of these same pressures on men and boys.[8]

Worst little boys – or not

There is a standard notion that boys will be bad. It is well known that being 'best at being worst' is a way for males, particularly young males, to achieve status. Yet it is a notion that can seriously sideline the possibility that the mindset that generates 'the worst little boy in the world' is a mindset that may develop out of anorexic deprivation. As they strive to be best at being worst, as they hold fast to their anti-hero status, the moral nature of their striving – the fact that 'badness' has to be worked at too and its achievement demonstrated – hides this possible source of their extreme thinking.

Men know they must strive and they must achieve. In terms of the requirements of the Protestant or work ethic, and the requirements of the male role, they know they have to prove themselves. All the worse for them, then, if they do not strive, if they do not achieve, if they cannot take their stand, if they do not show they are tough, if they do not demonstrate their success; the greater shame on them, and the greater the devaluation of their self.

They have the burden of having to fulfil these expectations, prove their relevance, show they are worthwhile as men, and sustain it. For the ethic is one which requires continual evidence of their adequacy. Best at being worst or best at being best, either way they know they are only as good as their last achievement. There is always another to be attained. So men banish feelings with a vengeance and get on with the job.

There are times when events allow fulfilment of role requirements, and times when they do not. Where straightforward achievement and anticipation of success in the workplace become uncertain, the pressure on males to strive, their particular obligation to make something of themselves, transfers to other activities, notably to sport. As they strive to achieve in sport, or physical fitness, their body can become a measure of their success. There is nothing in their system of values to serve as a brake on their physical activity or on their aspirations to achieve. There is nothing to prevent them moving to extremes as they crave certainty in their goals.

It is no real surprise then to find that anorexia nervosa/bulimia sufferers are by no means absent among the males who are lone cyclists, who spend hours running, swimming, weight training, putting in time at the gym. It is no surprise to find that these men have 'got to be lean'; that for them too 'fat is the enemy'; that they are concerned with 'dietary vigilance'; that they believe in endurance, in pushing themselves harder. It is no surprise to find that they too calculate calories, use diuretics to attain their particular food and body controlling aims, and perceive pain as proof of achievement; again, evidence that they are on the right road. These are men who just know they have 'got to strive, and must keep going', and, as their body is their measure of their achievement, it has to be fit, hard, trimmed, in control.

There is no surprise either in finding that their endorsement of physical activity has moral fervour. Their best is never good enough. The horizon here too is ever-retreating: 'Other people at the gym notice the results before me. But I'm very critical of myself. I'm never happy with how I look.' As they marshal information about food substances, about weight, about male physiology, as they compute every detail relevant to obtaining their goal, their mindset is no different from that of any other anorexic. Best is never good enough. An extreme example of this can be found among body builders.

I read up on new training methods, and tried just about every diet and natural supplement known to man. I seemed to train harder than anybody I knew, but was at a sticking point. I longed for the type of physique you saw in the magazines. Then I heard about steroids . . . after seven years my body was primed; steroids were just the missing link in the chain. [9]

Where the board game is concerned it is perhaps debatable whether exercisers at this point are to be seen as still in Square 2, or as having moved to Square 5. Either way, they are exercising and eating the 'right' food. Even as these food/body controllers are using 'performance-enhancing' drugs, they are, as the comment from Keith, a strength trainer, illuminates, definitely seen as being on the 'good' side of the moral divide: ' . . . the people who use these drugs are exercising regularly, have a good diet, don't drink or smoke and are doing themselves no more harm than the average Brit who smokes, drinks and eats junk food.' [10]

People may become informed about the changes in brain chemistry that take place with strenuous exercise and produce a sense of well-being. But as altered consciousness through fasting is seen in esoteric subcultures as a desired state, so in a sports subculture imbued with an ethic of striving, the endorphin high is advertised as 'positive', and sold as 'proof' of achievement. As, in validating food/body control, the vocabulary of biochemisty is subsumed, so 'sport' harnesses science to tag evidence of moral adequacy and personal goodness.

References

1 *The Lady*, 1 October 1896, in London, quoted in *The Lady*, 12 September 1985.
2 Orbach, S. (1978) *Fat is a Feminist Issue*. London: Hamlyn, 165.
3 Tawney, R.H. (1926) *Religion and the Rise of Capitalism*. Harmondsworth: Pelican, 124.
4 Slade, R. (1984) *The Anorexia Nervosa Reference Book*. London: Harper and Row, 119–21.
5 Ibid., 121–2.
6 Ibid., 125.
7 Eichenbaum, L. and Orbach, S. (1982) *Outside In Inside Out*. Harmondsworth: Pelican, 27–47.
8 Slade, R. (1984) op. cit., 197–9.
9 Shabi, R. (2001) *Guardian* Weekend, 21 July, 22.
10 Carlowe, J. (2001) *Observer* Magazine, 23 September, 4–6.

eight

On becoming a person: through food control

For the many reasons described in the preceding chapters anorexia nervosa/ bulimia sufferers constantly devalue themselves and pay little, if any, attention to their own emotional needs. Consequently they have little idea of what they want, and little idea of who they are. They are very uncertain in themselves. But they have discovered, usually inadvertently, what a superb solution food and body regulation provide to the problem of feeling so unsure, and how well it fits crucial moral standards and their important and closely held aspirations.

Being . . .

In the process of this discovery their ability to restrict food has become not just the difference between being good or being bad, being a success or a failure. It has become the difference between being and not being. It has become their solution to being at all.

This is how it is that sufferers feel they exist as long as they are in control of their food and body, and that, if their control goes, the sense of who they are disappears as well. It is this experience of the certainty of 'self' residing in food and body control that is the source of statements like 'If I don't control my food, I'm nothing. That's the only way I can get anything done', and

'I'm all right when I'm not eating. I have to have that organized. If I don't, I just go to pieces. Everything disintegrates (i.e. I disintegrate)', and 'I must get to the gym, then I've got myself sorted. If anything stops my training routines, I just cut out food. I've got to know where I am.' It is food and body control thus that is their core, that sustains them, that provides direction. The use of 'I', and 'I am', and the value they give these words is entirely bound up with what they see as success or failure in that arena, which then reflects on every other aspect of their life. This is the centrality that is evident in the characteristic 'anorexic attitude' (see Chapter 1).

'An anorexic is not simply a girl or young woman who doesn't eat and can be considered cured when she resumes eating. She is someone who doesn't know how to live except by non-eating'[1] is a statement that can be safely expanded to include older women, men and boys. Not knowing how to live 'except by non-eating' is not, nor ever has been, the preserve only of those who are young and female. Comments from females and males alike, such as 'Whatever I eat – it's a total must, I've got to be able to burn it', and 'I'm a body trainer. It's justified eating – that's what I do. It's my life' are made by who those do not know how to live except by physical exertion.

On becoming bulimic, sufferers are on a more obvious switchback between disintegration and chaos of eating and the certainty of control. While bulimic eating may lack order, and sufferers may describe it as chaotic, their certainty is that certainty of knowing they can do something: they can act to regain the control that is essential to their being. Cyclic episodes of stuffing–starving, or binge–vomiting temporarily provide a sense of order that stands in contrast to the confusion in the rest of their life; the confusion of which they are the more aware at their usually nearer-normal weight levels and/or whenever their food intake is meeting their actual day-by-day requirements. To this extent these episodes provide them with some relief, a feeling of having some direction. Control is still the locus of 'self'.

> At least when I'm going to have a binge it's something definite. I can start it, I can even enjoy it in a strange sort of way while I'm eating all this food, and I can finish it. There's an end to it. So I know where I am.

When they have been bulimic for several years sufferers can lose the sense of control achieved this way and so lose this temporary haven of selfhood. Then they find themselves in a state of total despair.

. . . and nothingness

Behind the conscientious, hard-working, committed exterior that supports the food/body control self there lies a hollow emptiness, a 'nothingness' so profound it is terrifying to experience. It becomes essential for them to maintain the food regulating, or the fitness, that is their protective exterior and to resist any suggestion that they might look further than this.

Anorexic [whose weight is currently 73 per cent AEBW, after eleven months in therapy]: But I still don't think there's anything wrong. I can go out of here and look perfectly all right. I'm efficient at work. I can get on with what I have to do.

Helper: Yes, you can do that. Concentrating on how you feel now, though . . . what feeling do you have, right now?

Anorexic [in a dead tone]: Nothing.

Helper: Nothing. [Affirming her] If you were to have a feeling now, what feeling would that be?

Anorexic [dull and hopelessly]: I don't know.

Helper: If there were something you'd like, now . . . What might it be?

Anorexic [pausing for some time, then wistfully]: I suppose I'd like to be loved . . . But (in a more definite but hopeless tone) there's nothing in here to love. Nothing. I am nothing. I'm just empty. I feel as though I've got a hollow glass ball here, in the middle of me.

It can also be frightening for a helper who is unaware of the nature of the problem, who accompanies the sufferer to this void, not knowing that it is there.

Sufferers are aware of this sense of nothingness, even though others are not. This for them is their real deep-down sense of who they are. This is the source of their angry, dismissive statements about themselves, such as: 'I'm not worth bothering about. I'm nothing. Nothing at all. A cardboard façade around a hole.' Equally it is the source of their despair: 'If you (the helper) were to take anorexia away from me, you know, draw it away with your hands [bursting into tears] there'd be nothing left.'

In so far as food/body regulation provides certainty, it creates a sense of self for anyone who is failing to gain and experience selfhood in any other way. This is the experience of becoming a person through food and body control, the experience that makes anorexia nervosa/bulimia in all its dimensions a solution to an existential problem.

How is an existential problem to be recognized?

There are many who might find it difficult to work with the idea of 'existence', or 'an existential problem'. To those who see themselves as essentially practical people, words like 'existence' almost invite dismissal. Or they might ask 'What does it actually mean?' Or 'How can you know that's what the problem is?' So there is a need to be specific about the nature of a fragile sense of self, and to consider more closely what counts as evidence of an underlying existential malaise, and the circumstances in which it is likely to be evident.

This is also relevant in relation to the problem of identifying or diagnosing the condition where the sufferer, male or female, appears so very plausible and shows a face to the world that is highly acceptable and 'right'.

Dither and indecisiveness

The clearest indication of sufferers' existential unease is their inability to choose and make their own independent decisions. This may not show so much in relation to decisions concerning a career or leaving home, for these are often taken care of at the level of cultural and family values, though inability to choose is still present.

> Everyone used to be going off to do exciting things in the summer, and I'd think about doing this, or doing that, write off here, get brochures there, and the end of term would be getting nearer, but I'd be no nearer knowing what to do. And in the end my father would step in and arrange it so I'd come back after the holiday and could say where I'd been and what exciting things I'd done too.

This indecisiveness is evident in the inability to order priorities over completely mundane matters. If there is a series of tasks to be done, they cannot decide for themselves which one of them to do first. They end up in a state of total, agonized dithering.

> It's over the smallest things, like having to decide what clothes to wear. Or I think I want to paint a wall in my room, but then I feel I ought to clear up the kitchen first, because my flatmate is on nightshifts and she doesn't get time. But there's the jumper I started knitting. I can't sit down to that but I ought to because winter's coming and I need it, but that feels selfish, so I go and feed the cat and start to clean the kitchen. But I ought to be writing all the letters I haven't replied to, but I haven't got any stationery and that means going out, and if I go out I'm not clearing up the kitchen, or painting my room, and I waste all this time going round and round in circles. A whole two hours starting things and not finishing them. Ending up making a cup of coffee and then not being able to decide whether I ought to drink it. [Sounding angry and frustrated] I'm supposed to be intelligent. But how can I be if I can't organize my life? When I can't decide to do the silliest little thing! I'm stupid, and that just proves it.

The nearer a normal weight they are, and the more aware of the numbers of options available, the more they have to dither about, so their indecisiveness becomes the more paralysing. This can become noticeable in their being completely physically immobilized, unable to decide whether to stand up or sit down, to stay in the room or go out.

> She said she was going out, and she seemed to make all sorts of preparations, but she ended up just standing there, door open, on the doorstep. She was there ten minutes or more, sort of hovering in a vacant, undecided way.

This is where their conviction of their own worthlessness and their pattern of responding to others' needs and obligations leave them. Denying their own needs and feelings, they deny themselves the information on which preferences are based, and on which choice and decision making depend.

With no immediate knowledge of their own personal preferences, they strive to apply logic, rationality and externally derived rules to every choice and every decision. But the demands, needs, interests of everyone around inevitably conflict. So they end up like an anxious accountant, continually trying to make absolutely sure the books are balanced.

> My parents are pleased I got into medical school. But it's difficult for my brother. He didn't get into such a good university. He scraped in. He's doing biochemistry, but it's a struggle. They've arranged for him to have private tuition. They make him feel he ought to match up to me and that's what I hate. We've always got on really well together. He's great, I really like him. But I'm a thorn in his side. I don't like hurting him. But if I give up, I'll upset my parents, and I don't want to upset them.

As they strive to weigh up every implication of every action, all they achieve is level upon level of intellectualization and level upon level of analysis, which does nothing to move them forward. For logic and rationality are but handmaidens to personal preference. They do not, by themselves, resolve conflict. It is sufferers' attempts to use them to resolve conflict that result in their coming to exist permanently in a state of confused indecision. It is this that creates the sense of 'intellectual wheelspin', the feeling of gaining no traction, of being unable to make any contact with, or impression upon, the world:

> When I push, nothing moves. It's like being a car with the engine really going, revving like mad all ready to go, but with the brake full on. You feel frustrated. So frustrated. And utterly hopeless.

Lack of spontaneity

It is paradoxical that the more visible face of this dithering indecisiveness is efficiency, organization and routine. The onlooker needs to be aware of the rigid tenacity with which sufferers cling to their routines, and to observe that these routines are but a limited part of their life. They are carefully related to maintaining food/body control.

Any situation that threatens them will result in the sufferer clinging to them with even greater rigidity. In this is the evidence of control-dependence. Changes of any kind will not be tolerated. Even the suggestion of change will arouse panic. This may reveal itself in small ways in the early stages. It will be noticeable in their reducing food. If they have lapsed and eaten, or had food forced on them, they will starve more strictly and exercise more relentlessly. They will be most calm where they have everything planned and predicted days in advance: food and meal times, work, bedtime, every detail of how to meet a day's worth of obligations.

It's terrible if you get asked to go for coffee after a lecture. It's anti-social not to go, and I don't want them to feel I'm rejecting them, but if you go you never know how long it's going to be, and when you've planned to go to the library, you know you've organized to be there at a quarter past eleven exactly, then something like that just throws you out. But I don't want them to think I don't appreciate that they've asked me to come for a coffee.

Tentative and fragile as they are, unless they have twenty-four hours to plan a change to their routine they feel in danger of being completely annihilated by people and events.

If there's any chance I have to eat when I'm with anyone, I make sure I don't eat the day before. That's what I did last weekend. The conference was on the Monday and I knew I'd have to eat with all the other delegates at midday. I ate a bit on Saturday; just an apple and some cheese. Sunday I didn't have anything at all.

It is necessary to be aware that the lower weight is, the more the lack of ability to make real choices will be masked by a sense of being 'quite decided'. Sufferers will be directed by their food/body-control self. Meanwhile, where they are bulimic, their panic at threats to their control can become desperately clear.

In an attempt to make her break the habit, my father tried to stop her (the speaker's sister) going into the bathroom to be sick, and she went absolutely wild. It was quite violent, and my father was white with rage. It didn't make anything any better. She just ended up in floods of tears, and totally refused to eat anything.

Controlling others . . .

The food/body control imperative, core to their own lives, leads to sufferers controlling the lives of others. This control may start with others' bodies explicitly, as is clear in the case of the trainers, sports coaches, nutrition advisers and so on who are often notably 'committed'. It may appear as 'having great clarity' or a 'strong personality', or come across merely as being 'really decisive'. But attention to the source of the impetus for control will reveal its anorexic roots.

We all decided to go for a drink. No one specially minded where. Someone suggested the pub on the corner, but what we actually found ourselves doing was trekking half way across town to a bistro where Susie knew she could get a particular red wine. That was the only thing she would agree to. She was really stuck on that. We didn't want to break up the crowd. So it turned out we went there, just because that was what she wanted.

As pointed out previously, relatives can feel as though they are being taken over by the sufferer.

> I asked her to wait till we'd finished the meal before she began clearing up. But she was determined to get everything put away. She had the knives and forks out of our hands before we'd finished the last mouthful. And my kitchen's not my own any more. She gets so tense if I go in when she's cooking. I feel completely overruled by her. My husband says I shouldn't let her, but his answer is to disappear into his study, or go out to play golf.

Others can just be drawn in.

> He had to have his session in his gym. We had to book a flight to take that into account. It meant a whole day wasted out of the time I'd taken off for the holiday, but that didn't matter to him. In the end I went to the gym too. I began to feel I was just lazy if I didn't.

. . . or follow-my-leader

Unable to choose and decide on the basis of their own real preferences, and so form their own opinions and initiate their own actions, sufferers attempt to resolve their own non-existence by following the examples of others. This will be more clear at higher weights when they are more aware of people and situations around them, though it can happen at quite low weight too that in subtle, and sometimes not so subtle, ways they are taken over by others' ideas and opinions. As one nurse observed of an anorexic patient: 'She's going round talking to everybody and just taking on the thing that every last person says and repeating it to the next.' This characteristic compliance, the flip side of the rigid control in relation to food, is evidence of their being externally controlled, of their following the rule, sensitively pleasing, doing the 'proper thing' whoever they are with, and whatever context they are in. Another sufferer said despairingly:

> I have to see how other people do things. They're all right. They've got themselves together. They get on with their lives. I'm really nosey, I've got to find out what they do. They've got the answers, and I haven't. So I have to copy them. But then I despise myself, because I ought to have my own answers.

Openly or otherwise, sufferers allow others to resolve their indecision and organize their life for them. Their conviction that everyone knows better than they do, that there is one 'right' or absolute way of doing things and that others have the key to everything, is a conviction that permeates every relationship. It can also render the unwary helper ineffective in quite subtle ways. The client who says 'But that's what Cara said, and Cara's my therapist, so she *must* know. She *must* be right about me' is handing the helper the task and the responsibility of defining that client. The helper who is unaware that the sufferer is following the helper's lead can unwittingly take on the task of leading and so become drawn into perpetuating sufferers' inability to initiate their own actions, or perpetuating their lack of capacity to feel who or how they are for themselves.

Even if sufferers are aware of what they want, or need, their ability to decide is still paralysed by conflicting pressures. They still struggle to be fair and reasonable, logically to balance the accounts, but end up with their fragile autonomy undermined, with no sense of achievement and nothing to lessen their confusion.

> When it came to choosing exam subjects I wanted to do domestic science, and they wanted me to do maths. They thought that was more important, but it wasn't important to me. I didn't want to do maths, but I ended up doing it for them. What I really wanted to do was do maths and fail, and that would have served them right. But I didn't want to fail for myself, so I had to succeed for me, and do the maths for them, and I ended up feeling like I'd achieved nothing.

Food/body control: a solution to confusion

In the context of the experience of having no sense of self, anyone, male or female, is in danger of discovering that they feel more real, more in command of their life, by avoiding or tightly controlling food, being frenetic-ally active, or both. Where every other action is fraught with the possibility of failure, where the rule is that failure and personal inadequacy are not allowed, where the demand is that the individual must be independent and strong, then a food-control self comes into its own. These acts of control are straightforward, uncomplicated. They give a sense of supreme autonomy. For they are independent of anyone. Success is measurable, immediate and belongs unequivocally to the person who has achieved it. Where personhood is food/body-control, personal fulfilment can be obtained from moment to controlling moment. The certainty of this 'self' can be gained here and now. Here is evidence of doing something 'absolutely right', of achieving socially approved ideals. So this food-control self is morally superior, tangibly realizing perfectionist aims.

> It gradually sort of happened. I found life was organized. In control of every detail. Whatever I ate I weighed. I didn't eat a single calorie more than I'd worked out. I was fine. I was still teaching. My lessons were going haywire. I couldn't understand why, but I was sure it wasn't my fault. I'd never done so much preparation for lessons than I was doing then. They said I'd lose the job. I was too thin. But I didn't care what anyone said. I'd got this thing. And nobody, but *nobody*, was going to take it away from me.

Whatever form it happens to take, food/body control is insidious in the way it gains hold.

I'd never really lost much weight, though I'd tried dieting, on and off. I don't think I ever lost more than half a stone (3.2 kg) like that. Then I discovered I could make myself sick, and that became something special for me. I didn't binge then. Not like I have been recently. I just used to get rid of the food after each meal, and that felt better. I had this secret thing. No one but me knew about it. But I felt I could cope when I'd got that. It sounds silly . . . but it was the feeling that I'd got something nobody else had, and I was going to keep it. I never got really thin. But I was more confident. Confident I wouldn't get fat.

Having once become control dependent the person's self-concept is anchored in this, and is so anchored, whatever their current weight happens to be. Thus:

I'm in a most extraordinary situation at the moment: even by medical standards severely overweight, bulimic in my eating habits, yet totally and completely anorexic in my mind. It's odd really, because despite the vast change in me physically, I'm just the same mentally as I was at my lowest weight. My mind is a complex, intricate tangle of problems, fears and difficulties. I am still struggling with the bulimia, although I feel I am getting somewhere now. In the last three weeks I have managed five days of fasting which is major achievement for me, as normally I binge every single day. My weight is still dreadfully high but I have lost half a stone (3.2 kg) recently. I just live for the day when I will be five stone or less again (i.e. 31.8 kg or less); it means everything to me, it really does. I will still have most of the problems I've got now, but at least I'll be a weight I feel safe with and that will help me bear the other things.[2]

The difficulty there is in expressing nothingness

As we have seen, there are cultural patterns, strengthened by events in the family's history, that encourage a sufferer to hide feelings (see Chapter 7). It has also been pointed out that the overwhelming confusion and paralysis of action experienced on gaining weight are in themselves sufficient to explain food/body control, were they not so hidden (Chapter 6). There is a particular difficulty, however, that obscures this crucial information. Feelings of confusion and nothingness are by their nature almost inexpressible. Hence oblique, vague and evidently self-deprecating comments such as 'It's just such a mess. You can't describe a mess. It's just confusing. There's nothing else to say . . . Nothing. You're utterly confused and a mess. It's hopeless.'

Sufferers can have a sense well beforehand that something is not right, and find it impossible to explain. 'For a long time I had a feeling there was something wrong with me. I didn't know what it was. It was something. But I couldn't pin it down. Like trying to get hold of something I couldn't grasp.' Likewise it is impossible for a sufferer who feels non-existent to assert or insist upon the significance this has in her or his life. Even though sufferers may try to express their sense of nothingness, because they appear so efficient and successful, they are rarely believed.

> I did once try to explain to my father that I didn't feel there was any-thing that was really me. You know, I didn't have any idea of who I was. No sense of identity. But he dismissed the idea. I was just being silly.

As the following account illustrates, being unable to express the nature of the problem has important implications in relation to asking for help at all, let alone obtaining help that is appropriate.

> I have been anorexic since puberty and had 'treatment' for 'something' when I was 19. I am now 39 and have spent the last twenty years in total isolation from my fellow human beings, not knowing why I couldn't make contact with people and feeling guilty about asking for help as I did not know what to ask for help for.[3]

Unable to express the self she or he is deepens the despair, increases fellings of hopelessness. Sufferers are frustrated, and all the more so as others fail to understand how it is to feel as they do.

> You get to the point where you can't do anything. You sit on the floor, leaned up against the wall, not knowing which way to move. So you just sit there, paralysed. And there's this stupid counsellor saying, 'You've got to be true to yourself.' But [wailing suddenly with frustration] how *can* I be true to myself when I haven't *got* a self to be true to? There isn't a feeling of being me!

Compared with the profound existential unease there is in the sense of 'never knowing what to do, never knowing whether what I'm doing is right; constantly feeling if it's all right over here, it's not all right over there, and I can't get it right in both places, so I'm wrong whatever I do', a food restricting, body controlling self is comforting and safe.

Their strong commitment to Protestant or work-ethic values plays a significant part in the structuring of sufferers' understanding of the confused, paralysed, empty self they experience. All human beings can feel these ways at some times and in some circumstances, but the food/body controllers' moral code denies them a way of accepting such feelings in themselves, and denies them any language in which to express those feelings 'positively'. So their paralysed action becomes 'laziness', or 'time wasting'. Their dithering confusion becomes 'sloppiness', or 'not having a grip'. Their ineffectiveness becomes 'a failure to achieve', or 'a lack of standards'. The actuality of the experience of nothingness, and the potential for this really to become a problem where it persists and perpetuates itself, is then dangerously obscured by being overlaid by intense and enduring feelings of guilt and self-blame at 'being wrong'.

It is their moral stance, together with the very intangibility of the experi-ence that is nothingness, that contributes to their dismissing the suggestion that they have a problem at all, no matter how great their distress. If they sense something is wrong, they believe that whatever it is, it is entirely their fault, and their values dictate that it is their responsibility to put it right. Yet this too is an impossibility where it is so difficult for them to know what it is they have to put right.

Meanwhile as they turn to food/body control as the only remaining way of doing anything correct or getting anything right, cherished values cast a gloss of virtue on the gathering effects of starvation and physical exertions. So, by the time those around a sufferer have begun to be alarmed by the severity of the control, they are meeting an individual whose sense of identity has already formed around restricting food intake, and being 'single-mindedly' active.

The significance of indecisiveness

It is difficult to exaggerate the importance of the sufferer's indecisiveness and the lack of a sense of self that lies behind this, for they provide the impetus and the rationale for food/body control. Both practically and theoretically they are at the core of the illness.

The failure to appreciate the direct link that exists between the need for effective action of *any* kind as a confirmation of self and the use of food/body control to provide this confirmation has led to the proliferation of theories that miss this central point. Again dangerously, such theories readily draw helpers' attention away from the quality of experience that the sufferers' control, or continual attempts to re-establish control, are, every moment, warding off.

The helper who begins, on the other hand, to work with their indecisiveness and with their sense of confusion will tend to obtain immediate confirmation, in the way they respond, that this is the core problem. Meanwhile, provided they are not very severely constrained by the effects of starvation – which they generally will be when body weight is below approximately 70 per cent AEBW – they will usually begin to feel a glimmering of being understood, and the helper will begin to have a sense of having a grasp of the problem, and some leverage to assist change.

A feature of most theories of anorexia nervosa is that they incorporate reasons why sufferers should not be expected to accept the proponent's view of their condition – i.e. the reasons for their behaviour are held to be buried in their unconscious, or shielded from them by a phobia, or distanced from their understanding by their arrested intellectual development. The assumption is that only much later will they come to realize the correctness of others' theoretical views. But as we have said, theoretical ideas that do not depend for their validity on a sufferer's own experience can be oppressive to that person. Because of the real uncertainty of self that sufferers endure, because of the difficulty they have in trusting and believing in their own feelings and in expressing anything of themselves that is perhaps felt, they very easily feel put upon, construed, interpreted, analysed, taken over, invaded by others' views, fenced in by others' predictions. This is how anorexia nervosa/bulimia sufferers who typically are highly intelligent, well educated and articulate come to be so defenceless in the face of academic theorizing about their illness.

Sources of confusion

Dithering indecision would melt away, had they any feeling of what they wanted for themselves. But because their own wants are precisely what they will not, or cannot, allow, they have no basis inside themselves, no ground on which they can come to their own decisions (see Chapter 14).

It is not that a fragile self on its own creates a problem as destructive as anorexia nervosa/bulimia. People who have a poorly developed sense of self are certainly vulnerable to external control. But as long as the received values and priorities are consistent with each other, it is entirely possible for such people to act effectively, to engage with the world in terms of those values and priorities and maintain a sense of self-worth. Such people may endure the cost of never reaching their full human potential, but they are spared the profound sense of paralysis experienced by the anorexia nervosa/bulimia sufferer.

Rather it is that the standards and expectations which anorexics/bulimics try to fulfil are contradictory. There is conflict between the work ethic requirement to strive, and the expectation that women will be sensitive and caring that springs from the requirements of the female role. This tension, together with the experience it brings of 'being wrong whatever I do',[4] results in some degree of value conflict being a common experience for women. Boys and men are not immune from value conflict or role confusion either. They are not immune in principle, or in practice; a point which tends to become particularly clear at times when economies falter, and when social and political landscapes undergo change.

In the case of anorexia nervosa/bulimia sufferers, however, these experiences are particularly severe. The histories of their parents, grandparents and great-grandparents have certainly resulted in their passing on highly ambivalent or 'mixed' messages to their children, but gender roles themselves provide an illuminating example of conflicting expectations as they beset both males and females.

Gender roles

Gender roles are important because they provide one of the ways in which people order their priorities. The requirements and expectations of the male and female roles guide people's choices and shape their decisions, particularly in situations where conflicting responses are possible.

For instance, faced with a situation in which one could be either sensitive or assertive, males responding in their gender role would resolve the conflict by being assertive; a resolution typified in such attitudes as 'We'd like to be nice guys, but we've got the world to run.' Females responding to the requirements of their gender role would resolve the conflict by being sensitive; a resolution typified in such attitudes as 'I'd like to tell you what I think, but I don't want to hurt your feelings.' This latter is an example of what has been referred to as 'the compassion trap'.[5] These are expectations that press on men and on women. It is not that men by their nature cannot be sensitive, nor that women by their nature cannot be assertive. But the influence of gender roles on personal development is so strong that this frequently seems to be the result.

When psychological tests were used by one of the authors (RS) to examine gender role in female anorexia nervosa sufferers, it emerged that none felt they ought to conform to the conventional female role. Some described themselves in terms of male role characteristics, and others in androgynous terms – androgyny being a way of referring to people who ascribe characteristics to themselves which are drawn from both the male role and the female role.[6] This result was perhaps hardly surprising in view of the extreme commitment to the work ethic and other circumstances of their family history, as described.

Again it is not the fact that girls and women who become anorexia nervosa/bulimia sufferers have adopted male or androgynous roles that seems to be the problem, for both are compatible with a woman living her life in a way that is highly effective. Rather, as the same psychological research has shown, these sufferers seem to have taken on contradictory halves of each gender role.[7]

Trying to make bricks without straw

Each gender role usually describes certain desirable ends together with certain characteristics which make it possible to attain these. Thus men are expected to be competent, independent and successful in the world, and they are allowed, and expected, to be assertive and single-minded in order to achieve this. Women are expected to be sensitive and caring, and to do this they are allowed a certain freedom of emotional expression.

Anorexia nervosa/bulimia sufferers meanwhile take on some of the obligations from each role, yet either way deny themselves the means to fulfil them. Convinced she ought to be strong, effective, independent, emotionally controlled, which are male role characteristics, the female sufferer also knows that, according to her rules, she must not be assertive because assertiveness is selfish and hurtful to others. So she is conflicted here. She both wants and believes she ought to be sensitive, caring and responsive to others' needs but, while emotional responsiveness both requires and is enhanced by the expression of feelings, she does not permit herself this. True to the particular half of the male role requirements she adheres to, she believes allowing herself feelings is self-indulgent and weak. So she denies herself essential ingredients for effective action within the female role too. Either way she tries to make bricks without straw. Forbidding herself the tools that are needed to achieve either goal, she ends up feeling ineffective and inadequate whichever way she tries to act.

This pattern of taking on some of the expectations from each gender role, whilst ignoring those other aspects of each role that would enable the expectations to be fulfilled, applies equally to male sufferers. But in their case the parts of each role that are assumed and parts that are denied are generally reversed, so, for instance, they believe they ought to be assertive, but actually feel sensitive and caring, and likewise they end up feeling ineffective and inadequate whatever they do or do not do.[8]

The danger in resolving sufferers' conflict for them

In theory, if the problem has its roots in conflicting expectations, a solution could be to remove one side of the conflict. Progress might be made if a sufferer, happening to be a girl, were for instance to scale down her career aspirations and take on a more straightforward and conventionally female role. Alternatively she might develop her more male-role interests and capabilities, pursue a career, and do this at the cost of being sensitive, caring and nurturant. The same solution, removing one or other side of their conflicts, could equally be put in hand for those who happen to be male.

Sufferers, male and female, do in fact quite often find that people who try to help them advise them overtly or covertly to relinquish one or other set of values or expectations, the recommended one depending on the helper's own particular inclinations and prejudices.

> The consultant seemed to think it was my duty to put on weight and get my periods back so I could get married and have babies. When I was talking to one of the nurses afterwards, she let it out that he'd like a family himself, but his wife can't have children.

But neither approach is likely to be satisfactory because both sides of the sufferer's conflicting values are strongly supported by the culture and the experience of their families.

If it were possible for sufferers simply to drop one set of expectations in favour of the other, they would have done this for themselves long ago, as girls can do in their teens when they give up trying to be competent and qualified in favour of being decorative and nurturant. This is a well-documented explanation of academic under-achievement and failure in adolescent girls.[9]

This is not to deny that there are sufferers who make some recovery by just dropping one set of expectations. The illness is so protracted that, while the sufferer is bound up in it, the family's values and expectations may themselves alter or modify over the duration in such a way as to make this a possible solution. So it is always worth helping the sufferer to check whether this might be so.

While, in terms of recovery, it again has its limitations, there are others who achieve some change by taking on a set of rules or external controls which they can use to guide them in their decision making, which provides a focus for their existence that is not explicitly food/body control. For some this involves turning to a religion. For others caring for animals becomes a central preoccupation. Others find a way of living that provides food rules for them. 'I do keep to a strict vegan diet. But it does the trick. It does the controlling for me. I'm aware of what I'm doing. I'm not stupid. But I can't manage any other way.' Work evolves as some form of solution for many. A job or career provides a programme, it structures time, it creates demands – rules – that can be responded to, and if one job is not sufficient in this respect a sufferer will take on two jobs, or even three. Thus while work can be an important step in creating some change, it can also indicate the degree to which the illness is still present.

Meanwhile for helpers to exercise their own prejudices and blindly encourage sufferers either towards particular role expectations or towards another set of external controls or rules is to fail to address the problem. It is to leave them in the position of saying, as one girl said of those counselling her: 'That's all right for them, but I still don't know what *I* want.' It is to perpetuate the sense that 'Whatever I have, I always seem to want more', and 'I'm never satisfied. I always want too much. I *ought* not to want so much.' So they will remain deeply dissatisfied still, and with no understanding of how they come to feel this way. The root task of therapy is to foster in the sufferer a sense of his/her *own* selfhood.

At the same time, since food restriction is potentially life-threatening, the specific problems created by anorexic/bulimic behaviour must be addressed. The lower weight is, the greater the difficulty there will be in reaching the sufferer through the barriers that this creates. These are topics we will return to in Chapter 10 and subsequent chapters, however. The prior task is to consider the way helpers may feel towards the sufferer, and towards the problem. For there is always the possibility of their being drawn to the same style of thinking themselves, and anyone who is so will be the less able to help.

References

1 McLeod, S. (1981) *The Art of Starvation*. London: Virago, 182.
2 Anorexic Aid Newsletter (1986) *Contact*, High Wycombe, Bucks, September.
3 Ibid., December.
4 Baker Miller, J. (1978) *Towards a New Psychology of Women*. London: Pelican, 52–63.
5 Dixon, A. (1982) *A Woman in Your Own Right*. London: Quartet Books, 54–9.
6 Slade, R. (1984) *The Anorexia Nervosa Reference Book*. London: Harper and Row, 192.
   Bem, S.L. (1974) The measurement of psychological androgyny, *Journal of Consulting and Clinical Psychology*, Washington, 42(2): 155–62.
7 Slade, R. (1984) op. cit., 194–6.
8 Horner, M. (1972) Towards an understanding of achievement-related conflicts in women, *Journal of Social Issues*, New York, 28: 2.
9 Ibid.

Part III

nine

Perspectives that maintain the ability to help

By its nature anorexia nervosa/bulimia has great potential to disturb those who attempt to help. The condition is remarkable for the extent to which it challenges the helper's own personal beliefs and lifestyle. This is because the ordinary standards and values that many people cherish play an essential role in creating a potentially lethal illness.

Comparing starvation effects with the effects of alcohol, and the attitudes that are held in relation to each, is probably the clearest way of illustrating how helpers' beliefs are challenged. For lack of awareness of the role that values, attitudes and beliefs play can render attempts to help totally ineffective.

Food/body control and the use of alcohol compared . . .

Chapter 2 showed how self-starvation and excessive exercise are like alcohol in that they induce certain psychotropic effects, or altered states of consciousness, that can be experienced as a sense of well-being. In much the same way as a few drinks can give a person 'courage' to face a difficult or uncomfortable situation, so the high or speedy state induced by restricting food can create a sense of well-being, and prevent awareness of those aspects of the person's life that are difficult to countenance, by inducing a feeling of being confidently active. The psychotropic effects of undernutrition, as we have said, occur more rapidly than is generally realized. A relatively few hours without food can create a sense of euphoria. Like the excessive use of alcohol, continued starvation also gradually disrupts the biochemical basis for normal intellectual functioning. (In the case of starvation in people who are already physically mature this effect is reversible, but with sustained alcohol abuse the damage may be permanent.) Thus food restriction and alcohol are both potent means of changing the way people think. Decisions to continue are in both instances made from a different physical and psychological position from the decision to begin. Thus both have the capacity to entrap their users into a spiral of personality deterioration.

Because, when a person's weight is below approximately 70 per cent AEBW, further weight loss of even quite small amounts can bring about major shifts in mood and further changes in thinking, food restricting, like the need for alcohol, is likely to become a permanent lifestyle.

. . . and contrasted

The difference between food/body control and alcohol lies in the way their use is valued. Except in limited subcultures, such as certain groups of young single men for instance, excessive drinking is regarded as undesirable. But people who maintain extreme self-control in relation to food, or are 'totally committed' to exercise, persistently attract considerable admiration. It is true that the moderate use of alcohol is tolerated, particularly as a way of easing social situations. But this has long been tempered with an awareness of the possible dangers. So campaigns are launched against drinking and driving. People are aware that drinking leads to going out of control. Children are warned about the hazards of alcohol. But no similar effort is made to warn of the hazards of sustained food restriction and the biochemical changes wrought by excessive exercise, and where warnings are attempted they are hard to sustain. There is a way in which they ring hollow. For being restrained in relation to food or being obviously physically fit are seen as achievements attained through self-control; self-control is virtuous, and being virtuous can hardly be wrong. The visible consequences of self-regulation are used to proclaim to the world the moral qualities of the individual.

The different values we place on the use of alcohol and on dieting or food regulating and exercising would appear to derive not so much from what may happen to the individual as a result of these activities as from the implications they have for social order. Individuals who drink to excess may suffer personal harm. As a disinhibiting drug, however, alcohol can lead people to neglect their social responsibilities. So its abuse is a potential threat to significant institutions such as the family. Similarly, since caring for the home and for children is a designated female responsibility, drunkenness in women persistently attracts far greater disapproval than drunkenness in men. The need to combat such threats is constantly reasserted by politicians and moral leaders in the community. Thus the burdens and privileges that go with such social arrangements are maintained.

Food and body regulation, meanwhile, not only fit dominant social values. Whatever harm they may in fact do to the individual, they are seen to pose no threat to the established order (except possibly in the case of hunger striking). Under the banner of 'health' or 'fitness' they are extolled as preconditions of national well-being.

Symptoms of excessive virtue

The person whose body is thin and lithe is not easily construed as greedy, slack, self-indulgent and given to wayward appetite. Even the marked symptoms of undernutrition that occur with anorexia nervosa are interpreted positively. Hyperactivity suggests a busy, committed, achieving person; not indolence or slothfulness. So even where people are quite emaciated, it becomes difficult to see their hyperactivity for what it is. Sleeplessness likewise readily lends itself to positive interpretations. Getting up early is seen as good for the soul. It distances people from any accusations of laziness. The person who goes running at 5 a.m. elicits admiration and feelings of guilt: 'I'd feel better if I could get up at that time. I should be organized like that.' Thus the fact that the early rising is the result of hunger-induced restlessness, and the running is part of a compulsive exercise routine the runner dare not break, is lost in a blur of moral approval. Withdrawal from social situations, although a symptom found in all starving people, loses its symptom status because isolating oneself is often taken as the mark of a person going places. 'Going it alone' signifies individuality and ultimate success. Thus those intent on self-starving and other controlling routines easily obtain not just permission to be alone, but approval for their 'independence'.

Although the harder sufferers work the more they may succeed in driving away thoughts of food, although their perfectionism is the expression of their polarized thinking, although organization and ritual are essential to the maintainance of food restricting routines, these are not easily seen as symptoms. This is merely someone who is 'very thorough' and at this stage 'very reliable'. Hence the success of many a business or organizational enterprise may well have been achieved on the back of a ritually underfeeding anorexic.

> I must admit that a lot of our success in the early days was due to the girl who worked here when we were getting the business off the ground. She was amazing. She used to be in here at seven in the morning – regular as clockwork. You've never seen such organization. We were always up to date on everything. She was the most efficient secretary I've ever had, and she didn't leave this office till seven or eight at night either. Then I believe she used to go and do a shift for the Samaritans. A real worker. It's a pity she's not here still, now the company's bigger. I'm

looking for a personal secretary. I'd have given her the job. Of course, we didn't know then she had this anorexia thing . . .

Hoarding is also symptomatic of the totally controlling anorexic lifestyle. At low weight, or in 'control mode', sufferers are likely to save everything from money to the sticky edges on postage stamps. 'Saving' or hoarding usually gives little cause for concern, particularly to members of their own family. It is quite consistent with the belief that resources should be used 'sensibly'. But this means choice and making decisions. Unable to do this, they accumulate sometimes very considerable sums when weight is low and food is in control, characteristically running through equally large amounts with apparent recklessness in a bulimic phase of the illness: 'I couldn't tell Mummy and Daddy why I had absolutely nothing to show for the £1000 that came from my grandmother. They expected me at least to have bought myself a sewing machine.' Legacies amounting to thousands of pounds have been known to last sufferers only a matter of months as a result of food and other shopping binges. Using credit cards for endless buying, sufferers can also run up endless levels of debt.

The preference for physical explanation

Because it is disturbing to realize and acknowledge the extent to which the extreme actions of anorexia nervosa/bulimia sufferers grow out of ordinary values and everyday notions of moral goodness, many parents find more comfort in believing their offspring is suffering from an as yet unspecified brain disorder or endocrine disturbance, or that it is a genetic illness. This is easier than countenancing the idea that the standards they live by are implicated in the development of the condition that is causing them so much distress.

An instance of the wish to believe in the existence of a simple physical cure was illustrated by the enthusiasm there was at one stage for the suggestion that a specific mineral deficiency might be involved in the aetiology of anorexia nervosa. 'This led to hundreds of anorexics asking their family doctors for zinc salts and to some practitioners actually prescribing them, in the absence of any scientific evidence to demonstrate their efficacy.'[1]

Nor are parents alone in the preference for physical explanation. The predominance of physiological research into the problem has gained much of its plausibility from the general unwillingness to accept the idea that moral goodness can have undesirable or bad consequences. Indeed, the history of research into anorexia nervosa is an intriguing example of the subtle way in which society's cherished beliefs shape scientific hypotheses. There is a cruel irony in the persisting notion that anorexia nervosa is a mysterious illness. It is not so much a mystery as a case of organized blindness. There seems to be no point at which the preconceptions with which people approach anorexic illness enable or encourage them to see what is really happening to the sufferer.

Seeing what is there

Though ready social approval attracts attention away from falling weight and other signs that a person is entrapped in food and body control, it is nevertheless essential from the point of view of help that onlookers recognize and acknowledge these signs for what they are. There are otherwise very few safety nets in which sufferers can be caught before they plummet into low weight and land on Square 1, or on another square on the board (see Chapter 3).

It is especially important for those professionally concerned with the pastoral care of young people – hostel wardens, teachers, ballet teachers, sports or games coaches, university and college lecturers and counsellors, school nurses and so on – not only to recognize warning signs, but to be aware of how their own values and attitudes may be received by those under their guidance or in their care, whose sense of self may be more fragile than appearances would suggest.

> Cathy's coach passed a comment after a disappointing race about her being a little too heavy. As a well-ordered, introspective perfectionist, she began a rigid diet next day. Her weight dropped from $8^1/2$ stone (54 kg) to $7^1/2$ stone (47.6 kg). She parted from the coach, and to this day he does not realize the misery his chance observation caused. Cathy's promising career as a runner ground to a halt. As later she wrote in her diary 'It's gone on four and a half years now, and I'm so frightened. I stopped going to athletic club because I hate the idea of racing. But I feel lost without running and scared I'll lose my identity if I don't run.'[2]

Just as we make allowances for the effects of alcohol when listening to a person who is drunk, so we must also learn to listen and allow for the effects of underfeeding and exercise dependency in anorexia nervosa. In much the same way as expressions of bravado are understood as 'the beer talking', so commitment to being positive, or being active, having willpower, being rational, being controlled needs to be understood as the starvation talking, or, indeed, the over-exertion talking.

There are great disadvantages in waiting for a sufferer to become obviously emaciated or to begin to incur accidents and injuries at low weight just to 'be sure this really is anorexia nervosa'. Inevitably, because of the way thinking alters as weight drops, communication is diminished. To wait until weight loss alone is severe enough to appear to justify action is to wait until the best chances for initiating therapy have been lost. The over-lean, well-exercised body meanwhile provides a useful camouflage for the illness. Hence it is also important to be aware that the muscular body, primed for 'burning', does not look food-deprived. Either way the changes in personality that accrue with persistent undernutrition are not easy to alter once they become well established.

From praising control to imputing madness

Conventional values and standards also create certain difficulties in the way sufferers experience changes in attitude towards them. Eventually, instead of receiving approval, albeit unjustified, for being very slim, self-starvers find their slimness abruptly redefined as emaciation – as a symptom of mental or sometimes physical illness. 'People can be so cruel when they realize you're anorexic. They'll have been all nice, and kind, and helpful and then suddenly – well, they treat you as if you're mad!'

It is when this category change occurs that it can be felt to be no longer necessary to talk to them about their actions. There have been cases too where treatment has been imposed without a sufferer's consent (see Chapter 4). Sufferers experience this redefinition as a devastating betrayal. It does nothing either to help their feelings of confusion, or worthlessness.

> I was getting thinner, but no one said anything. The staff at school used to come into the library at lunch time and find me there, working. But they never said anything. There was a sort of conspiracy of silence. Then one day, after my exams – O-levels they were in those days – they announced I was going to hospital for tests, to find out what was wrong. I felt a thorough hypocrite occupying this hospital bed, especially while I had this great sense of well-being.
>
> Then I was *told* I was going to have insulin treatment. That was one of the few times I broke down. I actually cried in front of my father. The doctor said, 'Yes, they do get hysterical. That's one of the symptoms.' The thing was – it never occurred to me I was doing anything wrong. Or that I was in any way crazy. Eventually I found out what was wrong with me from a textbook belonging to another patient – actually with a certain sense of relief. Because at last I had found out what I was being accused of.

It is far more constructive for others to tell the sufferer about their concerns or their suspicions as soon as they arise, and to express those concerns repeatedly.

> It felt like being down a long dark tunnel. Mum used to shake me and cry at me, saying I would die. But she was so far away. And I could hear my therapist saying the same. But it was safe down here in the dark. Life looked easy, I was so far down this tunnel. (73 per cent AEBW)

It will seem that, whatever anybody says, the sufferer will not listen. The reality is, however, that this person is so biologically and psychologically altered, he or she cannot hear with any understanding. Nor, because of the way underfeeding works, will a sufferer be able to reverse the whirlpool process merely because others are persisting in voicing anxieties and providing observations. Even so, where concern is expressed, and expressed early and repeatedly, this tends to avoid the more destructive later experience of being suddenly betrayed. There is also just the chance it might be directly constructive.

> What was important was the letter from my friend. She said she knew I wasn't eating, and she was very worried because she cared about me. She said she'd already seen her cousin go through anorexia and it was a terrible experience, and please would I be careful what I was doing. I was already right in it by that time, and I didn't know what I was doing. I just knew I didn't want to stop – and didn't know how. But Vicki's letter meant a lot to me. My therapist helped me see that much.

Admiring the anorexic

Helpers are likely to find they share many of the sufferer's values and aspirations regarding food regulation and self-control. They commonly come from the same social background, share the same attitudes, the same cultural ideas concerning body regulation, and likewise take this as a valid area in which to achieve success. The sharing of values will be most evident where the sufferer is straightforwardly underfeeding or exercising rather than enduring the complications of bulimia, and raises crucial issues in terms of providing effective help.

Like the alcoholic or drug addict, bulimics tend to elicit negative judgements. There can be a horrified fascination, a voyeurism about the activities they resort to, but bulimics 'evidently' are out of control. Generally there is no wish to be like them. Those attempting to help bulimics are more easily able to see themselves as different. They more easily feel they can identify 'the problem' as something apart from themselves. More clearly, the bulimic is ill. Similarly where muscle already developed to groteque proportions is referred to as inadequate: 'I'm nowhere, compared with these guys', or where steroids are then taken as a quick fix – a response that parallels that of the inadequate dieter who fixes by reaching for the laxatives, or by vomiting – the same kind of distancing occurs. Again here there is room for the idea that something is wrong.

Where helper and sufferer do share the same strong values in relation body control, the patient or client will often appear to the helper as having gone further along the same path and as having achieved more. Thus the extremity that has been reached may easily be perceived by the helper as this person's greater success. This means that even at quite low weight sufferers can maintain the ability to call out approval for their actions from helpers who then find themselves in the confusing position of approving of the means whilst being professionally obliged to disapprove of the ends. Particularly, but not necessarily exclusively, in relation to female sufferers, hospital staff, for instance, whilst appreciating the idea of illness, may nevertheless be unable to prevent themselves construing it merely in terms of 'somehow having taken things a bit too far', and find themselves otherwise sympathizing with the patient, admiring her and wishing they were thinner themselves. As they are required to feed her or monitor her intake, young nurses can feel the amount the anorexic is being asked to eat is 'far too much' because their own dietary intake is inadequate and patchy. Their doubts are clear to the perceptive anorexic and contribute to the difficulty she already has in believing she ought to eat as much as is being asked. As, with increasing weight, restlessness and the urge to exercise become more desperate, again a doctor may suggest the jittery sufferer goes to the gym because that would be his or her own valued solution to feeling restless or agitated and needing to feel more in control of these feelings.

Many attempts to help are undermined by the sense of hypocrisy there is in a helper's feeling obliged to work in opposition to his or her own values and aspirations. During a ward round an anorexic patient was met by a team of hospital staff and her problem discussed sincerely and professionally. But walking away from her bedside the social worker turned to the ward sister and confessed: 'I wouldn't mind a bit of anorexia myself. About a stone and a half's worth. That would do me nicely.' With this comment the social worker illustrated her own lack of self-acceptance and made it clear that she valued precisely the same actions as the anorexic. A helper who is slim and elegant will (unless she is evidently at home with her body and not fighting to keep it that way) commonly make little headway with anorexia nervosa sufferers because she too signals that her values are consistent with their own. Whatever a helper may say, the sufferer will perceive from the way the helper presents herself or himself that this helper has the same beliefs and aspirations in relation to thinness, success, self-control and so on, and where such contradictions exist, the helper's response to the sufferer can hardly be unambiguous.

Contradictory attitudes also make it difficult to obtain a consistent approach to an anorexic patient where professional helpers are working as a team. An instance is provided by a debate that arose over whether a new patient (a smart young woman who had carefully been restricting her food intake and whose weight had fallen to 76 per cent of her AEBW) was primarily depressed or whether she was anorexic. The reaction of both the newly arrived male senior registrar and the skinny female student social worker on placement to the team member experienced in working with sufferers was: 'But why do you think she's anorexic? She's not thin!'[3]

Many people who have an enduring sense of their own personal failure are drawn to the feelings of power and success that come with restricting food intake and the pursuit of fitness. Nor is anyone necessarily free from such a sense of failure, or exempt from the possibility of being drawn to these ways of making themselves feel 'better' just because they have taken on a helping role, professional or otherwise and of whatever status.

Attitudes in a helper that are consistent with the defining 'anorexic attitude' invariably reinforce sufferers' commitment to their own food/body controlling.

A helper's longing to eat less and lose weight or get fitter, whether spoken or not, will fuel sufferers' need to feel better about themselves. Their worthlessness is so profound, any helper must, by definition, be better than they are. So where a helper admires anorexic control, this works as proof that this helper is inferior, and proof therefore of their own superiority. They cling to such proof to sustain their pride, and to maintain their image in their own eyes. It is this same pattern that leads to their dismissing anyone they consider to fall short of their standards of excellence, which are so high as to ensure that everyone must fall short. This is the way they trap themselves into finding no therapist, doctor, counsellor or friend who is *really* good enough for them.

Meanwhile they will also swiftly dismiss the helper who demonstrates the same perfectionist standards as their own, who has the same attitude towards control as the anorexic, yet who ignores this fact about himself or herself whilst at the same time trying to persuade sufferers to lower their standards, and break their precious control. They will judge such a helper not just as extremely lacking in perception, but as two-faced as well, and will take only moments to rumble the helper's inconsistency. Painfully aware of their own false pride, anorexia nervosa/bulimia sufferers are characteristically ruthless at debunking hypocrisy in others. Their moral victory here is essential. The only alternative they have if they fail to 'win' this way is to fall into their pit of worthlessness.

Helpers may be envious or stand in awe of anorexics not only because they are able to be so controlled over food, and thin, but also because of their academic qualifications, career, social status, wealth, artistic talents, practical skills and other successes. This too can leave sufferers feeling even more deeply unworthy. To them the helper's awe is undeserved and misplaced, and the envy as confusing, as isolating – exacerbating the already profound sense of not being understood. Their thinking will be:

> I manage to look clever, but I'm not really. I'm just despicable and low. It's all false. I'm just a liar and a hypocrite. You wouldn't feel inferior to me, not if you *really* knew what I'm like underneath.

Becoming drawn in and ineffective as help

Anyone who takes the anorexic or the controlled, apparently recovered bulimic at face value will be of little help. The more anyone is seduced by the ideas and beliefs sufferers express concerning the importance of being rational, having willpower, being determined, hard working, self-controlled and independent, the more anyone is impressed by the person the sufferer appears to be, the less likelihood there is of that person actually being able to help.

Extreme examples occur quite frequently of would-be helpers getting sucked in by sufferers' persuasive beliefs and attitudes, and by their alluring values. Delia's mother, for example, became so drawn into the arguments her daughter used to justify her adamant refusal to eat that, even when the girl was admitted to hospital as a medical emergency, weighing only 30.8 kg (4 st. 12 lbs) – i.e. 58 per cent AEBW – she was quite unable to help. She hovered at the bedside, clearly anxious and caring, but could not bring herself to pick up the glass containing the prescribed fortified milk drink and feed it to her obviously dangerously emaciated daughter. The drink stayed on the bedside cabinet while mother stroked her daughter's forehead and, by her presence, kept the nurses away. As she commented to one of the nurses, who had to ask her to go outside so that the patient could be fed: 'Delia is so strong-willed, I can't help admiring her. When she's so determined I can't really bring myself to break her will.'

Respecting what she saw as evidence of admirable attributes, this mother was effectively blind to her daughter's physically dangerous state.

Intervention: problems and strategies

The above problems stem from a fundamental misinterpretation of the actions of a self-starver or dedicated exerciser. But it is understanding that such a misinterpretation exists that provides the rationale for the informed helper to intervene.

Unwelcome to the sufferer, and often in opposition to what many consider to be praiseworthy behaviour, intervention is generally fraught with conflict and emotional upheaval. Having found in food/body control a solution to dissatisfaction, uneasiness and previous uncertainty of self, sufferers will rarely experience what is being offered in the name of help *as* helpful. Resistance can be particularly strong in the initial stages of the illness when the feeling of being in control has been newly achieved and weight is drifting down for the first time. Self-starvation is at this stage a heady new experience. So sufferers will resent anyone who attempts to interfere or prevent them from persisting with their newly discovered lifestyle, and they will be distinctly impervious to criticism.

Knowing self-control and thinness are by definition good, sufferers typically assume that anyone who is critical on these issues is merely jealous of their success. Schoolfriends' comments that a classmate has lost enough weight and ought to stop dieting are discounted as expressions of envy. Many girls who have started dieting with their friends or mothers, or, as it also turns out, have started running with boyfriends or fathers, and who have subsequently become anorexic report that they, for the same reason, ignored all warnings and entreaties to eat, or to ease up on sport and exercise.

> There were times when I was at school and I hadn't eaten much. Some-
> times I'd eat nothing at all for a few days; though I never did that for
> more than six days running. Then my mother and I went on a diet
> together. She couldn't stick to it. I could. It was easy. I knew how. She
> kept saying I ought to stop, I'd lost enough weight; but I just thought:

she's saying that because she's jealous. I thought she didn't want me to succeed because she'd failed.

Where they are convinced they have no need of help, or fear their control will be attacked, sufferers will naturally not seek help themselves. Concerned others do this, though this then leaves the difficulty of persuading them to agree to meet the helper and characteristically they will make use of any chink in the situation to avoid change. A particular headmistress, for example, aware that one of her students had become anorexic, saw the girl's examination prospects as likely to be affected by her obvious weight loss; but all attempts to help were frustrated by the parents' conviction that their daughter's isolation and preoccupation were simply a consequence of her working hard to achieve the required examination grades so she could take up the place she had already been offered at medical school. Their view was, of course, endorsed by the girl herself, and the school staff were helpless in the face of the family's conviction that no problem existed.

Another girl leaned on her boyfriend's appreciation of her thinness to reject her parent's worries about her picking at food and avoiding all set meals.

They kept on about me seeing the doctor, but I got Pete to say I'd had a meal with him. He didn't think there was anything wrong with me, and I knew if Pete said I'd eaten they wouldn't get at me too much. My brother and his girlfriend had just split up, and that caused them enough trouble.

Yet another avoided help because her mother had no faith in the general practitioner's ability to help and favoured seeing a counsellor, while her father thought the general practitioner should 'do his job and get the girl to eat', so no appointment was made with either possible helper. Where opinion is divided, the sufferer's routines persist.

The only approach to the problem of resistance that is likely to succeed is one where sufficient time and discussion are allowed for prior agreement to be reached between all those involved that the person in question does indeed need help. Only after this has been done is it productive for their concern to be expressed clearly and directly to the sufferer, until she or he gives in to pressure created by this unambiguous statement of joint concern, and reluctantly agrees that help should be sought. Sufferers may see no need for the concern, but where those around them are unified in expressing their anxiety, and in their strategy for dealing with this, there is more chance that the person in question will actually reach help, and sooner rather than later.

Teachers or employers who are uneasy about a student or employee's preoccupation with food/body control will be helpful if they ensure they carry out the personnel-management aspects of their own job effectively; if they carefully but persistently request for instance that the suspected sufferer meets the requirements or demands inherent in the particular work or school situation rather than being allowed to avoid them. It will in the long run be more beneficial if an employer does not tolerate the inefficiency that follows a low-weight anorexic's growing inability to remember the tasks that the job involves, and if teachers of perfectionist anorexic students require essays to be handed in after an appropriate number of hours' work rather than let them take extra days over them, and if the suspected bulimic is confronted with the fact of patchy attendance at work or school. Thus the problem may begin to be brought into the open and eventually helped. Onlookers who perceive something is wrong can also help by voicing their discomfort to their superiors, as one university lecturer did when he bluntly told his professor he could no longer teach his second-year seminar group 'with this appalling skeleton sitting in the same room'. The sight of her made it impossible for him to concentrate on teaching. It was only at this point that notice was taken of the girl's plight and the resources of the university health service called upon to help her with her 19.0 kg (approximately 3 st.) weight loss.

Different professional views about the causes of anorexia nervosa/bulimia, and differing opinions as to the appropriate treatment, make it difficult too to negotiate a unified approach. Again sufferers will take advantage of any lack of cohesion, slipping adroitly between different professional groups in their search for 'help' that does not make them confront the centrality of food/body regulation in their lives, and so does not threaten their anorexic control. Hence a useful strategy is for everyone concerned to reach an agreement for a sufferer to see one named helper. Meanwhile shame and embarrassment may prevent those who are 'out of control', that is, bulimic, from seeking help. Though where, for a bulimic, help still means 'the anorexic solution', a helper who challenges this craved position will be seen as no help.

Justifying intervention

Working with resistant clients can raise moral and legal issues that do not occur when people seek help willingly. With anorexia nervosa this problem is particularly acute. This is not only because of the positive moral connotation that is placed on the effects of food/body regulation but also because, unless the helper takes careful steps to avoid it, any intervention can seem to be in opposition to that very conscious, directed, and systematically organized behaviour which is the hallmark of ordinary, responsible human action, and which is also the key to recognizing so many aspects of the illness. It is in this ambiguity over the 'illness' status of anorexic control that the potential lies for attempts to help to degenerate rapidly into destructive confrontations.

There does need to be some justification for a therapist, doctor or any helper to work in opposition to the clearly expressed wishes of the client. But in this helpers are not simply pitting their view of correct conduct against that of the sufferer. Rather they are using their knowledge of how conflict and confusion, together with food restriction and relentless exercising, can create behaviour that looks as if it arises from personal or moral strength. With experience, a helper can obtain a sense of when such processes are taking place. There are, as we have shown, clear indications in sufferers' polarizing between rigid control in relation to food and exercise, and dithering indecisiveness in every other area of their life. There are clear indications of the early effects of undernutrition.

There are times when helpers will find they need to explain these indications, perhaps to counter the charge that they are perversely attacking the sufferer, attacking deeply held personal beliefs or flying in the face of cherished social values. Where such a situation arises, helpers will find the comparison between food restriction/exercise and the downward spiral created by the effects of alcohol can usefully be drawn upon.

Self-interpretation and virtue

Anorexia nervosa would not exist if it were not possible for a person to welcome and value the gathering effects of starvation. When changes thus wrought are taken morally and physically to be an improvement, it becomes extremely difficult for any onlooker to counter this, to get the message through that others are concerned.

The problem the onlooker faces is that, in terms of sufferers' understanding of self, the physiological information they have and their moral standards are entirely conflated. Sufferers meet expressions of concern, therefore, with frank disbelief or with the conviction that the facts of physiology have no relevance to their situation. The sufferer's view is, characteristically, that physiologically he or she is unique. Thus even after stating correctly that 1400 calories is the daily minimum requirement for an unconscious head-injury patient, an anorexic nurse will firmly insist: 'I'm different. Three hundred calories a day is plenty for me.' The attitude is: 'Whatever you're saying, it doesn't apply to me.' Evidence is not based on physiological facts relating to food requirements but on the experience of euphoria, on the 'good' or 'positive' feeling that results from altered brain chemistry.

Different languages and their implicit values

Physiological terminology has its own clarity and precision, yet relying on this terminology alone can make it more rather than less difficult for a helper to understand the subtle blend of physical changes and interpretations of these changes that the sufferer creates through lowering weight, or being relentlessly active, or through vomiting and purging.

There is a clash where the language of symptoms, which a helper may use, meets the language of personal virtues used by the person dependent on food/body control. It is very easy for anorexics to feel their precious control is being dismissed when their feelings are referred to as 'merely the result of her low blood sugar'. Even if a dismissive attitude is avoided, the words themselves are inherently evaluative. Symptom language has strong negative connotations. Personal virtues are positive by definition. To refer to someone as being 'anorexic' is to pathologize a person who, in the language of personal virtues, is 'striving to hold on to his or her moral integrity'. Thus the more attuned helpers are to the subtle implications of value there are in the words they use, the more effective they are likely to be.

The well-fed helper does not share the experience of the consistently underfed sufferer, and this, together with the different ways these experiences are valued, is sufficient to prevent helper and sufferer ever agreeing about what the problem is, or indeed whether there is a problem at all. Thus the condition gains its reputation for being intractable.

Certainly many therapeutic skills are needed, even to establish a working agreement about the task in hand. But the first step is for the would-be helper to appreciate the sufferer's position fully. It is *to begin where the sufferer is*. Helpers must also appreciate what the consequences are in terms of feelings, emotions, sensations and understanding of self, should a sufferer, at a helper's request, eat even a little more food; or should control slip so that more is eaten by accident. Helpers must appreciate and allow for the fact that, when starvers or persistent underfeeders eat, this switches off some of the pleasant feelings they have grown accustomed to and at the same time switches them rapidly into other feelings they do not like. From being on a starvation high they experience themselves plunging into deep depression as the effects of undernutrition-induced alterations in brain chemistry are reversed. Even taking a quite small amount of food is sufficient to produce this 'mood crash' or 'food hangover'.

Anyone who has just eaten a meal will, for a while, feel less energetic and perhaps rather sleepy as their body diverts blood away from their muscles towards their stomach in the process of digestion. But self-starvers experience this fatigue as extreme. The thinner and weaker they are, the more unacceptably tired and heavy they will feel after eating. The 'solid lump of food' in the stomach is a physical discomfort that reinforces their emotional discomfort. They are not easy-going or forgiving about these feelings and sensations, even though they are normal experiences, and quite predictably happen when any underfed person takes in anything but the most insubstantial amount of food. They are unwelcome and frightening sensations for a person dependent on the 'right' feelings which are obtained from non-eating. A drop in energy, a 'full-stomach feeling' and the sense of having a hangover are all the 'proof' needed that eating is wrong.

A helper recognizing the sufferer's experience of having a 'mood crash' or 'food hangover' enables its terrors to be shared. These descriptions are usually accepted by sufferers as fitting exactly their understanding of what happens when they eat. Eventually, as they begin to take in the idea that a 'mood crash' is an ordinary if worrying event, they may feel able to be a little more accepting over its occurrence.

There are also other changes that take place on eating that are likewise unwelcome and frightening, such as an increase in heart rate and temperature that results in feeling hot, flushed, sweaty, uncomfortable and possibly rather dizzy. These changes are often particularly marked in sufferers who are nearer normal weight, who have been starving and then massively overeat. A stomach that is extremely full can also be excessively painful. Those who regularly vomit and/or purge to relieve themselves of food eaten will also experience subsequent weakness and lethargy. Again these are feelings and sensations that follow normally where food is controlled in these ways. They are brought about by the loss of chemicals from the body with the elimination of body fluids. Whether or not sufferers know this, they do not easily engage with the information. From their experience of themselves after vomiting episodes, and in their persistent use of purgatives, they are convinced they are lazy, good-for-nothing. Quite simply, everything would be better if they could avoid food altogether. The road to breaching this conviction is long and hard.

Sufferers typically monitor their body states very closely. They are usually aware of the most minute changes. But they are effectively prevented from comprehending basic information about the way their body works because their physiological experiences and moral values have become so fused, and because the 'adrenalizing' effects of food avoidance and being relentlessly active have become so intimately bound up with self-worth. So they do not have appropriate interpretations of their body states, nor of the changes that take place in relation to eating and not eating. Hence an important task is to assist them, if they will, in separating out, gradually, facts from values and to provide them with such basic practical information as will help them do this. It involves both helper and sufferer attending to the fine detail of the sufferer's experience in specific episodes of taking in or not taking in food, and the same care will be required in relation to exercise reduction or restriction. A helper will need to accept that it will take considerable time before sufferers are able to modify the assumptions they are working on about their own body, and this applies particularly to accomplished self-starvers and to those habitually working their body to achieve ever higher levels of physical prowess.

References

1 Cockett, A.D. (1968) 'Zinc deficiency and anorexia – cause or consequence', Ipswich: Institute of Family Psychiatry, paper no. 85.
2 *The Sunday Times* (1987) London, 22 February.
3 Welbourne, J., personal communication.

ten

Getting through

A number of points have emerged so far that are of paramount importance, particularly as we turn now to consider the kind of interventions that are of direct practical help.

These points are that:

(a) Because physical starvation is involved *the helper must respond differently at different stages of the disorder*. There is no single counselling or therapeutic approach that is appropriate or sufficient throughout the whole spectrum of the various manifestations of anorexic illness.

(b) *All interventions must be calculated to foster a sense of self*: to increase, not decrease, the sufferer's self-respect. This applies even when some weight gain is urgently required for the sake of physical safety.

(c) Since restricted eating or non-eating and body regulation are central to a sufferer's idea of self, and weight change constitutes changing this 'self', *weight gain needs to take place only as fast as the sufferer is able to cope with it*. This can be expected to take months, if not years, as she or he is helped towards a self that is not a food/body-control self.

To these a further point can now be added, which is that:

(d) If the above are to be achieved, the helper will need to get through to the sufferer in a direct and effective way. *All alternatives to coercion depend on communicating*.

Whatever their connection with the sufferer, few people want or like the destructive confrontations that arise, usually when stores of patience and goodwill have been exhausted. Nor is anyone against communicating. Indeed its value is an article of faith, particularly to those in the helping professions. But the injunction to communicate with the anorexic or bulimic will ring hollow to those who have tried and failed.

The problem here is that feelings of goodwill and a commitment to communicating are not enough. To be effective, a would-be helper needs information about the nature of the condition.

Acknowledging the sufferer's style of thinking

In addition to being informed, helpers must also be prepared to make certain mental adjustments, or efforts of imagination, as suggested in Chapter 5, if they are to place themselves in the sufferer's position, particularly when weight visibly has been lost. To meet a sufferer where she or he is, physiologically and psychologically, a helper will need to change the basic assumptions on which conversations usually proceed. Only then will helper and sufferer find they are talking about the same thing.

In the practical task of getting through, these necessary changes of assumption merge together. A helper, with some practice, will be able to make the adjustments automatically, rather like simultaneously translating into a different language. But to be clear about the changes involved, it is useful to set out the ordinary assumptions that are usually made and compare them with sufferers' understanding of their own experience.

	Ordinary assumptions	*Anorexic/bulimic experience*
(i)	Regulating food and body is one important thing amongst many in her/his life.	Regulating food and body is the only important or significant issue in her/his life. It is the sole measure of personal worth. (Centrality of food and body control: Chapters 1 and 8.)
(ii)	The sufferer is intellectually and emotionally the same person as she/he was before losing weight.	The sufferer has changed her/himself through food and body control and feels a better person, as long as she/he remains in control. (Altered thinking and feelings: Chapter 2.)
(iii)	The sufferer has the same kind and range of physical experiences as the helper.	Some of his/her physical experiences are outside the experience of the adequately fed helper. (Different physical experiences: Chapters 2 and 5.)
(iv)	The sufferer's personal skills and achievements must be as valuable to her/him as they are judged to be by the helper.	The sufferer believes her/himself to be utterly worthless in every respect. (Low self-esteem: Chapter 6.)

(v) Helpers tend to assume that the values implicit in the words they use are shared by the sufferer; that she/he must believe emaciation, intellectual 'shut down' and emotional distance are undesirable.	While the helper may use negative words about her/him, the sufferer uses words with positive connotations. Emotional distance and intellectual 'shut down' are, for the sufferer, clear thinking, a sense of calm, the ability to be decided. (Different implicit values: Chapters 5 and 9.)

It is this mismatch that exists between the assumptions others make about them and anorexia nervosa/bulimia sufferers' different but undeclared understanding of their own position that creates the breakdown in communication. So accustomed do they become to this breakdown that, having been previously shut off, sullen or superior and distant, they can become surprised, wide-eyed, when a helper demonstrates an awareness of how they are thinking and feeling. A working relationship between helper and sufferer can often grow from this point.

For anorexia nervosa/bulimia sufferers, feeling isolated and separate is a core experience; as if they have passed through a glass beyond which others can see them, hear what they are saying, but seem incapable of understanding them.[1] Many images of separateness occur in autobiographical accounts of the illness. The sense of being divided from the rest of the world by a sheet of glass is an image that occurs frequently, and not necessarily only at low weight.

Because the personality changes wrought by starvation are cumulative, and because they are usually well established by the time food/body control has come to be seen as a problem, it is the helper who has to adjust for the sufferer's different perceptions and different understanding, who must make the effort of imagination to pass through the glass and make contact. For imprisoned as they are in what one person referred to as 'her glass fortress', and another as 'this steel wall', they cannot make the adjustments themselves to reach back. Yet once a helper has imaginatively made this transition, 'passed through' the glass, she or he will begin to comprehend the remarkable simplicity, the completeness and predictability of the world sufferers inhabit where they are successfully underfeeding/over-exercising, how it becomes essential to them to protect this world from being destroyed, and how this task of protection can seem so much simpler and easier, the thinner and more cognitively constrained they become.

It is by adjusting for the characteristic style of thinking, and for the way its changes are weight-related, that the helper will be able to appreciate the truth for sufferers of the statements they make, to see how it is they are neither lying, nor mad, nor incomprehensible to themselves. Yet while making these adjustments, it is imperative that the helper at the same time stands firmly on this side of the glass, securely in a non-anorexic, non-food/body controlling world. This tends to require a high degree of self-awareness on the part of helpers, the ability to separate themselves from the sufferer's style of thinking and evaluation of personal experiences, and the ability to avoid becoming drawn in (see Chapter 9). It is essential to appreciate the sufferer's position and style of thinking, but equally, to do this in such a way as to retain the freedom to promote change.

It would be wrong to give the impression that, once a helper has learned the skill of translating for an anorexic or food/body-control perception of self and the world, easy cooperation and harmony will prevail. On the contrary, many of the helping strategies we will describe necessarily involve some conflict. But the helper's skill here will lie in drawing out and working with the conflicts that already exist within the sufferer and paralyse effective action, whilst not becoming part of those conflicts. The difference is in the nature of the conflict, and between an approach that seeks to impose change on the sufferer, 'whatever she (or he) thinks', and an approach that suggests changes because of the conflict in the sufferer's own thinking (see Chapter 9).

Returning to the stepladder

Though it can, at some stages and in some situations, be quite difficult to detect, it remains the case that whatever a sufferer's weight, centrality of food control is always present. Though it may home on different activities, and present very different appearances at different times, the defining attitude is always the same.

Sufferers whose weight is around their average expected body weight and whose current pattern is stuffing–starving or binge–vomiting will at this stage be totally focused on the problem of how to avoid food and eating, and how to regain the control they lose in their continual and humiliating cyclic failure to do so. Nevertheless they have the capacity to think in complex and varied ways. At low weight, on the other hand, it is the total preoccupation with food and the contraction of intellectual capacity that together create the inability to think about anything else. Centrality of food control at this stage is the consequence of an actual inability to conceptualize much beyond food, and of the polarized thinking that renders this person incapable of grasping the possibility of there being intermediate positions at all.

Those who are not at a very low weight can respond to appropriate therapy far more rapidly than those who are emaciated and very constrained intellectually. The way in which it is possible to hold conversations with a sufferer who is 75 per cent AEBW and still in full employment, for instance, is different both in content and in process from the more concrete, limited colloquies that can be had with the sufferer at 60 per cent AEBW who is exhausted and in crisis. Where intellectual potential is not so closed down by starvation, new experiences in the course of therapy are more readily held in focus, and there is some capacity to process them.

Therefore the adjustments listed at the beginning of this chapter require different emphases at different stages of the illness. Since there is not one, but a number of tasks involved in getting through, so, depending on where a sufferer is, a helper will need to tailor these adjustments to the requirements of each individually. Just as there are clear levels that can be differentiated physically, in terms of bands of weight and related appearance, and psychologically in terms of intellectual capacity and emotional experience, so there are levels that can be differentiated in relation to getting through to the sufferer. In other words there is a stepladder for communicating too.

Working with this idea, the last four chapters are organized around four different stages of the condition. For anyone reading this book with a particular person in mind these steps should provide at least one picture they can recognize. The task of this present chapter meanwhile is to point out some aspects of communicating that apply in general.

Adjusting for the centrality of food control

As we have said, the centrality of food/body control is the key to diagnosing anorexic illness, and necessarily so in its underweight stage. It is the presence of the core attitude that will confirm that it is anorexia nervosa the helper is meeting in any particular case.

> I must absolutely plan what I eat, I must know in advance, otherwise I can't organize anything else. Once I've done that I'm all right. Then I know where I am. I don't often eat out, or anything like that. I usually prefer my own company anyway. (At 85 per cent AEBW)

With practice helpers and others can quickly learn to tune in to the authentic ring of the anorexic conviction that life is possible only as long as food and body are in control. Statements about food/body regulation will tend to be delivered with a confident assurance. A sufferer can also have a certain social poise that tends to deflect questioning, that turns suspicion aside.

Illustrations were given in Chapter 8 to enable a helper to begin to clarify the existential quality of the content of 'anorexic' statements. It is useful to be attuned to hear, as well as see, evidence of the sufferer's characteristic attitude: 'I never miss my running. That's too important. Whatever the weather's like, it doesn't matter to me. I have to go out for my run. I wouldn't feel right if I didn't' (at 90 per cent AEBW). Similarly, 'I don't mind if it's muscle I gain. But it *mustn't* be fat. That would totally panic me. I can't do that. But I know I'm safe, as long as I get to the gym. I'll eat what I need to eat to get to the gym. You know, the right food. I'm always very careful about what I eat' (at 96 per cent AEBW). It is also useful for the helper, and concerned others, to be aware that there can be a hidden agenda in statements such as 'I always get so involved in my work, I find that when I'm working I really don't need to eat . . .' (at 89 per cent AEBW). Further questioning is likely to reveal that the speaker regularly goes all day without food, and then considers:

It's not worth the trouble preparing myself anything when I get home late in the evening. I might just have a slice of bread and a piece of fruit. I can't be bothered at that time of night. Besides, I don't like to have too much food in my stomach when I go to bed. I hate going to sleep feeling bloated.

A person's extreme thinness will, of course, make it easier to hear the central importance of food and body control in the things she/he says. But as we have said, sufferers are not always identifiable by their thinness.

Because anorexic commitment to food/body control is in the nature of a lens or prism through which every comment, question, observation, encouragement or suggestion passes, all the 'being' or life statements sufferers make about themselves need to be translated by the helper into food statements, or equally, food-burning statements. Conversely, where the helper uses life statements, he or she must be aware that sufferers will receive and understand these as food statements. Thus when the helper asks how a sufferer is feeling, and the reply is 'I'm feeling fine', the helper must understand that this means 'I'm in control.' In other words, this person has not eaten anything she/he did not mean to eat, has probably eaten less than the amount she/he planned to allow him/herself, and is currently feeling 'good', and 'safe'. The underlying account will run something like: 'I haven't eaten all day, so I can allow myself salad this evening, and a slice of cold chicken (8 cm square) and still be in control.' There are probably familiar and reassuring aches being felt, because there has been time to run the two miles to the appointment with the helper, instead of taking a bus, and more calories burnt off than would otherwise have been.

Conversely statements such as 'I don't feel very good today', or 'I feel terrible' translate as 'My eating is out of control.' The experience, and underlying account, in this case runs something like:

It's 12.30 and I've eaten a whole 200 grams of cottage cheese. I only ever eat 100 grams at 12.30. It's made me go completely to pieces. I'm terrified. I might eat and eat and never stop. I hate myself when I can't stick to what I know I ought to.

It must be remembered too that statements about 'feeling terrible' will be made with most urgency and greatest conviction by the hospitalized 28.6 kg (4 st. 7l bs) sufferer – i.e. 59 per cent AEBW – who has just gained the first 0.5 kg (barely one pound) of weight.

Helpers who, by translating thus, can step imaginatively into the anorexic world will more easily understand the situation from its perspective and so genuinely be able to accept the positive statements sufferers make about themselves as being true for them, however unlikely that may seem from the way they currently look! Genuine acceptance, which will be felt by the sufferer, is fundamental in assisting change.

The helper's position described here contrasts with that of the onlooker who sees the sufferer – usually female in this instance, though by no means invariably so – as fashionably skinny, who agrees with her when she says 'I feel fine', and is drawn in because there is no mismatch at all between the sufferer's anorexic views and the onlooker's own views. It also, equally and oppositely, contrasts with the position of the onlooker who sees an anorexic's stick-like appearance, notices the bluish-mauve hands, hears her say 'I'm feeling fine', does not believe her and dismisses what she says. Here there is a complete mismatch between the sufferer's and the onlooker's views. Sufferers will always notice the hearer's disbelief and dismissive attitude. They can become angry and hostile at not being believed, and feel totally unjustly treated.

This response they will take as one more judgement against them; one more failure; yet another instance of not being understood. Where no adjustment is made for the anorexic mindset, attempts to reach a sufferer rapidly arrive at their uncomfortable impasse.

Helper: I wonder if there's anything worrying you?
Anorexic [blandly]: No.
Helper: Nothing at all?
Anorexic: No. Nothing's worrying me. [Translated: I've really got my eating under control, and I'm not worried about anything when I've got that sorted out.]
Helper: You look rather worried.
Anorexic: No, I'm all right. [Translated: The only thing that's worrying me now is you. I'm scared you're going to start pressuring me. I've got it organized and I don't want to be undermined by you or anyone else.]
Helper: But other people are worried about you. Your parents, for instance. That's why you're here.
Anorexic: Yes, I came because I know they're worried, but I don't see there's any need for them to feel like that. I'm OK.
Helper: I'm rather concerned about how thin you are.
Anorexic: But I'm not. I'm fine. There's no need for you to worry about me. You can see I'm all right.

Here the helper thinks: 'But she's skeletal. What does she mean?' and conversation grinds to a halt. A helper on the other hand who continually adjusts for the sufferer's perspective has the possibility of moving into that world and communicating with the sufferer in her or his own terms. This not only avoids an impasse. It demonstrates to the sufferer that the helper understands the position. It is a way of really meeting this person. Thus the above conversation might instead take the following course.

Helper: Is there anything worrying you?
Anorexic [blandly]: No.
Helper: Nothing at all?
Anorexic: No. Nothing's worrying me. [Translated: I've got my eating in control, and I'm not worried about anything when that's all right.]

Helper: You look a bit worried to me . . . [Deciding to try a 'move' towards her] I imagine the people who think you're thin pressure you a lot to eat more. And I'm wondering whether, right now, you're worried I might start pressuring you like everybody else?

Anorexic [appearing startled, and then finding herself agreeing]: They're always trying to make me eat all this food. But I don't want it.

Helper [indicating acceptance of her last statement by mirroring her determined tone]: No, you don't want it. But it's probably very hard to make them understand that you feel much better when you don't eat. You can get more done, perhaps?

Anorexic [still rather surprised that this therapist appears to understand]: Yes. I do, but they won't believe me.

Helper: And I guess you do eat something?

Anorexic [opening up]: Oh yes, I eat the things I like. [Translated: I like eating a small range of low-calorie foods such as . . .]

Helper: What kind of things do you like?

Anorexic [enthusiastically]: Vegetables. I love vegetables. And cottage cheese. I eat a lot of cottage cheese. [Translated: That is, a small amount which is always exactly the same so I still feel safe.]

In meeting the sufferer by adjusting for this centrality, it becomes possible to help bring the detail of the need for control into the open. This is one essential step towards sufferers eventually allowing themselves to experiment with risking some change (see Chapter 12).

Helper: How are you feeling?

Anorexic: Fine.

Helper: You're feeling fine. So I guess you've got your eating organized.

Anorexic [brightly]: Oh yes.

Helper: Would you like to tell me about that? What have you eaten today, for instance?

Anorexic: Well, I don't eat anything till the evening.

Helper: So you haven't eaten anything so far today.

Anorexic: No, I never do. I don't need to.

Helper [noting last comment, but letting it pass in favour of bringing in a suggestion of change]: Suppose you'd eaten a slice of toast for breakfast before coming here . . .

Anorexic [looking alarmed]: I couldn't do that.

Helper: No, but suppose you had. How d'you think you'd feel?

Anorexic: Terrible.

Helper: Yes, I agree. You'd feel terrible. Like you'd let yourself down?

Anorexic [pausing before risking admitting this]: I'd be a total failure . . .

Helper: And my guess is you wouldn't eat for the rest of the day.

Anorexic: No. [Looking panicky] Not if I'd eaten that for breakfast.

Helper: You took as though the very thought of it makes you panic.

Anorexic [relieved the helper has noticed her panic, but doesn't seem to blame her, or think she's silly]: Yes, it does. [Pause] It seems silly to get into a panic over a slice of toast . . . but . . .
Helper: At the moment that's what you do.
Anorexic [firmly]: I would if I ate it – but I don't. Not if I can help it.

Adjusting for altered thinking

As starvation progresses sufferers think about a smaller range of things, they think about them in an increasingly polarized way, and everything that is thought about is thought about in non-food, or food-burning terms. These are the main intellectual changes created where food intake is persistently inadequate for daily requirements (see Chapter 2).

The changes intensify as weight falls, and become less severe as weight rises. This means that, of the adjustments the helper needs to make, the exact adjustment required for altered thinking will depend utterly on *this* person's weight level on *this* day, and how it has recently altered: whether it has gone up or down, and how fast.

Intellectual change can be masked for a considerable length of time by habitual performance. For instance, while weight drops, sufferers are likely to continue to obtain high marks for academic work at first because they will make up with many hours of dedicated, repetitive learning what they cannot do by abstraction, or by the creative synthesis of new ideas. How well they perform will also depend somewhat on their particular history within the illness, the significant factor usually being the length of time they have been maintaining a low-weight state and at the same time fulfilling day-to-day obligations. If they are studying medicine, or geography, or any subject where the task is to assimilate material in a predictable, pre-organized form, sufferers will be able to continue to do this even at quite low weight. But if they are studying A-level or university mathematics, or another course where problem solving via new decisions is required, or the flexible and creative reorganization of ideas, then they will begin to fail much sooner. They will not be able to perform even after a relatively small drop in weight below 85 per cent AEBW. The ability to understand and assimilate new information will be restricted and this will become increasingly apparent as they become more emaciated. As one ex-sufferer said:

It showed a lot when it came to doing essays. You sit in the library and make notes and more notes till you're drowning in notes. But you can't handle them. The last thing you can do is turn them into a coherent well-argued essay. You can't decide where to begin, or what to put in, and it seems impossible to leave anything out.

It is for this reason that it is pointless for a helper to present low-weight sufferers with the 'grand analysis' in the hope that, by telling them their starvation is progressively impairing their intellectual capacity, they might be encouraged to eat. Attempting to get through by rational argument is as unproductive as attempting to discuss complex issues with a person who is continually under the influence of alcohol. They only have the capacity to respond in the most simple, polarized way, and in any case will not want to believe anything that is out of line with their own rigid views, or contrary to their 'improved' experience of themselves. They do not take kindly to anyone who attempts to deprive them in any way of their greatest achievement, i.e. their recent or sustained weight loss.

It is far more effective a strategy for the helper to make adjustments, and so talk about specific deficits that can be judged as most likely to be happening to each sufferer at their particular current weight in the hope that they themselves will be able to recognize that those things the helper is mentioning have begun to occur in their own life.

Helper: You've lost another pound. I know that's not worrying you . . .
Anorexic: No.
Helper [aware that the girl is now around 72 per cent AEBW]: I'm aware it's easier for you not to eat. Your weight's gone down again. But I wonder . . . Have you noticed yourself changing any other way?
Anorexic [silent, and looks blank]: –
Helper: I wonder if you're feeling the cold much more? And taking longer about doing things . . . Because perhaps your concentration might be a bit patchy? Or as though you've got gaps in your memory?
Anorexic [in a changed tone]: Funny you should say that. I don't concentrate as well as I did. It's hard to keep my mind on things. When I'm at work . . . even writing letters, it takes ages.
Helper: You're noticing that yourself.
Anorexic: Yes. I don't remember things. I have to keep asking.
Helper: It wasn't like that a few weeks ago . . .
Anorexic: No.
Helper: So as your weight is going down, you can't work as well as you did.
Anorexic [grudgingly]: Mmm. I suppose so.

Such an intervention can be risky unless the helper is sure she or he has recognized the appropriate stage. Sufferers will be highly offended at the idea that they cannot concentrate if they feel they can. Yet when there is a bland denying of any problem at all, an appropriately judged intervention that homes in on a specific deficit may make its mark.

A helper may find it useful to imagine polarized or altered thinking as a template that is set on every aspect of the person's experience. It is a template that can help make sense of the totally assured, holier-than-thou attitude the sufferer has at one time (i.e. when all is organized and feels in control), and the total self-hatred and self-disgust the same sufferer experiences at another time (i.e. when control has been lost). There are no intermediate positions. A shift from one extreme to the other can occur as a result of unplanned eating of an amount of food that, to anyone not anorexic in their thinking, will seem insignificant – such as four grapes, or a single bite of a sandwich – or it can occur as a result of not getting to get to the gym *exactly* at 12.45 p.m.

Such a template also gives coherence to statements about weight – 'It's all right if I'm five stone thirteen. Then I'm thin. But I couldn't possibly be six stone. That's fat!' – and to every other statement concerning quantity and measurement. 'In that exam? I only got 99 per cent. So what if the pass mark's 70. That's not what I ought to have got. Of course I've failed! I should have got it *all* right.'

Again these are statements that, should the person who hears them lack the necessary informed understanding, can be dismissed as nonsense or madness. But to those aware of the changes starvation creates, their meaning is clear and, in relation to the sufferer, informative.

The perceptual changes that take place, and that have the effect of making sufferers feel fatter than they actually are, are in fact an example of a quite normal psychological process that occurs whenever a particular distinction acquires a great significance for any person.[2] This process (perceptual shift) is exploited every day by price tags advertising £6.99 rather than £7, or £18,950 rather than £19,000. It works by exaggerating the difference between two points on any scale that are in fact quite near each other so that they seem importantly different and far apart from each other. Because of the effects of starvation, such perceptual shifts are very much more exaggerated at low weight.

Adjusting for low self-esteem

Anorexic or bulimic sufferers' extremely low self-esteem may not be in the least apparent. Whether they come across as entirely confident and superior or as depressed and self-effacing will always be tied closely to their current sense of being in control of food and weight, or how exercised they feel.

Whether or not their low self-esteem is evident, a helper will assist by allowing for its presence, by adjusting for it from the first moments of meeting and actively engaging in ways likely to promote a sense of self-worth. Simple measures such as acknowledging their presence by greeting them by name, giving eye contact in so far as they seem able to cope with this, talking *to* them rather than *about* them, listening to and genuinely acknowledging what they say, and giving them plenty of time to express their position are all helpful in this respect.

A particular adjustment that will need to be made is for the way absence of self-worth colours the way sufferers relate to others, ensuring a pattern of either finding every possible fault with other people, dismissing others as worthless and inferior, or finding every possible fault with themselves and dismissing themselves. Either way, low self-esteem serves to protect and defend anyone feeling deeply worthless from the burden of engaging with anyone, including any helper (see Chapter 9).

Sufferers who have tried to express their feelings of worthlessness and inadequacy will have been used to having these feelings dismissed. They will be accustomed to others seeing them as highly talented, as confident, poised, well-qualified, as socially advantaged. So they anticipate that this helper too will see them the same way. A helper who does take this view will create an impasse as the sufferer feels obliged to sustain the 'false front'. If on the other hand a helper can gently demonstrate awareness of the mismatch that exists between the way the world sees the anorexic/bulimic and the way sufferers see themselves, this again can provide an awakening, a point of genuine meeting and understanding that might stir the possibility of developing a helping relationship, or assist in keeping a fragile or incipient relationship alive.

It is important to appreciate how sufferers fear being 'really known', or found out for being 'such a really hateful person'. Believing then, 'that'll be the end, so I'd better stop this therapy before *that* happens'.

Equally it is important to avoid carelessly triggering defences. Any hint of criticism or judgemental comment at this point is fatal to the development of any therapeutic relationship, as is vicariously laughing, sniggering or joking. Being straightforward is essential.

> *Helper* [at a first meeting with a sufferer who appears resentful, silent and withdrawn]: . . . and your parents seemed proud to tell me you've just got your degree . . . I guess most people see you as very successful . . . I suspect that's not quite the way you feel yourself . . . (Watching the girl's face colour slightly) . . . even though you got a first.
>
> *Sufferer* [rapidly]: I didn't deserve it.
>
> *Helper*: You don't believe you deserved it . . . You feel a fraud?
>
> *Sufferer* [quietly]: Mmm . . .

Though they will fear being 'so transparent' it can, even so, be a great relief to meet someone who seems to know just how worthless and ineffectual they feel, and how much they loathe themselves, yet who does not blame or chide them for feeling like this; who in fact seems, bewilderingly, to accept them, though they cannot see why.

Even when they are low weight and successfully starving, sufferers will be terrified of losing control. So, though they may dismiss the helper's 'inferior' attempts to communicate with them, it is on the issue of losing control that the helper is likely to find a chink in their armour of 'superiority'. However, while aiming to help them bring this greatest fear into the open, it is also appropriate to accept their superior or dismissive attitude straightforwardly, as current. So a helper may say:

> It seems clear you think I'm pretty stupid and misguided to go on believing you need help when you've made it quite plain you think it's

unnecessary. You seem sure you've got your life organized. And I'm not going to deny that [Pause] but my guess is that a lot of your organization hangs on keeping a tight watch on what you let yourself eat . . . and trying not to eat . . . which is usually very hard work . . . [Noting a slight, inadvertent nod]. I wonder whether you always feel so sure about yourself? Like when it gets difficult to avoid food. Or you seem to find yourself eating by accident [Noting she is looking panicky]. You look a bit scared . . . [Gently] Has that happened? Or is it that you're afraid it might?

Like any other human being, an anorexia nervosa/bulimia sufferer is quite normal and ordinary in wanting and needing attention, acknowledgement, respect. Indeed, all of these are essential if a person is to begin to allow the development of a self that does not depend on food/body control. But their feelings of unworthiness prevent sufferers from taking the attention and acknowledgement they need. These are undeserved, in their eyes. They also create obligations and responsibilities. They must prove they are worth acknowledgement and respect, but at the same time they are afraid they will be unable to fulfil the obligations these generate. They fear the uncertainty too of not knowing what the obligations and responsibilities might be. Hence the dilemma is that they both want and do not want attention. Where the helper empathizes accurately, and gives appropriate attention and acknowledgement even in recognizing this ambivalence and the tangle of feelings it creates, then communication can become effective.

Adjusting for different physical experiences

The helper will need to be aware of, and adjust for, the many physical sensations familiar to sufferers in their starved state, but outside the experience of the adequately fed person. The detail of these was described in Chapter 2. It is also essential to bear in mind the very distinct contrast there is at low weight between the physical feeling of being empty and the changes to this feeling when even quite small quantities of food are eaten. Larger amounts eaten regularly will leave a sufferer feeling 'like one great big digestive tract'.

Failure to appreciate that at low weight the sufferer is speaking from a place that is physiologically different from that of those who are adequately fed has vitiated many medical research projects and investigations, and there is no progress to be made in terms of therapy by making the same mistake. Where the helper allows for different physical sensations, then statements sufferers make about 'feeling disgustingly full', or 'being swollen and bloated', when they have eaten as little as half an orange become quite coherent and intelligible. A helper who understands them as accurate expressions of their physical experiences at low weight is more likely to be able to keep communication open.

Anorexic: I couldn't eat at lunchtime. I never eat till evening. That's my rule.

Helper: You'd feel swollen up, even if you ate say an apple and a biscuit . . . You feel much better not eating at all.

Anorexic [looking suddenly relieved, as if discovering 'Here's someone who knows; someone I don't have to pretend to!']: Yes . . . It's always much easier not to eat.

Helper: If you don't eat, then you don't get that terrible depressed feeling afterwards.

Anorexic: Yes.

Helper: Like a kind of 'mood crash'? Does that describe it for you?

Anorexic [more alert]: Yes. That *is* how it feels . . . [Opening up] I got really upset I felt so awful yesterday after supper [This sufferer's only small food intake in the day]. I'd been really cold and I knew I had to eat – but I felt terrible about it. My brother found me crying in my room, and my parents just thought I was being stupid. But it does make you feel so disgusting and really low when you eat. No one understands that.

Helper: No. They don't. [Pause] The trouble is . . . till you've eaten a little bit more and put up with having these terrible feelings afterwards for quite a few more times, there is no way you can get on top of these feelings. At the moment slight shifts in your blood sugar are going to change your mood catastrophically.

The experienced helper knows that this, or something very like this, will have to be said to the anorexic *over and over again*.

Adjusting for different implicit values

The helper's difficulty in communicating with sufferers about the way they experience their bodily states does not arise only because at low weight they are making statements about their physical experiences from a different physiological baseline. Like everyone else anorexia nervosa/bulimia sufferers use their mental faculties to understand and creatively interpret their bodily sensations in terms of their values and their beliefs about themselves. So they interpret all the physical experiences they associate with non-eating and exertion as morally positive, and all those associated with eating or rest as morally negative (see Chapter 9).

When a self-starver is obviously too thin and still rigidly refusing food, there is the greater temptation for the helper to assume that the sufferer here 'must be able to realize that she cannot go on like this'. It can be useful, as with polarized thinking, for the helper again to imagine a template set on the sufferer's values that completely reverses the ideas of good and bad, safe and unsafe. This helps adjust for the fact that the sufferer is using these ideas in a topsy-turvy way.

Nurturing a sense of self

No helper can work with anyone, anorexic/bulimic or otherwise, without their being willing to come to the next appointment. This most minimal cooperation is more likely to be given to the helper who, by making the appropriate adjustments, conveys an accurate and genuine understanding of the way the sufferer feels. There is a balance to be achieved between creating the appropriate safety and engaging a sufferer's curiosity, which may occur initially as a result of the unusual responses received from a helper who is informed, even though such responses also open up risk. Either provides a point from which minimal cooperation can be negotiated, such as coming for a next appointment.

Acknowledging the need for control and thus at first not breaking down the little self-esteem a sufferer has is, in the long term, far more conducive to recovery. *The person who dismisses what the sufferer says is dismissing the person she or he currently is.* Interventions that attack control destroy the only thing the anorexic or bulimic wants, and, in so doing, destroy all that this person is. Such interventions ensure the continuation of hopeless feelings, despair, confusion and failure. They perpetuate the sense of being 'something less than human'.

Whatever their current weight level, sufferers need to find out for themselves in quite practical ways how destructive is their style of thinking, or mindset. As they discover this, they will need support and practical information about how they might begin to change. Such information will be the most valuable and enduring where it is learnt gradually through their own first-hand experience. Meanwhile the kind of beginning that can be made in setting this process in train will always depend on each sufferer's physical state, current weight and pattern of food/body control, the circumstances in which they are living and the speed at which weight is falling. Given that the natural progression of the illness is for weight to drop, an assessment of the amount of time there is available before it becomes dangerously low is crucial to the helper's decision about what, at any point, should be the immediate focus of help.

References

1 Slade, R. (1984) *The Anorexia Nervosa Reference Book.* London: Harper and Row, 10.
2 Ibid., 97–100, 113–14.

eleven

Good medicine

We have said the single most important piece of information a helper can have about an anorexia nervosa/bulimia sufferer is that person's current weight. It is this that gives a ready guide to the kind of communication that is possible, and information about how urgent the need is for increased nutrition. Different weight bands – and we will identify four of these – typically present a different cluster of problems. Identifying which band applies to a sufferer at any point is an essential first step in adjusting help to individual needs.

While these four weight bands, or stages, reflect the most commonly occurring patterns within the condition, the time at which some symptoms occur varies. Although some self-starvers keep themselves at dangerously low weight levels by vomiting everything they eat, and others regularly take large amounts of laxatives, and some do both at once, this persistent, simultaneous use of all the possible forms of weight and body control is usually only arrived at after several years. For the sake of clarity, problems associated with vomiting and laxative abuse will be discussed in Chapter 13 where issues that usually arise at higher weight bands will be considered. The point to note here is that the combination of binge eating and vomiting, together with habitual misuse of laxatives, provides the greatest threat to survival when the sufferer resorts to these at low weight.

The lower weight is, the more constrained communication will be, and conversely the more pressing the concerns aroused by the person's debilitated physical condition. How physical needs in the lowest band of weights can most constructively be met, given the rigidity of thinking that will also be met here, is the subject of this chapter. As weight increases, and as long as care is taken to sustain, as far as possible, the sufferer's sense of physical and psychological safety in relation to food and weight, and the pressure felt to exercise, so the focus of therapy will gradually widen to include other aspects of experience. This widening of focus will be reflected in the content of each subsequent chapter.

50–65 per cent AEBW: emaciation and medical help

We have also pointed out that there is, strictly speaking, no medical cure for anorexia nervosa/bulimia. The medicine required is food, and the problem is how to provide this in a way a sufferer can accept. There are techniques for refeeding a person emaciated by the illness available to those who are medically trained that are not available to other helpers; though the medical options for refeeding are much more limited than many people believe or indeed hope, particularly when the more inappropriate and/or destructive approaches have been discarded.

It is not just because some refeeding must be achieved that hospital is the best place for the very low-weight or emaciated sufferer. Emaciation can bring about medical crises that only a hospital has the facilities to cope with. Once such hazards have been successfully avoided, the techniques for refeeding in a way that reduces the threat that food presents to the sufferer can in principle be used inside or outside hospital. Which context is the more appropriate is a pragmatic decision and can go either way, depending on the circumstances in each individual case.

It should not be assumed, on the one hand, that using these techniques at home is necessarily easier or more humane if, in practice, this means giving extra tasks and responsibilities to a family already reeling from years of coping with the illness. The sufferer also may find it easier to make some initial changes in a different situation, away from home. On the other hand, it can be easy to exaggerate the capacity of hospital institutions to provide food in the non-threatening way the sufferer needs.

How much time do we have?

A helper's priorities must change as a sufferer's weight falls. In the 65–50 per cent weight band the thresholds of physical change become critical. It is not possible to engage in psychotherapy with a corpse.

Those who are controlling their food intake by starvation alone, and whose weight is falling slowly (around 0.5 kg /1 lb. a week) are usually medically safe until the point where their weight reaches 60 per cent AEBW, *provided that no other factor is influencing that person's health*. Injury or illness rapidly alters the picture for the worse (see Chapter 3). However determined, or content, sufferers sound when they are severely emaciated, hospital admission will be necessary at or below this point. Should weight fall as low as 50 per cent AEBW death may occur within days. (These levels can be calculated, as shown in the Introduction to this book, from the tables in the Appendix.)

There are important qualifications to these thresholds, however. If weight is falling at a more rapid rate (1.5–2.0 kg/3–4 lbs a week), then 65 per cent is the level at which the condition must be considered medically dangerous. All of these percentage weight levels must be calculated from the original body weight rather than the average expected body weight (AEBW) if the sufferer's rapid weight loss began from a point where the sufferer was substantially overweight (see Chapter 5 for examples).

If food intake is markedly reduced and vomiting is occurring (either self-induced or, more sinisterly, spontaneous vomiting, i.e the elimination that has come to be a 'quite ordinary' event; not 'sought' or provoked), then hospital admission at once is the only safe measure. Electrolyte imbalance and dehydration, in addition to malnutrition, are a lethal mixture. Dehydration and constipation can lead to gastric or bowel perforations due to gas pressure occluding blood flow in the wall of the gut, and so producing gangrenous patches in the gut wall. Infections in severely undernourished patients do not produce the same signs, such as feverishness and raised white cell count, as they would in a normal person. If patients cannot spare the resources to make the protein antibodies in response to an invading bacterium, they may have fewer symptoms, but they are the more gravely ill. An observer's impression that a patient is ill, and more ill and listless than she/he was the day before, should overrule laboratory results and thermometer readings.

From the point where weight falls to around the 70 per cent level it is essential that the helper should keep a close check on the degree of emaciation. Between 69 and 65 per cent AEBW the probability is that, unless the sufferer soon comes to the point of deciding to attempt the task of feeding with the therapist's help, medical help will be needed. This probability will be all the greater where an emaciated sufferer has no previous relationship with the helper that she or he has been brought to see.

An unpractised helper, or one without ready access to medical support, will need to prepare at this level of just below 70 per cent for the possibility that medical care will be necessary, and be aware of the length of time referrals through a general practitioner can take.

The helper must not assume either that, even if weight loss has been slow but steady before, it will continue at a steady rate. The lower weight is, the greater the preoccupation becomes with food and non-eating. All other matters fade into the periphery of consciousness, or they are expressed only in terms of food/body control. Thus with a very reduced range of ideas left at this stage to work with, there is the tendency for food restriction to intensify just when its consequences become serious. So weight may plummet suddenly. This must be responded to urgently. If a 0.5 kg (1 lb.) per week loss suddenly becomes a 1.5–2.0 kg (3–4 lbs) loss in the most recent week, then the helper should act immediately by calling in medical help. Any changes in behaviour at this point, such as moving from solid foods to liquids only, or losing interest in a beloved pet, must be taken seriously. At this stage sufferers may well stop eating or drinking altogether. If this happens, it is an emergency. There are only ten days or so in which to get eating restarted. If a person stops taking all fluids as well, then a critical point is reached in only 36–48 hours.

50–65 per cent AEBW: communication

Sometimes life-saving measures must be the first consideration but, handled with appropriate care, these measures need not entirely alienate the sufferer from those providing the needed medical help. However severe emaciation may be, the sufferer is not just a body.

> *Anorexic*: They don't believe me when I say I feel better when I don't eat. But I do.
> *Helper*: Yes, that's right. You do feel better when you don't eat.
> *Anorexic*: The more I tell them about how I feel, the less they believe me. The less they trust that I'm telling the truth. It's difficult if they don't believe me.
> *Helper*: You want to be believed. [The girl nods] And the truth is you feel really bad when you eat.
> *Anorexic*: Yes . . . but *why* can't they believe me?
> *Helper*: They see you now as so starved you could die from starvation any time. And they're treating that as more important than you feeling better when you don't eat.

Even when emaciation is so severe it is crucially important to meet sufferers at the specific point where *they* are, to acknowledge genuinely what they are saying of themselves from this position, and appreciate that their extreme statements are accurate because they are speaking from within a situation where all perspectives are extreme. Anything else here is felt by sufferers as their being opposed, and, as we have shown, opposition or confrontation works in a curious way to confirm the validity of extreme thinking. When this happens, a helper becomes as stuck as any sufferer.

The task, certainly when thinking is so constrained, is to hold the more intermediate position the anorexic cannot hold. While demonstrating genuine understanding and acceptance of the sufferer's position, the helper can encourage very limited moves away from this extreme, which at this stage will focus on moving in the direction of eating a little more food. For helpers this means getting the information across that, while they understand and accept the sufferer's way of thinking and feeling, and believe the truth *for the sufferer* of what she or he is saying, they do not share the anorexic view of the position that person is in. The message a helper needs to get through is 'I understand, but I don't agree.' A helper who demonstrates genuine understanding and who also genuinely disagrees will not fit conveniently in either of the sufferer's categories. Yet being a different kind of experience, it can arouse curiosity, and assist the helping relationship.

The lower their weight is, the greater difficulty sufferers have in following even quite simple conversations. Any verbal communication at this stage must be direct, clear, repeated and repeated often. Anything complicated merely creates confusion and does so very quickly, or it provokes panic and/or anger about losing control on non-eating. Sufferers will often look far away and rather blank, and will easily be overwhelmed by attempts to communicate because they are unable to cope intellectually with the ideas that others are trying to get through to them. Everything has to be repeated, because they rapidly forget. Preoccupation with non-eating will be so extreme at this stage, it will be difficult for them to keep any other thought in focus.

Not only the way of talking, but also the content of conversation must be simple – acknowledging their views, feelings, sensations, should these be expressed; giving facts truthfully; dealing with *one* item of any topic at a time; dealing with food issues because this is their central concern. It is vital at this stage that only one person engages a sufferer in conversation at any one time. That is, unless the purpose is to overwhelm on a particular topic. A statement such as 'You cannot leave hospital tonight. The last bus has gone. It's raining. It's cold. You are too thin to walk home, and it isn't safe anyway' will be more effectively made by two or three staff together.

Whatever the message, it will be conveyed as much by a helper's attitude and bearing as by what is said. The helper's own body language and tone of voice will support or deny verbal statements. If there is a mismatch, if at this or at any stage a helper does not believe what she or he is saying to the suf-ferer, the sufferer will sense this and will become dismissive, or more confused. Where a helper does get through, and obtains even minimal cooperation, the task of caring for the sufferer's physical need for food will, to the same degree, be less fraught.

Refeeding the anorexic in hospital

Essential nourishment can be given by intravenous drip, or using a nasogastric tube (a tube that goes from the nose through the gullet to the stomach), or a liquid diet, or eventually a mixture of normal meals and additional fortified drinks, or normal meals and a bedtime drink. Obviously the first two of these methods are possible only in hospital. The procedure that is appropriate will differ in each individual case and will depend on the extent of emaciation and the sufferer's physical condition.

Whatever a self-starver's weight, it is psychologically more beneficial to start the process of refeeding slowly and increase nourishment by small steps. The lower weight is, the more essential this will also be from a physiological point of view. Thus the total daily calorie intake will also vary from individual to individual, and will depend on the amount of nourishment required for the task in hand. The first step is to work out what the particular sufferer will need to take to gain weight – for example, 3000 calories per day – and then (given there is one calorie per ml for most proprietary tube feeds) to start with one sixth of that amount (500 calories) at half strength (plus 500 ml water) the first day, increasing to one third at half strength the next day and so on till the full volume of fluid (i.e. 3000 ml) which at this point consists of 2000 ml tube-feed plus 1000 ml water, has been reached. Then from here, and by exactly the same steps, increase the strength of the feed but keep the volume the same. If the patient is not sick and normal bowel sounds can be heard, then the whole process can be accomplished over four to six days. But should the anorexic be ill, then the more ill she/he is, the lower the initial amount of nourishment that must be given, and the longer it will take to work up to giving the full amount the refeeding process requires.

Intravenous feeding

Intravenous feeding carries risks so it is usually only employed when a severely ill patient has developed a condition, such as gastric dilatation or paralytic ileus, in which the digestive system cannot absorb food. These are two conditions which are unfortunately likely to be produced by refeeding a sufferer who has a low serum potassium level and who has stopped eating altogether for a few days. Sometimes the intravenous route has to be used because emaciation has reached the point where there is not enough time left to reach an adequate intake any other way. The risks arise because food substances in solution are an irritant. This means a large-calibre vein has to be used to introduce them, and any infection inadvertently introduced will therefore spread very rapidly, a serious hazard, especially in a severely emaciated patient.

Nasogastric-tube feeding

Nasogastric-tube feeding, once an awkward last resort, is a procedure which is nowadays easier to implement. Cooperative patients will find that, once the tube has been gently introduced into the nostril and pushed until its tip is at the back of the throat, as they swallow a large mouthful of water, the end of the tube will curve and slip down into the oesophagus almost under its own weight. A gentle nudge from the nurse's hand and swallowing a little more water will have the tube in place down the oesophagus into the stomach. This may be used for the patient to be fed with the entire amount of the necessary food which, with the aid of a pump, goes down at a slow, steady trickle.

Alternatively, because of the ease, speed and relative comfort with which a nasogastric tube can be introduced, it is possible to encourage a sufferer who is even marginally willing to make the attempt to try to drink either the whole or some part of the prescribed liquid diet during the day. This can be done in the knowledge that, whatever the extent to which this has not been managed by bedtime, a nurse can put down a nasogastric tube and let the amount that remains infuse overnight.

Nasogastric-tube feeding ties the sufferer to a drip stand, so its use effectively means bed rest. In our view the extra effort involved in letting the patient have a bath when one container of tube feed has gone through, and before the next one is started, is well worthwhile in terms of maintaining morale. It would be foolish, however, and unkind to let a sufferer bathe with nutrient liquid still going down the tube. For a frightened and desperate self-starver the temptation to disconnect and let the fluid food run into towels or dirty bath water would be too hard to resist.

Much less nursing time is needed in using this method, which is significant where ward staffing levels are less than generous. It also permits a flexible approach to feeding that gives scope, where there is the necessary psychological support, for sufferers to attempt to feed themselves and therefore retain some sense of autonomy, even in this situation. It can be used permanently or intermittently until a weight level is achieved that is medically safe.

Liquid diet

The next level is where the sufferer takes a wholly liquid diet consisting of prescribed amounts of a fortified drink. A variety of these is available. The kind of drink can be tailored to the needs and taste of the particular sufferer. A protein powder may be prescribed, for instance, for those who cannot tolerate milk because of lactose allergy, or firmly held vegan principles. The problem here is that a great deal of nursing time and effort will be taken up at this stage, but this is a point we will return to.

Ordinary food, with or without liquid supplements

It is unwise, if not impossible, for sufferers to switch in one step from a wholly liquid diet to three normal meals per day. It would be a move inconsistent too with the process of gradual change at all stages that, in the long term, is more beneficial.

The introduction of one meal at a time is the change that is most appropriate to start with. Sufferers usually know which meal they feel able to begin with, and the dietician's expertise can be used to reduce the liquid diet by an equivalent amount of calories. The aim will be to graduate slowly to three ordinary meals and three snacks or fortified drinks per day. A pattern of meals which will maintain weight, plus drinks between these meals to provide extra calories needed for weight gain, has the advantage of teaching a sufferer to eat the kind of meals that, with the aim of keeping weight stable, can be continued safely after discharge from hospital.

Moderate aims for weight increase

It is both unrealistic and misguided, as we have said, to bring weight up swiftly to a near-normal level and then expect that a sufferer will feel better or be 'cured'. Weight gain by itself is not a cure. Recovery depends on change of mind, on change in way of being. Necessarily this is a lengthy process. Weight gain, as a treatment on its own, and particularly if it is rapid, neither gives time for sufferers' fundamental beliefs about themselves to alter, nor encourages in them any inclination for the therapeutic work involved.

An aim that is more appropriate to the condition, and one that can be more straightforwardly justified to them, is to bring them up to a weight that is medically safe and which provides a margin, two to three kilograms perhaps, which can be lost without immediate medical risk. Where they have the support of an informed helper, and where circumstances generally are likely to enable them to maintain the recovered weight, or at least not to lose it again rapidly, then weight gain to 70 per cent AEBW can be enough for the time being. Alternatively where a sufferer has little emotional support, refeeding to 75 per cent will give an extra margin of weight that can be lost without hospital admission having to be repeated at once.

While increasing weight to this level draws self-starvers away from the extreme of life-endangering emaciation, it does not enforce upon them the real extreme of bringing them rapidly to a normal or near-normal weight level that brings with it more emotional change than they are ready or able to cope with. As such it is both a demonstration of the possibility of middle positions, and an intermediate solution to the practical problem of their emaciation having reached the point of endangering their life.

While, from the perspective of the adequately fed, non-anorexic person, this can readily be seen as a moderate approach, helpers must bear in mind that for any sufferer an increase of 'a single pound, or even one decimal point of a kilogram' is the 'other extreme'. An anorexic will be highly disturbed still by the minimal increase involved in being brought to a weight level that is temporarily physically safe. Nor will this intermediate step remove the state of starvation. It will, however, bring the sufferer to a point where others will be able to relax a little, simply because they know their relative/friend/ patient is not in immediate danger of dying of starvation.

No one who has been involved in helping an anorexia nervosa/bulimia sufferer has not, at some time, wished for an instant cure and for all anxiety to be over. But it is important that parents, doctors and others concerned to help are moderate too; that they are realistic rather than polarized in their expectations. Sufferers cannot 'get better all at once'; but when they are at least physically safe, there is a margin of time gained in which important steps can be made in continuing to assist them towards a degree of psychological change which will match the enforced physical change they have just undergone. Where relatives are less anxious, the likelihood is that such help will be the more productive.

Helping the sufferer feel safe

Since the sufferer's thinking is extremely simple it is generally helpful to keep the context in which refeeding takes place simple too. Units specializing in in-patient treatment for eating disordered patients may have this as their aim, yet how it is contrived can vary, since approaches differ. Admitting a sufferer to a medical ward is a different approach, not without problems, but worth consideration. The predictable order and routine to be found on a medical ward is appropriate to rigid thinking, and the necessity of this order here is not contrived. Admission to a psychiatric ward might seem a more obvious course, but this is a much more complicated environment, and will be experienced as such. There is a wider range of unpredictable behaviour among patients, which, along with the less formal organization and less easily perceived routine, can easily overwhelm. It can feel like more of the chaos and confusion that already terrifies the sufferer. If a sense of order is lost, non-eating is the more rigidly clung to.

As a patient in an ordinary medical ward, the consequences of non-eating and the body's need for food can be presented at a simple and straightforward physical level, as encapsulated in the following statement made by the medical consultant to a newly admitted anorexic patient – at 29.9 kg (4 st. 10 lbs) and 57 per cent AEBW.

> I am Dr X, your consultant. It's clear to me you're very malnourished and at risk of dying. I don't understand too much about why you are not eating. But it's my job to see you receive enough nourishment to stay alive. We won't give you too much. It'll be hard for you to trust us, I know. But on my ward we don't let people die of starvation.

There can be difficulties of course. It may not be possible to contain a disturbed, frightened and therefore impulsive or recalcitrant anorexic in this situation. Pressure on hospital beds for ordinary medical patients, and on the resources of the medical team, can be problematic. In some circumstances, though, the disadvantages might be less about the practicalities of running a busy medical ward and more about attitude to the patient. Some ward staff may not see their job as including the rehabilitating of a self-starver, and the existence of eating disorder units may lead to the condition being seen as 'too specialized' and therefore its treatment in a medical context as 'inappropriate'. For other staff, conscious of their own preoccupation with food control, the presence of a very low-weight anorexic/bulimic patient might be just too close for comfort.

There are also advantages. Where the actual task of refeeding is concerned there is the possibility that – where they are able, willing, and appropriately briefed – staff may handle this as another of the relatively matter-of-fact medical treatments that are carried out on this ward at prescribed times. Refeeding will seem ordinary, since for all the patients here the emphasis is more specifically on bodily needs. The kind of help that can easily be given using a nasogastric tube is an unremarkable procedure here too, and so more comfortable psychologically for the sufferer. In this, as in any other situation where they are being refed, sufferers are likely to need a nurse sitting with them until all of their 'food' is taken, and for half an hour afterwards to see that they do not vomit. If there is a danger of self-harm, or running away when sectioned under the Mental Health Act and therefore legally bound to stay put, a sufferer may be 'specialled' thus all the time. This level of nursing can be arranged while sufferers are on a medical or psychiatric ward, just as it can in a unit or clinic specifically for eating disordered patients, and can be accompanied by psychotherapeutic support on a one-to-one basis.

Refeeding in a simple environment such as this, to approximately 70 per cent AEBW, can provide a useful beginning, as necessary, moving to a psychiatric ward or unit afterwards to continue with an entirely liquid diet, and eventually a mixed diet of fortified drinks and ordinary meals.

Admission to a medical ward makes it much easier to convey the message that it is, at this point, physical safety that the hospital staff and family are worried about. Sufferers being admitted to hospital for the first time are likely to be strongly resistant, and possibly very confused about why this is necessary at all. They believe there is nothing wrong with their actions. They cannot believe what they are doing has anything to do with anorexia nervosa. They have been praised and admired for being self-controlled in the past, and they feel better for being in control of food now. They are only being active, as they ought. All this, together with the confusion of experiencing their good behaviour being labelled as bad, or mad, or both, can undermine them even further. It is proof again that, however hard they try to get things right, they always end up getting everything wrong.

Symptomatic of their anorexic thinking, they are also likely to insist that other patients are far more in need of the bed than they are. It can come as quite a shock, and a constructive one, to be told by the consultant physician that their need for medical help is as urgent as those around them.

When weight is at, say, 57 per cent AEBW a doctor can tell a sufferer straightforwardly, and genuinely, that the refeeding treatment being arranged is to prevent their collapsing, or collapsing again, and their soon dying of starvation. Although there may still be violent rejection of the idea of being refed, the message may get across, again particularly if the necessity for refeeding can be related to a specific deficit that the self-starver in question is aware of. 'I knew I was weak when I was down that low [in this case 61 per cent AEBW]. I remember when Martin [the speaker's husband] brought me up to the clinic, I could hardly put one foot in front of the other to climb the stairs. But I still thought I was all right.' This relating is easier when a sufferer at this stage has already, for instance, fallen off a bike, or has bruises from bumping into doorframes or tripping over the kerb as a result of being so underweight.

Where their physical state is not immediately endangering their life it is helpful if the doctor is genuinely honest about this too, and provides them with the actual reason why they are being admitted to hospital to be refed at, say, 69 per cent AEBW.

At this moment you're not immediately in danger of dying. The danger point will come if you carry on doing what you are doing without increasing the amount of food you eat each day. Right now your parents/

husband/children are so desperately worried, I feel I have to admit you to hospital because they can't cope. I want to see that for a while you take more nourishment. And I think it'll be helpful to you if everyone around you becomes less anxious, knowing you're here and having more food. Would you agree with that?

Sufferers will not be overjoyed at the prospect of having no escape from a more adequate food intake. They will, however, characteristically, be aware of the anxiety they are causing to those close to them and will dislike themselves intensely for creating so much worry. Reducing this anxiety will make sense in terms of their being sensitive to others' feelings. They do not get what they want in terms of maintaining absolute control over their eating, but they are nevertheless pleasing others.

This is an example of the way in which it may be possible to help a sufferer by bringing into focus some of the other cherished values that starvation effects will, at this stage, have pushed further and further to the periphery of consciousness. It is an example of working with sufferers by working with their own conflict, rather than setting up a situation that feels in absolute opposition to all their values. Their response will always depend on how emaciated they are, the previous experiences they have had of being treated in hospital, or hospitals, and how realistically they feel they can trust the helper.

Where the situation they find themselves in is to some degree understandable to them in terms of their own values, there is the possibility of their maintaining some minimal composure. Where, on the other hand, the situation seems entirely incomprehensible they will feel the more confused, frightened, angry, and will be very much more resistant. This happens when they sense they are being lied to (as when a person denies being angry with them, yet they sense that person's anger) or when they feel that in some way they are lacking information that is important to them (as when their family fails to explain why a hospital admission has been arranged). Low weight they may be, but they are no different from any other human being in these respects.

Refeeding and the need for predictability

Whatever their feelings about hospital treatment, and in whatever kind of hospital situation they may be, the need to feel in control of what is happening in relation to food and eating is absolutely paramount. Here too a great deal can be gained by working with rather than against the illness, acknowledging and acting upon sufferers' need to know exactly what food they are being given, how much, how frequently, and why. They will feel safer and more understood if as much as possible in their life can be made completely predictable. So whatever information nursing staff can get through to them about what is happening is helpful, particularly if they can at the same time acknowledge their real terror at the increase in the amount of food they are being required to take.

The need for predictability has a very practical side. They will always, for instance, feel safer when their menu is organized around complete sachets or containers of the prescribed fortified drinks. To bring a sachet that is twice the size of the prescribed amount, that they or a nurse has to divide in half, is to introduce uncertainty. They will not trust the amount they are having to take is *exact*. Likewise, where ordinary meals are their prescribed food, these must be delivered as named, pre-arranged, standard portions. Sufferers must *know* that if a 125 gram portion of cottage cheese and one medium-size jacket potato with salad is what is on the list for a specific meal, then that is what they will get. It is useless to present them with 100 grams of curd cheese and three small boiled potatoes and tell them it amounts to the same thing (which is roughly true) because for these people it is not *safe*. More than this, it demonstrates to them that the hospital staff are not to be trusted, because they do not understand. The feeling is: 'If they understood how I felt they *couldn't* bring me the wrong food.' Meanwhile it has been found to be helpful for the nurses on the ward, the dietician, the doctor and the patient each to have a copy of a previously agreed and mutually signed menu so that misunderstanding can be prevented.

Reliability and exactness are essential support where eating is concerned, and this also includes having prescribed food presented at the pre-arranged time. If hospital staff can grasp this, they will make the extra effort needed to bring the fortified drinks exactly on time and not keep this patient waiting for something she or he does not want. The nurse who forgets the 2 p.m. drink until 3 p.m. and then says 'Why didn't you ask for it?' adds insult to injury. As one sufferer said, 'They know I don't want it. Why the hell should I have to beg for it! It's not as though they're doing me a favour when they bring it.'

Where minimal cooperation has been enlisted and a sufferer has agreed to take pre-arranged amounts of liquid food if these are presented by the staff, this minimal cooperation must be recognized for what it is. More will be achieved by appreciating just how much has been agreed to in this, rather than by stretching willingness to cooperate beyond its current limits. Such a situation is exemplified by the sufferer who said 'No. I haven't had anything all day. No one brought it. I'll drink the stuff if you give it to me. I won't ask for it. I never said I'd do that. I only said I'd have what the staff gave me.'

To achieve the kind of security or containment that sufferers need, it is appropriate, and often quite explicitly helpful, for their pre-arranged food to be entirely 'boring'. It does not matter if, as a balanced menu, they eat exactly the same items of food every day. If they are feeling even minimally safe about food, they will to the same extent be less anxious and more able to give whatever degree of attention they can, in their low-weight state, to therapeutic help of a slightly wider nature – if this is offered, or possible, in the context they are in. But where anxiety or terror overwhelms them, as easily it will, there will be absolutely no room for any thoughts but those concerning food/body control. They will feel absolutely threatened, and totally panicked.

Food as medicine

Whatever the context in which amounts of food are being increased, whether in hospital or at home, it can be helpful for all concerned if food is seen and treated as medicine. For sufferers it is helpful not only from the point of view of their emaciation, but also for their need for ease of mind. This is a conventionally understood way of saying 'I appreciate you don't like it; but your body needs it.' Nor is it only a useful first step. In relation to the anorexic need for complete predictability where food is concerned, the analogy can be followed through.

To present anyone with a green pill one day, a blue pill the next and a yellow pill the day after, while insisting there is no difference between these pills, 'they are all just as good for you', would be a very effective way of inducing extreme anxiety in any individual: a sense of not knowing what was being given, or what was being done, an experience of having no control over one's own body, or own safety, or indeed life. Yet this is precisely the experience sufferers have in relation to the food they are required by others to eat.

Likewise where the stated and agreed prescription has, for example, been two red pills three times a day, it is equally anxiety-inducing for someone, already afraid these two red pills really *are* bad for them, to find that suddenly, and with no previous negotiation or agreement, they are expected to take three red pills, or two red pills and a blue one. Hence sufferers' resistance to much of their treatment. One girl's ability to confide in her doctor during a ward visit shows how this applies.

Anorexic: I said I would drink half a pint of fruit juice and 50 grams of Caloreen. But I'm sure they're giving me more than that.

Doctor: What gives you that feeling?

Anorexic: I never know how much it is. The first day they gave it to me in a glass. But the nurse brought it in a cup last night, and the one on duty this morning gave me a bigger mug . . . [Then as one uncertainty has arisen, further doubts are stirred] . . . and I'm sure they're putting in more of it each time. It's thicker today than yesterday. [This doubt was in fact unfounded, but the sufferer would have been less likely to have been anxious about viscosity, had the volume been always visibly the same.]

An unhelpful but all too frequent response here is 'Don't be so silly. Of course it's the same amount. It just looks different because it's in a different container.' But knowing the anorexic need to be absolutely sure of being given no more and no less than the agreed, pre-arranged amounts of any food, this doctor was able to respond in a more helpful way.

Doctor: Sometimes it looks as though they've given you more than we agreed, and sometimes less. [The girl nods] And you'd feel more comfortable if it always came in the same thing, wouldn't you?

Anorexic: It wouldn't make me so panicky if I could be sure how much liquid they were giving me.
Doctor: Does the glass feel safest?
Anorexic: Mmm. I'd rather have the glass. That's what it came in first.
Doctor: Okay. I'll write it on the menu. Your drink should always be given in a standard hospital glass. So it's there for everyone to see.

The increments and alterations necessary to gain weight must also be made in gradual steps, and sufferers will need to be consulted over these so they are assured of knowing what is happening. They will also feel more comfortable with increases in the food they are already agreeing to take, rather than having to cope with items of food that are different – for instance, where two slices of bread are already being eaten, increasing this to three slices, rather than introducing a small potato to the meal at this stage. The menu may seem unexciting in the extreme, but, as we have said, the task is not to give sufferers a varied and exciting diet. It is to enable increased amounts of essentially balanced food to be eaten. Sameness and predictability create the necessary security early in therapy at higher-weight stages equally.

Avoid offering choices

Since it is in the nature of the condition that sufferers cannot easily make choices and decisions over the most minor matters, it is not helpful for hospital staff or anyone else to persist in presenting them with choices about food, either in an unthinking way, or from the mistaken assumption that it is 'kind' to offer them the freedom of choice. The need for any spontaneous decisions, however small, catapults them into the very confusion that is the core problem, and which they will always resolve by not eating. 'A nurse came up out of the kitchen and said "What do you want with your salad? Cheese or egg?" And I was gone. I ran away. It was too much. I didn't come back, not for hours.' A less panic-inducing approach in this instance would have been for the helper merely to have said to the sufferer in question 'Here's your salad, like you agreed with Dr Y. You said egg or cheese was okay. You had cheese yesterday, so I ordered you egg today.'

Discovering preferences and making decisions are part of therapy (see Chapter 14), but the primary task of the staff in any hospital or treatment unit is to contain sufferers in such a way as optimizes the possibility of their taking in food, and minimizes their fear and confusion. Even without being given food choices, their level of panic will be very high in a situation where they are being made to eat. There are many ways in which this will become evident. Some were illustrated in Chapter 4. They may staunchly refuse to take their prescribed liquid food. They may switch off the pump attached to the nasogastric tube. Yet resistance, however manifest, is a measure of the terror they are experiencing at losing control, and/or the anger they feel at their control being violated. Sufferers' actions need to be understood thus rather than ignored or used as a cue for blame.

Making hospital staff comfortable

Hospital staff at any level and in any location can feel more comfortable when refeeding can be handled as a straightforward medical procedure. All who are involved work better where they know what is required of them, where their task is clearly defined. Whatever the procedures used, where staff are comfortable and informed it is easier for them to give anorexic/bulimic patients the needed support and reassurance, which is as important for their eventual well-being as implementing increases in food.

In the course of their duties, nursing and other staff quite normally talk to those in their care. The least that is required for anorexia nervosa/bulimia sufferers over and above this is that staff talk to them in a way that demonstrates some understanding of the way they are likely to be feeling, and so create some chance of relating to them rather than alienating them. For example, the nurse who is helping a sufferer, routinely, to suck an ice cube or swallow some water so the nasogastric tube can slip down, so that she can be fed whatever part of the planned intake she has not been able to take during the day, is making an important contribution if she or he makes the effort of imagination to see the situation the way the sufferer is seeing it, as for instance:

> You look terrified (angry/upset). I appreciate you'd rather not have it at all, but really it's your medicine that's going down this tube. Can you think of it as medicine? You'll die you see, if you don't have it. Look, all you need tonight is that carton, as we arranged [indicating the prescribed fortified drink]. I'm *not* going to give you any more than you need. I promise you I won't. [This is, of course, a promise that must be kept!]

If it is borne in mind that an increase of even 0.25 kg ($^{1}/_{2}$ lb.), however it comes about, is a weight change that utterly humiliates, that devastates, a sufferer, then communicating along the above lines can be seen to be far more appropriate than interacting in a way that further destroys; such as implying 'there is real stupidity in all this', or making accusations of 'unreasonableness'. Staff are not being helpful who say, or infer by their attitude: 'This is unnecessary stubbornness. I'd have thought you could have managed to drink this during the day.' Even saying 'Try a bit more' can seem like being accused of not having already tried. Saying 'Well done' when they have eaten or drunk the prescribed amount is even worse. The more emphatic and enthusiastic the praise, the greater is the certainty that, whatever has been taken, it was too much. The anorexic reasoning will be: 'If they didn't expect me to have it all, it *must* have been too much.'

A high level of psychological support is needed when sufferers are taking the required nourishment. It is commonplace for them to find it quite unbearable even to pour prescribed liquid food from its container into a cup. If one-and-a-half small slices of bread are put on the supper tray instead of the pre-arranged single large slice, weeks of painstaking confidence building can be undone.

Considerable emotional resources are needed to sit with a frightened, angry and unwilling anorexia nervosa/bulimia sufferer without becoming angry or blaming, and firmly sustain the certainty that the 'food' will be taken because it is vital. Whether or not staff have been trained in psychiatric nursing, or specifically in working with 'eating disorders', or with addiction generally, it is not difficult, particularly under pressure, to be brusque or dismissive, or resort to cajoling, or to judgemental approaches.

Generally any moral qualms about 'persecuting' the sufferer that may arise from unexamined beliefs that food intake should be a voluntary or a pleasurable activity make it impossible for any helper who holds such beliefs to succeed in feeding a convinced anorexic. Food has to be seen as essential medicine, and the helping task as supporting the patient to face, and manage, the fright and anger at eating it.

The importance of psychological support cannot be underestimated. Nor should this be conditional on whether or not a sufferer eats. Conditional support is nothing new to anorexia nervosa/bulimia sufferers. Nor is deferring their own wants or needs until they consider the fulfilment of these needs to be sufficiently deserved. This is their own pattern of response. They will learn nothing from a helper who behaves in the same withholding way. On the other hand, enabling them to feel they are worth talking to whether they eat or not is to provide them with a different experience, and one that may instigate change.

The use of sedatives in hospital

Sufferers can become extremely upset at being admitted to hospital for refeeding. They can be highly recalcitrant in their refusal to eat, and their behaviour can become very distressing and alarming, particularly where in their desperation they resort to self-harming. Doctors may consider it appropriate to sedate them therefore, as part of their responsibility of caring for them.

Medication might be considered necessary in order to save a sufferer's life. It can be useful while tube feeding is in progress, to counter rage or panic. But where such measures are employed, communication can be hampered. Certainly, if sufferers are sedated they are 'safer' and less distressing patients. This may be useful to those nursing them, and fellow patients or sufferers need to be considered. While panic can be talked through, there may not be enough staff available for anyone to have time for this. Temporary medication may be better than leaving a sufferer alone and terrified. The important question is how long such emergency strategies remain in place before some attempt is made to reach the sufferer as a frightened and angry human being.

The nature of the condition is that disturbance increases as weight rises. Consequently, where sufferers are being treated on an in-patient basis, their medication is often adjusted accordingly. So as sufferers 'get better' physically and become more aware mentally and emotionally, their prescribed doses of antidepressants and tranquillizers tend to be increased. Hence they are shut down, anaesthetized again, but by prescribed drugs rather than by starvation. If drugs are used for anxiety, the *minimum* effective dose is always the best choice.

Problems of communication are difficult where thought and feelings are affected by drugs, just as they are when they are affected by starvation, and the more so where both effects are combined. There also seems little point in increasing sufferers' weight at such a rate and to such an extent as necessitates having to resort to drugging them in order for them to be able to 'manage' emotionally at the achieved higher weight. A prolonged need for such measures would usually indicate that weight gain is proceeding too fast. Even in this lowest 50–65 per cent weight band, once a sufferer is not actually dying of malnutrition, help needs to be given for that person to catch up psychologically with the enforced physical change, and the time allowed that this necessarily takes. It is communicating at this stage that is important, allowing sufferers even here to begin to express rather than suppress their food/body control self; securing the stepladder that will eventually enable them to move away from their illness.

We have indicated the possible necessity, and some of the drawbacks, of using sedation while the minimum amount of weight is gained that will bring sufferers part of the way, or even all of the way up to the level where they are medically safe. There need be no obligation to endure the extreme emotional discomfort that is involved in eating and gaining weight. It may be more comfortable in some ways if feelings of panic and terror can be temporarily suppressed, for instance over a period such as a bank holiday weekend when a particular doctor or allocated helper will be off duty, or there are fewer staff available than usual. However, there is a great difference in the experience of those who are sedated against their will and refed and the experience of those who feel they have had at least some say in their treatment. Sedation will always be more useful, therapeutically, where sufferers give their own genuine consent, where they are helped to feel they have some control over what is done to them, and how long it is continued. Whether this can be achieved will, particularly in the case of new and very frightened patients, depend on the helpers' ability to get through to them.

> *Doctor*: You found it difficult last night, lying here with all this food going into you.
> *Anorexic* [silent]
> *Doctor*: Look, I know it's terrifying. Staff nurse told me you managed to switch the pump off five times during the night.
> *Anorexic* [sullen, but also scared]: I don't want to get fat.
> *Doctor*: No. I appreciate you don't. That makes you really panicky. [Pause] You must have the food. That's to keep you alive. But panic is very frightening. I don't think your fright is helping you at the moment. How about having something to help you have some sleep?
> *Anorexic* [looks dubious, but says nothing]

Doctor [anticipating a possible fear]: No more food. Only as much as we arranged before . . . But how about a night's rest from the panic, and all the other feelings? Try it just for tonight? And I'll come and see how you feel tomorrow?

Anorexic: I'm scared about the weight.

Doctor: Yes.

Anorexic [quietly, and after a long silence]: OK . . . because I am terrified . . . but I do need sleep. [Pause] Just for one night though.

'Experienced' self-starvers who have become familiar with their pattern of weight loss and the emotional turmoil that refeeding creates may, particularly if they have an adequately long-standing and trusting relationship with a helper, feel able to negotiate 'not feeling' for a period during the required refeeding process. Thus:

Doctor: Your weight's drifting down. It's 64 per cent now, and with all the pressure you're under you're not going to be able to eat more yourself, are you? And you seem so much more exhausted. How about coming into hospital for a while? We'll take you back up to 70 per cent, and then see how you go from there. Maybe things will have settled down a bit . . . elsewhere in life . . . And we can refresh the plan for your menu as well while you are in. You may be ready to move on from baked beans on toast for supper by now?

Anorexic: I don't want to, but . . . Well. I suppose so. Oh, I can't bear it. If I did come in on Friday could I have something . . . something so I can pretend it's not happening, just for the first weekend. I don't really want to be too awake the first couple of days – till I get used to hospital again.

Though this situation has happened, it does not happen very often, but it is worth bearing in mind as a possibility where there is a genuine relationship between sufferer and helper.

Help: dividing the task: providing continuity

Sufferers can be very unwilling to enter into a therapeutic relationship with those who are or have been involved in their gaining weight. This is another reason why it can be useful when emaciation is severe, or weight is in a very low band, for this particular task to be undertaken by those whose concern is clearly medical, and therapy to be undertaken with someone with else. Ideally such a relationship with an informed non-medical helper or psychotherapist would be fostered from the beginning of the refeeding process, or, even better, before this, and continue beyond the point where, having reached a medically safe weight, the sufferer moves to a psychiatric ward or other unit, and eventually beyond this again as essential reconnection with everyday living takes place.

Such an arrangement is difficult to obtain in an ordinary hospital context since a large proportion of therapy is conducted by fairly junior staff whose careers move them at six-month or shorter intervals. Hospitals and other centres offering extended in-patient and outpatient provision, even with specifically dedicated multidisciplinary teams, generally remain better geared to providing intense short-term care in an emergency or crisis, or support for the medium term, rather than the continuous, long-term therapeutic relationship that anorexia nervosa/bulimia sufferers ultimately need for the fine-grained work that is involved in their own individual recovery.

There are those who find a route out of the illness, not usually without specialist help, but certainly without either in-patient or outpatient care. Yet by its nature the illness generates crises, it can lead to emergencies and has overall a recidivist pattern, and this is so even where progress is being made. There is a need, therefore, for a safe location at certain times, and for informed staff. Contrary perhaps to expectations, however, hospital programmes cannot solve the problem in its entirety. They enable some sufferers to stay alive, but not others. They may enable others again to find a way of steadying themselves, so they no longer need repeated hospital admissions. Institutions can provide needed stepping stones, but it is usually wise to sustain or foster other resources beyond their walls. A continuous, long-term, therapeutic relationship can be valuable to easing the way through every stage of recovery, and valuable in the process of reconnecting with the world. It is important that the need for intermittent hospitalization does not jeopardize either possibility.

twelve

Turning around

This chapter deals with the tasks of helping when weight levels are between 65 and 75 per cent AEBW.

Where weight is falling, the weight loss, by the time a sufferer is 75 per cent AEBW, must no longer be ignored. The trend is a real cause for anxiety, and is so even though there is still some way to go before a level is reached at which life-saving medical help becomes urgently necessary. Personality changes will certainly have taken place, and the sufferer, dependent in every way upon the effects of food/body control, will respond to any adversity, any perceived threat to that control, by tightening it.

At this stage, and however hopeless they may feel, relatives and friends are not without the means to gain some leverage on the problem. In this band of weights there are real deficits in performance, and these can be used to initiate action. Others should *not* make allowances for diminished concentration, for the longer time it takes a sufferer to perform ordinary or usual tasks, or for the tell-tale accidents. To make allowances is simply to collude with the illness, and enable the situation to get worse. There can be an insistence upon the legitimate expectations that accompany the relationship others have with a sufferer. Where physical health is concerned too it is usually possible to insist that a doctor is seen for an opinion at least.

It is always worthwhile informing sufferers about the nature of the path they are on, even though, however carefully and repeatedly they are told about the dangers of their lifestyle, it is unrealistic to expect that this will bring about an immediate change in attitude. Sufferers' disbelief is often one of the helper's first problems.

> Everyone kept saying I'd have to go into hospital, but I knew they were wrong. I was sent to see a counsellor. She said the same thing. But I thought I was OK. I stopped going. My parents were still getting at me. It went on nearly a year like that. Then in the end they made me go into hospital, but I didn't believe I was ill.

Though a helper may know it can take a long time for sufferers to acknowledge there is a problem, their disbelief can still be startling. Someone who has been severely restricting food for at least ten years, who has been admitted to hospital several times during this period to be refed, can still say 'I don't believe I'm anorexic. I was reading an article about it. I don't think I'm like that.' However, by the time weight has fallen to 70 per cent or below, the belief in food/body control will have taken on a rather desperate air. Any alternative but to continue just as they are will seem the more unacceptable and terrifying. Food restricting or relentlessly exercising, sufferers dare not believe their control is a problem.

How to begin working together?

Where there is refusal to accept there is a problem, and such great terror of change, it is difficult for help to get started. Substantive areas of agreement are needed so that both parties can begin to talk about the same thing. At the beginning a helper may have very little to work with except an ability to demonstrate an understanding of how the sufferer feels (see Chapter 10). From any point of agreement the helper must build outwards until more and more aspects of the condition become shared knowledge between helper and sufferer. This takes time, several months at least. It also requires close attention to the detail of the sufferer's experiences, and how these relate to weight and eating. This will be a genuine two-way learning process. There are many subtleties in the way in which feelings and sensations vary with changes in intake, with ingestion or otherwise. Depending on what is being or has been done in the name of control, each individual sufferer's experience will be a little different. The helper must aim throughout to provide an adequate feeling of safety. Those who become entrapped in anorexic/bulimic illness are easily overwhelmed and terrified of going out of control, and terrified people do not change. In their fear they fail to take in or assimilate information.

Working with rather than against control

As indicated, a greater sense of safety can be provided by working with the need for control. This is not mere strategy. It is a responsible approach from a helper who is aware of the ease with which loss of control and desperation to regain it can move a sufferer from square to square on the board described in Chapter 3, and who recognizes the more complicated dangers that follow from control by means other than food avoidance.

The nature of anorexic control is the first thing sufferer and helper must come to agree about. For while the helper knows that, where food is restricted and there is increased restlessness or activity, the natural course is for weight to fall, and knows this person is trapped, sufferers believe they are regulating their food/body appropriately, believe they are doing so entirely of their own volition, and believe their efforts are *right*.

Offering an experiment

The way to build common ground over what is actually happening is for the helper to suggest the sufferer tries to hold weight stable at exactly its current level; to aim for the time being not to increase weight, but neither to let it fall any lower than it is. To suggest this as a first step is equally appropriate at weight levels above the 65–75 per cent band of weights. But where sufferers are here within this band it is a particularly relevant exercise in terms of enabling them to avoid the need for being refed in hospital, if this is what they want. It also allows other crucial therapeutic issues concerning choice and decision making to arise.

Whether weight is falling, has risen from a lower level or, yo-yo fashion, is swinging up and down, it is within this band of weights that it is still, or again becomes possible to suggest a sufferer engages in this experimental task of holding weight stable. For at this stage the necessary degree of communication can be achieved, despite low weight.

Within the 65–75 per cent weight band there is a narrower band at 71–69 per cent AEBW where sufferers tend to notice changes themselves. If they have previously been more emaciated, they will find, as they come up to this threshold, that they are more generally aware, but also that they feel more disturbed and uncomfortable. Conversely where weight has previously been higher by just a kilogram – a mere pound or two – they will sense themselves as more distant and psychologically more comfortable from 71 per cent downwards. Meanwhile the practised helper, while accommodating the greater disturbance, will find it somewhat easier to get through to the slightly more aware sufferer compared with the kind of communication that was possible when the same sufferer was only marginally more emaciated; or conversely will find it necessary to be even more simple and repetitive than previously, when this person was the kilogram heavier.

Suggesting an experiment helps anorexia nervosa/bulimia sufferers grasp a working understanding of what it is they are being asked to undertake jointly with the helper. This is something that tends to elude them, particularly when weight has been very low. The idea of a scientific experiment provides a familiar structure that is not too complex to cope with, and a framework that clearly maintains the position of their being in control. Experiments by their nature run for a limited time span. This is also useful because, where there is no setting of this kind, their all-or-nothing thinking leads them to feel compelled to hold 'for ever and ever' to any change they do introduce. Effectively an experiment can also be free of ideas of success and failure, for whatever happens during it or afterwards there will be something to be learnt.

Helper: My idea is that you try to have an extra 200 calories a day, just for this week. As an experiment. For you to see whether this amount of extra food stops your weight falling quite so fast. We can talk about exactly what the 200 calories can consist of in a minute. What do you feel about the idea of doing this experiment?

Anorexic [shrinks back and says nothing]

Helper: It's awful even to think about, isn't it? And it won't be comfortable to do. But how about trying it, just for this week? You may not be able to manage it all; or you may. But whatever you do or don't manage, it'll be part of the experiment. Will you try it?

Anxieties of parents/partner/friends may be reduced if they understand a sufferer is engaging with the problem at least to this extent. A helper may give encouragement by indicating this as a possibility. It can also be directly supportive if, with the sufferer's permission, the helper negotiates to stop pressure being exerted by relatives and others while an attempt is being made to keep weight stable. The suggestion to experiment, if adopted, will not only enable sufferers to find out more about themselves. It will also allow them, and the helper, to discover how much control they actually have at this present time.

Discovering anorexia nervosa is in control

It can be startling for sufferers, convinced they are in control, to discover that, despite their belief that they could maintain their current weight at a stable level, it still continues to fall. They can be shaken to find self-starvation does not provide the total, secure control they thought it did. For example, Anya had been low weight for nine years and had been refed in hospital twice in this time. She was enduringly convinced she would not need to go into hospital again, even though her non-eating was clearly leading to the point where her emaciation would soon become physically dangerous. But, after being routinely weighed by her therapist at each meeting over the previous seven months, it was possible to show her in good time how, in spite of her beliefs, her weight had gradually fallen by rather more than 3 kg (i.e. more than 7 lbs) to 71 per cent AEBW.

Helper: What do you feel, about this graph, looking now at what's happening to you?

Anya: Well . . . Shocked. Yes. When you see it like that . . . I've gone into hospital before when I've weighed more than this, because everyone got worried. It was when you said, just now, it doesn't seem to be in control. That's what really shocked me. [Looking puzzled] I can see that. It doesn't.

The inescapability of choice

In such a case, where weight is falling relatively slowly and a constructive relationship has already been built, there is still time (a length of time that could be roughly calculated) during which it is possible for the helper to continue with support while either the sufferer gradually increases food intake by small amounts to hold weight stable at the new level, or alternatively continues on the slow downward path which would lead to a fairly predictable point in the not-too-distant future when refeeding in hospital would become necessary.

To start this process from scratch with a new client at this low-weight point would be more difficult. But it is not impossible.

Once sufferers have begun to discover that food restriction does not give them the control they previously believed it did, they are faced with an acute problem. Either they have to struggle to make some alteration to their pattern of extreme food restriction, with all this means in terms of the terror of losing control, or they can carry on as they are, knowing it will lead to their control being taken from them. They have to decide whether or not to change course and, if so, how. Not only is this exactly where they are paralysed (see Chapter 8). It is also a very highly charged decision point. These are people whose core means of conflict resolution is prolonged abstinence from food, or intensified physical activity, or a combination of both.

Though they will be very resistant, and find it very hard to move from the habitual safety of non-eating and to risk a suggested change, it is helpful to make it very clear that this *is* a choice point, and inescapable. It needs to be held in focus that, whatever they do or do not do, they are actually making a choice either way. To do nothing, to make no change in the pattern of non-eating, is still to choose, but to choose by default.

> My responsibility, as your therapist, is to see you have the care that you want and need. We both know your weight's gone down again this week, by another point five of a kilogram – that's a pound. I appreciate you really felt it wouldn't . . . If you lose x more though (which will bring you to a level of 65 per cent of an average weight for a person of your age and height), then we'll need the help of your GP to take care of you. From looking at you, and seeing how very thin you are, my guess is that he'll be afraid of you dying of starvation. He won't want that. (I don't want that either.) But at 65 per cent he'll see it as his responsibility to see you're admitted to hospital at once because you're so emaciated. That's the way you're going. Do you want that?

Focusing on the fact that this is a decision point, and indicating repeatedly the unavoidable implications of choosing by default, the helper is persistently drawing the sufferer's attention to the true position she or he is in. This is a very uncomfortable position. Either option will seem equally intolerable.

In being led to this point it is important that sufferers have adequate support, and that they are enabled to engage properly with the issue of the decision here, particularly since it is at this point that they invariably feel forced, or coerced. It is *not* helpful to bring a sufferer to this point and then adopt the attitude that 'This choice is entirely yours. Whatever you decide to do is your responsibility.' This is, in effect, to abandon that person, and to do so in a way that gives dangerous and misleading confirmation to the principle, so strongly held by sufferers, that they ought to be totally responsible for everything and ought to manage entirely on their own.

It is also to fail to take into account the critical changes that undernutrition and reduced weight create in the process of decision making. Rather, at this point, sufferers need continued support and encouragement in undertaking the enormous task of establishing or reclaiming a vestige of autonomy. They also need help to assimilate the idea that they do not have to be entirely on their own as they experiment with how to resolve this situation. They can be helped, particularly in being shown in practical ways how they might gradually move from their polarized, all-or-nothing thinking to a state where more intermediate positions are possible.

Since the task is to encourage sufferers towards making their own real choices, it is essential that the helper makes it clear too that they do not have to do as is being suggested; there are no 'shoulds' or 'oughts' involved:

> You only need experiment if you want to. My suggestion is that you make a small change for this week. Then when you come next week, we'll look at how you've felt, and at what's happened. But you don't have to make any change. I don't mind. Whatever you do, either way I'm still prepared to give you the support you need. But this *is* a choice here for you, though it might not feel like it . . . So I'm concerned that *you* know fully which way you are going.

The helper must also make clear exactly what the small experimental change is that is being suggested, as we will show.

While a helper may say that there are no 'shoulds' or 'oughts' in experimenting with change, she or he may sense that a sufferer is nevertheless feeling coerced, and it is helpful to check to find out whether this is so. It is safe to push, or coerce, providing the sufferer knows and accepts that the helper is pushing, and knows that the helper knows (see also Chapter 14). While there need be no obligation to make any experimental change, the facts of a sufferer's particular situation *must* continually be brought into focus. The lower weight is, the more frequently the consequences of anorexic actions remaining unchanged will need to be reiterated. For the more emaciated sufferers become, the more they will see food/body controlling actions as the only option, the more closed and unable they will become in relation to altering course.

It's difficult for you, I know. And you might feel it's easier to let the hospital take over. You can do that if you like. That's OK by me and, because your weight's dropping steadily, it's going to be necessary soon . . . Can you feel what your reaction is when I talk about you letting the hospital take over? Is that what you want? . . . It may be that it is . . . [Gently] What are your feelings about this? Do you feel a 'Yes' or a 'No' inside you?

Though obligations may be genuinely removed, it will still be very difficult for sufferers to make any decision. The pattern of the illness is such that, except where food/body control is concerned, they let others do the choosing. So the helper, often through her or his own unclear dithering or anxiety, may be drawn into making the decision to hospitalize the sufferer, thus taking responsibility for this decision, but with neither helper nor sufferer being aware that this is actually what is happening because the issue is so delicate or so fraught. So this possibility needs to be brought into the open, with the helper making clear statements about her own position, and what she perceives is afoot.

I don't want to make your choice for you. But I wouldn't be doing my job if I didn't say that you are coming to the point where *I* will have to make a decision to refer you for medical help. This point will come only if you stay with making no changes. Because then I will reach that moment when I consider it's no longer physically safe for you to go on eating as little as you are now . . . So you will be choosing, all the time, even by doing nothing. Choosing to reach the point where I make that decision. D'you see?

This will need to be said gently, slowly and in a manner free of all threat.

Allowing the necessary time to choose

It can take months in therapy for sufferers to accept that they are stuck, and to pluck up the necessary courage to act differently. Possibly the helper will need to stand by as weight continues to drop, while the sufferer learns about the inevitability of falling weight.

At all stages of the condition, and particularly when weight is very low, parents and others will be inclined to define weight alone as the problem and want to know why quicker progress is not being made in dealing with such an obvious symptom. They will also expect emaciation to be magicked away. They nurture the hope that, if emaciation is treated 'directly' by making the sufferer eat and gain weight, she or he will be able to continue at school or university, or with the career, and life will return to normal. There may be difficulty, therefore, in enabling relatives to accept that an approach that involves weight gain at a pace that matches psychological change is legitimate or useful, even though it is in fact more conducive to long-term recovery.

There are rare occasions when psychological change proceeds by leaps and bounds, then rapid weight gain can be welcomed and encouraged. Usually, however, the pace is tentative, and painfully slow.

During this process there will be crises: lost jobs, disappointed careers, difficulties with relationships, increased anxiety and impatience in family members and other key people, and the crisis of falling weight. Yet these are the very crises that can also bring sufferers to a point where they may begin to see the need, and eventually the possibility, of taking a different kind of action. These are the crises that give them the impetus to experiment with change. It takes practice and skill meanwhile on the helper's part to 'hold' a sufferer whilst allowing the crises to happen, so learning from these can take place.

Even so, while the constructive use of crisis can have a key part in the therapeutic process, the helper must not lose sight of the fact that anorexia nervosa/bulimia is a life-threatening condition. Complacency is dangerous.

Calculating safety: recognizing danger

When weight is around 70 per cent AEBW and falling, a helper must be alert to the possibility of the condition becoming physically dangerous. An accurate weight measurement is the most simple yardstick for judging the extent of concern that is needed.

Sufferers may resist being weighed. They may also try to protect their anorexic lifestyle by contriving to appear heavier on the scales than they actually are, by for instance drinking quantities of water before appointments with the helper, or carrying coins in pockets, or, as one girl did, going to the lengths of sewing fishermen's lead weights into the hems of her clothing. Like switching off pumps and pouring liquid food into empty drink cans in the hospital ward, sufferers here are not so much cheating or lying as indicating the extent of their fear/anger/resentment at what is being done to them.

A practised helper, using regular weighing as a structure for sharing information and as a focus for enabling sufferers to relate the minutiae of their experience to these facts, may learn to become aware of there being a mismatch between measured weight and appearance; to attune to their own sense of how the sufferer's appearance makes them feel. There are the obvious signs of increasing physical danger to be noted – hollower cheeks, more sunken eyes, more protruding collarbones; the bluish-mauve colour of hands and other extremities, sometimes extending to the lower parts of legs and forearms; the tell-tale 'wire coat hanger look' that clothing has. As weight falls, and day-to-day life becomes the more hazardous, bruises may provide evidence of increasing accident proneness. The development of puffy swelling in the ankles and legs (oedema) is a serious sign. Conversation may reveal that dizziness is being experienced, for instance when changing position quickly, because of increasingly severe postural hypotension – because, in other words, arterial blood pressure is abnormally low. The inability to sustain physical effort is a clear indication that the sufferer's condition has become dangerous. Although such weakness increases as emaciation progresses, the point where it becomes evident happens suddenly. *Its absence is no proof that the sufferer's condition is not serious.*

There are other important factors in addition to physical deterioration which are relevant to a helper's calculation of how much time is available before medical help with nutritional first aid becomes necessary. Any change or potential change of routine, such as that created by a holiday, by Christmas or other celebrations, by outings, or guests staying with the family, is a threat. Sufferers always respond to such threats by cutting back on food, or increasing exercise. Alterations in the weather must also be taken into consideration. Sufferers are at risk of losing weight more rapidly if there is a sudden cold spell. Examinations and journeys are also danger periods which disrupt precariously balanced eating routines. The kind of support or otherwise a sufferer has from relatives and friends specifically during these events, and generally, will also be significant in relation to losing further weight.

The helper must become closely attuned to each sufferer, even if their weight level seems not to be near crisis point. Patterns vary in each individual case. Depending on how few calories per day are being allowed, how much movement or exercise is being done, and on the rate at which weight is already falling, one sufferer may temporarily hold weight stable on less than 800 calories a day, another on the same food intake will lose weight steadily at the rate of a kilogram per week.

Anxiety in the helper

Encouraging a sufferer to adopt the 'experimental scientist' approach together with allowing weight increase at a pace that goes hand in hand with psychological change are slow processes, and can be nerve-wracking for the helper. However, like any other relevant factor, the helper's own anxiety can play an important part in assisting change, particularly where some trust has already developed. While a helper can create a context in which the sufferer feels safe, the extent to which this context should be anxiety-free must be based on a reasonable and informed judgement of the sufferer's person's physical condition and the helper's own feelings of anxiety. It is neither realistic nor appropriate to remain unconcerned, and it is actually dangerous for a helper to give an appearance which *looks* free of anxiety where a sufferer's weight is around 65 per cent AEBW and falling rapidly, and if there are signs that the food quantities eaten are being reduced.

On this evidence it is entirely appropriate for helpers to present their own anxiety as a fact relating directly to the sufferer's deteriorating condition. It is a fact that needs to be expressed straightforwardly, repeatedly, and in a manner that shows awareness of anorexic feelings but, at the same time, makes it clear that the helper's feelings and consequent judgements are based on different information about what is going on. For example:

I know you feel all right as you are. But I'm anxious. I'm worried because you've found it too difficult to start eating a slice of toast at breakfast time [the suggested small change]. You're looking more pinched. You've said yourself you're slower, taking longer to get things done. Right now I think we've reached the point where we should soon arrange for you to have some help. Looking at how your weight's falling, my view is we can only go on like this for two more weeks at the most. How do you feel yourself reacting to that?

The helper should wait for, listen to and clearly acknowledge any response the sufferer may give to such a question and restate, if it seems appropriate, that he or she is causing anxiety. The helper should not be afraid of being boring, but be gentle, firm and very repetitive. It takes a long time for information to be taken in.

I'm anxious about you because of the way anorexia goes. It doesn't stop by itself. You *will* keep on losing weight till it's dangerously low. Your present weight is on the edge of the 'danger zone'. Losing any more will tip you right into it, and then we'll need emergency action. That's what I'm worried about. How about you?

The helper's anxiety can be a constructive element in the crisis that this low weight level presents, hence it must be informed and well grounded. Where the helper is jittery and begins to be inconsistent, variable or swept into unreflecting panic this will not help at all. It will wipe out any trust there might have been, and the sufferer will certainly not risk any change. Guilty at being the cause of the anxiety and/or disappointed and betrayed by the helper's apparent inadequacy, the sufferer will end up immobilized by the helper thus being yet another person who is unable to cope with her or him – and will cling to control.

Choosing to change

Sufferers may not necessarily prefer or be able to make the enormous effort to refeed themselves. Nor should it be assumed that, if they feel at one point able to make this effort, they will consistently feel this way, or, in the attempt, that they will manage to take the necessary steps to increase intake enough to prevent weight from continuing to fall. This road is a hard one. They will be reassured to know a helper is aware how hard it is. Nor is it failure still to need medical help when they are in the position of having tried to go against the grain of the illness, but without effect. The helper must let them know this.

Helper: It can be too much of a struggle to eat enough. You get panicky, compensate by not eating at all, swim 80 lengths instead of 60. That's how anorexia nervosa goes – and so you keep losing weight. I don't see you as a failure if you can't manage the change to your eating that you need to make to stop losing weight, and so it happens you need help in hospital. It's a hard pattern to alter.

Anorexic: Mmm. [Thoughtfully] I've got to resist the resistance.

Helper: You're right. And that's hard.

Where they continue on the path downwards until refeeding in hospital becomes necessary they will need continued support. Anorexia nervosa/bulimia sufferers do not have the existential stamina to withstand too many changes of helper. Continued contact with the person with whom there is already a therapeutic relationship can enable them to feel, even though they have been admitted to hospital, that they have not been totally abandoned to strangers with no understanding of their needs.

Where on the other hand they express even the most minimal willingness to experiment, they will need to be shown step by detailed step what they need to do, either to keep weight stable or, where it is falling fast, gradually to level off the downwards curve.

Practical planning for experiment

A sufferer whose daily intake has been 300 calories would need to begin by trying to increase that intake from 300 to 900 calories per day by 200-calorie steps, in the first week attempting 500 calories per day, the next week 700 calories per day and so on. The suggestion should be that four small meals per day are attempted, adding the initial 50 calories per meal to the small amounts currently being eaten, and spacing meals regularly through the day, with the last meal near bedtime to assist sleep. Being unable to sleep, sufferers will usually not miss the point of this.

Discussing together and noting down what is to be the precise content of each small meal are essential parts of the experiment. Absolutely clear aims are helpful, as is encouragement to build towards a balanced diet initially on the kind of foods already being eaten, and that the sufferer likes. If breakfast has been reduced to half a slice of toast for instance, it will generally feel safer to increase this to one slice, with a quantified amount of butter and marmalade, than introduce something quite different, like a bowl of cereal. If food restricting has come to mean only taking liquids, then a first move would be to work out four meals consisting of soups that are not low-calorie soups, and of fortified milk drinks. Proprietary brands of dietary supplement can be useful in this instance. Carbohydrate powders and high-protein drinks can be obtained from chemists. Different food items, most helpfully the ones that a sufferer likes but currently is 'not allowing', can gradually be introduced after getting over the hurdle of the first experimental change. Sufferers will also cope better where the quantity or calorific value of food is easily calculable. Two digestive biscuits are always safer than one small homemade cake.

As in Chapter 11 it is useful to use the idea that food is medicine. Rather than a helper listing the agreed meals and their exact contents, and each week's adjustments, it is more helpful for sufferers to take charge, writing their own 'food prescription' with the helper alongside. This may seem a small point, but this arrangement potentially gives them greater sense of control, a sense of the possibility of becoming actually involved, which is lost if a helper writes out the 'food prescription' for their experiment.

Routine and predictability will be essential, as ever. So sufferers will need help not only to plan their eating, but also to timetable routines of work, exercise, rest and leisure. The more secure they are in these respects, the more they will be able to cope with increasing food intake. Empty or unstructured time is a great danger to anorexia nervosa/bulimia sufferers. Work will have acted for them as a defence against eating. Because they are so terrified that they will never be able to stop eating once they start, the helper can usefully suggest they can create their own safety net by using their known ability to stick to allotted periods of work and other specific activities, ones that they as individuals enjoy, and do this in a positive way to protect them from the fear of refeeding going out of hand.

It is also helpful if relatives and others can support a sufferer at each stage in not eating more than the pre-arranged menu. If sufferers are anxious or frightened because after the prescribed meal they still feel hungry, which will usually happen when a beginning is made in increasing food intake, it will help to discuss and organize a way to manage this potential danger-point safely; arranging for instance a planned top-up amount – a 'permitted' single item of extra food, like a piece of fruit or a carton of yogurt – that will be there to have in this event.

Where a person is clearly very emaciated, to onlookers such minimal increases may seem ridiculous. But small incremental steps of the order described are changes those who are severely restricting are more likely to be prepared to try, particularly where the helper is evidently willing to accompany them through the many feelings that even the prospect of these changes create and through the many experiences that even small increases in weight awaken in them. Where there is continuing help, support and learning, any gain in weight is more likely to be permanent. Permanent weight gain is also likely to be the result of regular meals. Weight gained by chaotic eating feels so messy, so guilt-laden and wrong, it is nearly always lost again.

It should be appreciated that for sufferers who have reduced their daily intake to 200–300 calories, which is by no means unusual, to suggest they begin by increasing this first by 200 calories to an initial 400–500 calories a day is to suggest an immediate doubling of that intake. Likewise to work towards 800–900 calories a day is to work towards eating three or four times as much food as their body has become accustomed to. Apart from the terror of instant obesity and chaos, even these small steps will usually cause a great deal of physical discomfort as the digestive system readjusts to this greater amount of food. Each goal needs to be realistic. Only when they are securely eating 800–900 calories a day will they feel safe to experiment with the next step of adding a necessary extra 200 calories to a current daily intake to bring it to 1000–1100 per day. Expectations of the likelihood of these goals being achieved must be realistic too. For the first week or so a sufferer may well not manage a food increase to the level suggested, or even to make any change at all. Alternatively a move from 300 to 500 calories may be achieved the first two days, followed by a return to the safety of the previous routine and lower intake. But within the framework of the scientific experiment this need not be seen as failure so much as a discovery of just how risky change is, or how frightening, or how much courage is needed, or whatever is the sufferer's experience.

Information relating to food, to body functioning and to alterations of mood can usefully be provided as it becomes relevant to the feelings and experiences that are current and a struggle. Where sufferers begin to feel that the frightening changes involved in eating more do not take them into a territory that is total and unmanageable chaos, where they find weight does not 'rocket upwards' but actually levels, and find the helper can give a predictable map reference of the many different feelings, moods and uncomfortable physical sensations being experienced, their sense of safety will increase. Where they begin to have the confidence that the helper genuinely can find them if they get lost, panicky and confused in making small moves to explore change, when they begin to experience the feeling that it is possible to be helped to get their bearings again, then they are more likely also to begin the attempt to eat and slowly to gain weight.

As with the need to please others, the strong moral attitudes that have taken a person into anorexic illness can be openly engaged to initiate the reverse process, to move out of the starvation whirlpool.

> I knew I was very independent, and stubborn, and I used that stubbornness to start eating. I was only drinking fruit juice and I started with one slice of toast. I was terrified. I was so terrified my stomach would stretch. I knew I didn't want to go into hospital, I was terrified of that too. But I was in such a panic that I'd eat and eat and never stop. But I didn't. Mum knew I was terrified, because my therapist had told her I would be, and that helped.
>
> My first proper meal was lasagne, and afterwards I nearly died. I went hot, and cold, and shook terribly. This happened after each meal for two to three months, but I was determined to do it.

Where sufferers are at risk of losing a job because they are slow and cannot concentrate, helpers may usefully point out the mismatch that exists between the expressed preference for being independent and efficient, and the likelihood of their job being lost and with that their independence. Similarly, where examination papers cannot easily be completed because they are slowed down by the chilblains on their hands as a result of poor circulation, the mismatch between the reality that they are crippling themselves and the desire to do well academically needs to be brought into focus, again to find out what is really wanted here. If sufferers are car drivers they must be told that if weight continues to fall it will be unsafe to drive any more. This again is a restriction on independence. Though low self-esteem will ensure sufferers ignore warnings about their own safety, they will usually be reached by worry about acting in such a way as might cause others harm.

A helper must not be afraid of pointing out these obvious connections. They are often news to sufferers, indeed they may be the only route by which information can get through to them that their position is untenable and they need to make some change, but it will be blocked if the information is given with even the slightest admixture of blame.

Learning points

A range of learning points emerges as the low-weight anorexic/bulimic begins to engage in the process of experimenting, and it will be helpful to focus attention towards these as they arise.

Sufferers do not realize how much more they need to eat just to keep weight stable. Again this learning takes time. In terms of their own subjective experience, if they begin to eat the minimal amount that might begin to maintain a stable level, they will feel they are 'eating like a disgusting, fat pig'. There is a mismatch too that can be drawn out between this experience and their actual measured weight.

They need to be shown there is not the simple, one-to-one relationship between eating and gaining weight that they think there is. An increase of 500 calories per day for anyone who is 70 per cent AEBW and who has previously been taking 300 calories per day will not necessarily produce weight gain. Indeed this increase may barely slow the rate at which their weight is falling. But an increase of this order in calorie intake will increase their metabolic rate. Their heart will beat faster. They will feel a little warmer. These are changes that sufferers may notice for themselves.

They are likely to be terrified at what appears to be an instant gain of a quite enormous amount of weight when they first begin to eat a little more, so it will be helpful to let them know that this 'carbohydrate effect'[1] may occur, and what actually happens when it does. When a starved person begins to eat, even a small increase in carbohydrate intake allows the body immediately to retain more water. This effect can result in the scales recording an increase of as much as 2.5 to 3.0 kg (6 to 7 lbs), although 1.5 to 2.0 kg (3 to 4 lbs) is the more usual range. This change is temporary. Within a short time most of the apparent gain disappears and weight falls again to almost its former level. Sufferers experiencing this upwards shift invariably panic and immediately cut food back. They find it hard to accept that the 'carbohydrate effect' is the ordinary and quite normal response of a carbohydrate-deprived body to a sudden, and even quite small, increase in bread, biscuits, potato or other starchy food. The effect can occur at any weight after a few days' near-total starvation, or a diet of lettuce leaves and cottage cheese only. Even if sufferers are given the information that this will happen, they will still find it very difficult to let it happen without instantly restricting food, or trying to restrict in the following days.

Then there was the week my weight didn't drop. The first time for six months. I was so pleased, because I had been trying, because I didn't want to go into hospital. But I was frightened. What would happen if I put on loads of weight? And by the end of the following week, when I'd been eating extra bread and a potato with my supper I put on five pounds – nearly two and a half kilograms – in two days. That sent me into a terrible panic. My therapist said try another week on exactly the same menu. Don't change a thing! I was *terrified*, but the week after when I saw her it had gone down, just like she said it would. Dropped right back. All I'd really gained was half a pound! (Around 0.25 kg)

Sufferers need to learn that their feelings and bodily sensations are directly influenced by food intake, as well as lack of it. They need to learn too that these feelings and sensations are not immediate indicators of their moral worth, but that there is an ordinary physiological component to that experience which predictably results in lethargy after eating, in loss of euphoria or mood crashing, in being 'low' rather than high. Having an accurate and testable account of body processes enables sufferers gradually to disengage their judgements about their own moral worth from these feelings and sensations. Being informed beforehand about their likely event can help them to stop criticizing and blaming themselves for predictable experiences. It is important too for them to realize these feelings are temporary.

Underfeeding, low weight or locked into cycles of stuffing/eliminating/starving and accompanying weight fluctuation, sufferers are continually and overwhelmingly preoccupied with thoughts of food and how to dispose of it. Yet whatever their current or persistent pattern within the illness, through experimenting they will discover that after they have eaten enough, regularly, they will, in the end, be less preoccupied with food and able to concentrate better on other things. With low-weight sufferers this will be an intermittent effect at first but, as weight rises, their general ability to concentrate will improve. Reading will be possible for longer periods. Where it was previously only possible to flick through the pages of a magazine, as they move towards 75–80 per cent AEBW they will be able to follow the whole storyline of a novel, or concentrate on the whole of a television programme.

It is important not to dismiss sufferers' physical discomforts after eating, or even at the prospect of eating, as irrational or silly. They can feel choked. They can have a grossly stretched stomach. They can feel heavy, or bloated, or puffy. These may also be expressions of panic at going out of control, or expressions of other feelings. But when they are very thin and beginning to take an increasing bulk of food that their body is not accustomed to, all physical changes will be felt very acutely. If they are able to talk about how they feel, physically and emotionally, and experience themselves making sense to the helper, then the fear and mistrust they have of themselves, and of relating to others, will slowly diminish. Helpers meanwhile can warn, even promise sufferers that they will feel terrible in every way after eating a meal, and promise too that the feelings will pass. Each time the helper accompanies a sufferer through a turmoil of change that even these first steps create and is present without criticism and without blame, each time it is discovered that the information the helper has given is an accurate reflection of the experience endured, confidence will increase, and the effects of this will gradually become evident in all other areas of the sufferer's life.

Reference

1 Slade, R. (1984) *The Anorexia Nervosa Reference Book*. London: Harper and Row, 102.

thirteen

Transition

This chapter deals with the stage where weight is between 75 and 85 per cent AEBW. This is a broad band between the levels of starvation that pertain from 75 per cent AEBW downwards and the nearer normal weight that pertains from 85 per cent upwards. It is a stage of transition.

Within this stage, at its lower end, the effects of undernutrition that have been described will not only be present, but clearly evident. They also equally evidently recede as weight is allowed to climb through its mid-point, that is, through the 78–81 per cent AEBW threshold. This is the threshold where the pull of the whirlpool has intensified, and the person is removed to a permanently altered psychological state. As weight is regained, the reverse takes place.

In terms of effective help, neither the alteration in thinking that takes place as the whirlpool motion intensifies, nor the changes that occur in the endocrine system that affect sexuality and reproduction that also take place at this particular threshold, constitute a reason that justifies rapid refeeding – i.e. food intake that increases weight faster than the particular sufferer can tolerate – to this, or to any specific higher level. For although the whirlpool motion loosens as a sufferer moves across the 82–83 per cent AEBW alteration, or intensifying point, the capacity to live without the 'direction' it has created will be non-existent. In this lies the reason for effective communication throughout the preceding low-weight stages, its continuation during the course of the transition stage, and why it will be needed after this, for a time that can be expected to extend over years.

When sufferers are at the higher end of the 75–85 per cent transition range, and where their food intake, however achieved, is adequate to sustain the weight level that is current, they will have regained most of their mental and physical potential. The transition is that stage where, as weight is gained, there will be few traces of the problem in terms of appearance, or behaviour generally, though sufferers themselves will feel confused and be unable still really to act effectively, except through food/body regulating. Extreme confusion, indecisiveness, ineffective action are the problems that, up to this stage, will have largely been hidden by the psychological effects of low weight. Yet they are the problems that underlie the need for food/body control.

How a helper can assist in sufferers' coping with confusion and indecisiveness will be considered in Chapter 14, which will focus on the weight stage from 85–100 per cent AEBW and above where these experiences are most present. The transition is a stage which creates difficulties of its own.

In the band of weights between 75 and 85 per cent AEBW helpers will meet a very much wider range of behaviour. As sufferers move through the transition stage, the uniformity that starvation or undernutrition create fades away and the person begins to emerge. The possibility increases for conversations to become deeper and more complex, and for their content to include a wider range of experience. But this greater variability also reflects sufferers' confusion and their dithering indecision. Here, as they move through the 79–81 per cent threshold, the honest comment will be: 'I've had enough. My head's finished. I've had about as much of this confusion as I can take.'

Bombarded by myriad possibilities for action, and having little or no sense of their own direction, sufferers can shift abruptly, and in extreme and often violent ways, between all the various possibilities. Hence their vulnerability to bingeing and other forms of uncontrolled or 'compulsive' responses to food and eating. Feeling 'all over the place', totally haywire, like the 'cork tossed in a sea of chaos' can produce impulsive behaviour of all kinds.

It is as weight moves up through the transition stage, even as they may be genuinely attempting to hold their weight stable 'this time round', or as they feel uncontrolled over food, or as they become too exhausted to exercise, that the likelihood increases of their turning to alcohol, nicotine, cannabis or any other drug, or combination of drugs, including medication, prescribed or bought over the chemist's counter. They may lurch or drift into sexual or other relationships. They may shoplift, or buy goods persistently or impulsively. They may run up debt. They may resort to burning or cutting themselves, to skin puncturing of any kind, or enlist plastic surgeons or tatooists to do it for them (see Chapter 3). They may become religious. Intermittently, hard work, hard sport, hard physical fitness will be grasped at and will provide some sense or semblance of control. Yet in these arenas there will usually be no shortage of personal trainers, and all kinds of 'mentors' and sales people ready to make sure they 'keep up to the mark', or 'push themselves to the limit' or beyond it, and otherwise make sure they remain 'committed', if not 'ecstatic' in their enthusiasm about whatever it is they are busily doing. As control is lost, or becomes uncertain, so opportunities to get any other kind of buzz will be all around.

Hence there are many ways in which anorexic illness can appear to disappear. 'I think I must've been around everything, pretty much, you know . . . like the song, "Life is a masquerade, old chum . . ." and all that.' The problem becomes more complicated, more fragmented at this stage. As it seems to be seen, despite its masks, so, here and there the illness collects a new name. These are the anorexia nervosa variants. Frequently, however, it is not noticed at this stage at all.

On the other hand, should weight fall, the picture will simplify again as food restriction and/or exercise reduce the indecision and the confusion, reinstate the experience of 'being more focused', the feeling of being in control, and a craved sense of peace.

In this chapter we will consider some aspects of the help that is needed where sufferers are on a switchback between control and chaos; when the inability to cope can manifest itself still in extreme and desperate ways. These considerations also apply when weight is in the 85–100 per cent AEBW range and above, certainly when sufferers have reached that average or near-average weight stage without having been given time or help to adjust and to develop a change in attitude that is in step with the gain in weight. But they are considerations that, clearly, will begin to be relevant as they move through the transition stage: from a low weight to a more viable weight, from not eating to eating adequately for the specific weight level and/or exercise level attained.

During this transition *help becomes more necessary rather than less so*, and in principle it should be easier to provide. For, as we have said, this is the stage at which it becomes markedly easier to reach a sufferer. In practice, however, the matter is not quite so straightforward. The problems and pitfalls are many.

Catching the sufferer on the way down

Sufferers may have entered this stage because their weight has been rising from a previously lower weight, or because it is falling from a previously higher level. Feelings and attitude will differ according to the direction in which weight is moving as they arrive within this band of weights. They will be more comfortable if they have been successfully restricting food, or avoiding eating, and more depressed and anxious if food intake has been increasing. Whether the increase has been agreed and minutely organized, or whether it has been as a result of chaotic feeding, it will feel out of control either way. Where weight is falling for the first time they will be adamant that they need no help. The helper should be ready to adjust to the sufferer's mindset, or style of thinking, as outlined in Chapter 10. This will certainly be necessary where weight is below 79 per cent AEBW and can still be useful at weights as high as 83–85 per cent AEBW.

During this 75–85 per cent AEBW transition stage male sufferers may be noted as having a frail, or perhaps rather delicate, look. Beyond this – and the possibility of their having been referred to as 'skinny', or 'puny', or pressured, in addition, to 'get involved in sport, build up some muscle, make a man of you' – their thinness will tend to be ignored. Traditionally it seems the etiolated male has tended to raise few eyebrows. Female sufferers meanwhile will look 'model thin'. Even as they drift towards the lower end of this band of weights their appearance can raise few questions and attract a great deal of admiration in a society that places a high value on thinness in women. In either case it can be difficult to appreciate the extent to which their visible organization is functioning to keep them away from food, and their mind away from thoughts of food.

As with social drinkers whose behaviour is seen as fairly unremarkable, yet who are biochemically dependent on alcohol and therefore 'feel better for a drink', the food restricter is at this stage already hooked. It is very difficult to issue warnings to a person who confidently dismisses these with self-assured, offhand comments such as 'I'm all right. You don't have to worry about me. I eat what I want if I feel hungry. I'm perfectly happy. In fact I've never been so happy. There's no harm in that, is there?' Or 'It's just my fitness routine, isn't it? Exercise is healthy, and I need to be healthy. That's what running does for me. Same when I go to the gym. You don't need flab. It's healthy to keep yourself good and fit.'

At this stage there is only very subtle evidence that the way of life they have become involved in is addictive, and thus constraining. Yet the evidence is there. Increasing amounts of time are spent alone. To adhere to their routines, sufferers must know precisely what is going to happen, and when. They will be increasingly prone to panicky or aggressive outbursts when things do not go *precisely* as arranged, or as anticipated. Others have a sense of always being overridden, of being controlled by them. These are changes that indicate this person's dependency on food/body control. It is by focusing on these aspects of their behaviour that sufferers at this stage may be led to realize that there is a mismatch between what they think they are achieving and what they are actually achieving.

Holding the sufferer on the way up

Where sufferers are emerging from low weight having had the kind of help described in the preceding chapter they may, by this time, begin to have a sense of being real, authentic, more genuinely present; a sense grounded in the experience of autonomy that has been gained so far. This is particularly possible where they have reached this stage as a result of feeling their way forward through decision making of their own; through alterations that have taken place to their attitude; through different perceptions that have been reached, perhaps at crisis points at a lower weight. Where real autonomy has developed in parallel with weight gain, they may, by this time, have obtained just a little confidence in themselves. They may have a germinal ability to trust or even like themselves, rather than feel absolute self-hatred. No longer will they feel so desperately that they must keep performing, that they must keep up the front. They may feel they can show more of themselves. Yet though some confidence may be growing, it will still be very tentative and highly fluctuating.

At this stage they will still be discovering, or rediscovering, how confused and indecisive they are. 'I may look normal. Everyone think's I'm okay. But my head's a complete mess.' They will still be very afraid of going out of control. They are likely still to need help and guidance over the detail, meal by meal, of what they eat, or how long and in what way they exercise. They will also still be highly sensitive to demands, pressures and obligations, and uncertain of their ability to assert, let alone maintain, their emergent self in the face of them. They do not know whether they can cope in this new way. They have not yet had enough practice to believe they can. So they are still very vulnerable to being overwhelmed by fright and confusion about relating with others, about handling situations differently and weathering events as they arise.

Although physically they may look as though they have recovered from their illness, the anorexic mindset is still there. They are beset with the same thoughts, they still scheme hard to avoid food, or at least cut back on it. If food is being eaten, then burning it up will be a must. The gears will be altered on the bike so more effort will be needed to pedal. It will be imperative still to run upstairs that extra time. Food/body controlling continues to provide the best refuge, their haven, whenever they have even the slightest sense of not being able to cope.

Recovery involves continuing practice at recognizing, discovering and enabling the development of their non-anorexic self in the hurly-burly of day-to-day life. A more protected or modified environment may have been needed in the past to defend against overload from external sources, or to contain their experience when they have been flooded by their own resurging thoughts, feelings and sensations, and may still be needed at times. But generally a less protected environment will provide sufferers with more learning experience. Chronic anorexics/bulimics who have achieved an isolated, static, sealed-off lifestyle do not have enough happening to them to learn from.

The early results of their newer experiences and ways of being will need to be affirmed by the helper they trust, if they are to persevere in their development. They still need that same helper who has learned to empathize accurately; who will still listen and respond openly and honestly; who will level with them. They need that helper who can still be a guide, continuing to provide signposts; who will not add judgement and criticism to sufferers' own judgements and criticisms of themselves; who will not tell them they are stupid, ridiculous, inadequate to feel so very fragile still, or that their feelings are 'unnecessary' or 'exaggerated'; who does not secretly believe that 'really, by now they ought to be able to manage on their own'.

It is easier to achieve this quality of help if the helper is not a relative, colleague, workmate, landlord, landlady, partner, lover or friend. Where one person has more than one role, not only are these difficult to keep separate, but others readily become overloaded in the attempt to be therapist as well.

Getting better feels like getting worse

To feel a way through enormous confusion and uncertainty towards a sense of being that is new and overwhelmingly untried takes a great deal of courage on the sufferer's part, and some appreciation of this courage will be needed. For there are many points at this weight or stage, as at any other, when getting better feels like getting worse.

This is not an unusual experience for anyone undergoing personal change during therapy, but it is an experience that is particularly frightening for those attempting to emerge from the grip of anorexic illness. They are already too well acquainted with confusion, chaos, uncertainty. The mere possibility of these recurring can trip them into instant panic. It was experiences like these that made reliance upon the ritual organization of food and body controlling so attractive in the first place. Yet they will need to re-experience the original difficulties to some extent if they are to have the opportunity to respond differently. Looking back over the previous five years during which she had made substantial progress, one woman described her experiences this way:

> When you're just becoming unfrozen, it's terrifying. You can go back to freezing up, but the further away you get from it, the harder it is to get back, and that's appalling – the uncertainty of it all. And living with that uncertainty. No one knows how terrifying it is. You die a thousand deaths on the way up.

Sufferers will not easily *be* convinced that re-experiencing some chaos is necessary for progress to be made. Their inclination, and practice, will have been continually to analyse, calculate, theorize, conjecture, plan, compute, every step in advance. For this is the way to avoid the horror of uncertainty, to overcome dread confusion, to stall change.

However, even the sense of getting worse can be marginally more tolerable if it can be seen as something to be expected, if warning is given in advance that there is a pattern in this, that it is an identifiable part of the process that is recovery. Again they will have a greater chance of coping with feelings of upheaval, and with the disturbance involved in the process of change, if they know their helper or therapist is aware that these are the kind of experiences they are going through; if they know there is someone with whom they can share the panic, the terror, even the rage. They will have a greater chance to mend if they know there is one person at least who will not become panicked, terrified or unhappy when they do go out of control, become chaotic or get confused; if they know there is someone who will not become critical, or abandon them when there are shifts and alterations in their behaviour, or when their confusion and chaos is reflected in the panic- or pain-fuelled impulses that can throw them wildly this way and that. Hence helpers must take their own need for support seriously.

Giving sufferers the appreciation they need

Once sufferers at any stage begin to move away from their totally food/body controlling lifestyle they will begin to perceive many small and promising changes in themselves, and they can become quite upset when family and/or friends appear not to appreciate what enormous steps these are. Indeed, feeling they deserve some appreciation and acknowledgement of such change is, in itself, an indicator of their growing self-esteem.

> What's really upsetting me is the way they don't seem to notice how I've changed. I'm eating a bowl of cereal for breakfast. I know evenings are still sticky. I get so edgy, and I still hide in the kitchen and hate anyone coming in while I try to make myself something, and eat it without taking a bite and throwing the rest away. But *I* had to point out that at least we don't have blazing rows in the morning now, and Dad can get off to work peacefully. That seems a real achievement to me, and it really makes me angry when they accuse me of not trying. They've *just no idea* what a struggle it's been to get even this far.

The kind of support they need, or would like, from their family or from friends may, for some, not be forthcoming. Sufferers' families in particular will usually have been very stressed for a long time by their anorexic or bulimic member. Even if the significance of each small change is pointed out to them, there may still be a deep well of antagonism, resentment and despair about the way they see this person as having wrecked the family's life. Whatever the sufferers do, however they change, there is the possibility that, for their family, they will not be getting better 'in the right way', or they will not be getting better fast enough, or the improvement is just too little too late.

To some extent the situation can be helped by providing the family with information about the kind of problem this is. Understanding that, where they are highly valued, food restriction and exercise obtain their own motive force, and understanding that because of this it is possible to become drawn into anorexic illness without realizing this is happening, can help to lift a great deal of self-blame from the sufferer, and from a family. Even so, family members or a partner may not recognize the signs of constructive change as such. So it becomes essential that at least the helper recognizes and appreci- ates the effort the sufferer is making, and appreciates the courage it takes by acknowledging the steps that have been made, however small these may have been.

Attitude changes, particularly those that lead sufferers to reveal feelings or perceptions that have previously been hidden, or to alter the way they behave, may be experienced by relatives as difficult, unreasonable or disappointing. Such changes will often be seen as an affront to their standards. Since argument, crying or the expression of despair does not look like progress, those who are close will almost certainly see sufferers as getting worse as therapy progresses. It can help, therefore, if they are forewarned that this is likely and usual, if uncomfortable. They may find this idea difficult to accept. The process of a sufferer's recovery can highlight certain areas of inflexibility in those around them. Changes to their own values and attitudes may be a price of a recovery from anorexic illness that others may be unable or unwilling to pay. Teachers may meet some of these changes with a certain wistfulness, or ambiguity. As a professor of psychiatry said of a recovering fourth-year medical student who was no longer working fourteen hours a day to get A grades all the time, 'It's very nice that she's getting better. But it's a pity she's only getting B grades now. She was always top before.'

The sufferer who begins to leave anorexia nervosa/bulimia behind may sometimes find it genuinely difficult to behave in the way others see as appropriate for a person 'of her (or his) age and intelligence'. But recognizing that development ends where addiction begins, a helper (usually more readily than family) can allow a 24-year-old recovering anorexic/bulimic to be more like, say, an 18-year-old, or a 12-year-old when needed, and allow the feelings and emotions that go with this experience, rather than erroneously assume that since this person happens to be 24 'one has a right to expect that she should behave like a young woman of 24'.

The constructive use of crisis

In relation to situations that arise at lower weights we described how crises can be used constructively (see Chapter 12), and during the transition stage too crises will occur. There will still be extreme anxiety about food, about 'eating too much', about weight 'going out of control', and this can erupt in fear and anger. There will be other crises too: total panic at unforeseen events, irritation where threat is sensed, impatience and self-hatred at not 'coping' and so on, and sufferers will respond to these by tightening their food control, or resorting to laxative use, or shopping, or bouts of desperate exercising, or frantic cleaning, drugging, drinking or any of the other possibilities that are part of the still cyclic but far more fragmented picture.

Sufferers learning to value themselves in ways that do not centre on food/body control is a matter of two steps forward, one step back. There may be a plateau every now and again where no progress appears to be made at all. Where sufferer and concerned others know these stages are to be expected, it can save a great deal of disappointment, and help prevent false hopes and unrealistic expectations.

When a crisis occurs, it is not failure. It is quite normal and ordinary for people to revert to old patterns of behaving when they are stressed, and it is essential that a helper lets the sufferer know this quite explicitly. Furthermore, much that is valuable can be learnt from these relapses, particularly as they

Frightened	Lonely
Ashamed	Guilty
Sad	Jealous
Excited	Edgy
Disappointed	Depressed
Hungry	Uncertain
Resentful	Pleased
Tired	Listless
Anxious	Tense
Vindictive	Longing
Angry	Bored
Hurting	Wistful

Figure 5: Checklist for feelings

become more isolated. Indeed, there is far more that can be learned from these times when everything seems to slip backwards than can usually be learned from long stretches of extreme behaviour, anorexic or bulimic. They enable different perpectives to be obtained. Sufferers may themselves note the kind of events and situations which render them, as individuals, particularly vulnerable. By having a checklist (see Figure 5) to mark whenever they find themselves withdrawing from food, or crashing into a binge, or feeling desperate to exercise, most find, after several such episodes have occurred, that there are one or two feelings or states that receive significantly more ticks than the others. In this way, wherever they are on the games board, they become more aware of their chief areas of vulnerability and, with this, more swiftly alert to the possibility of falling into their particular or current trap. It may become possible to formulate alternative strategies for diverting into a safer activity, including having safe people to contact, instead of bingeing or starving or exercising when these situations next arise.

Self-knowledge of this kind tends to increase confidence and, with this, self-respect. Learning to acknowledge how they feel, and to perceive the value of feelings and emotions that render them vulnerable rather than despising them or feeling guilty about them or both, can be an important step towards finding other ways of satisfactorily expressing those feelings, or constructively containing them, instead of immediately resorting to food restriction, or exercise, or any other similar solution.

Because sufferers will still be very uncertain of themselves they will be prone to see, in any crisis, incipient or actual failure. So it is helpful not to let them lose sight of the steps they have made. These will need on occasion to be brought into focus, so they can keep in perspective the fact of being a person who can allow, even possibly like in some respects, the person they are. They will need to be reminded of ways, however small, in which they have been and may again be self-directed, autonomous in matters other than those related to food and frantic activity.

Likewise, if a sufferer seems to have reached a plateau, it needs to be made explicit that in therapy there is no rule to say that progress should be continual and unremitting. As they need or want to, anyone in therapy is entitled just to stand still and rest, including those still finding their way out of anorexia nervosa/bulimia. They too are entitled to take the time to reflect, time for experience to become integrated, time to appreciate how far they have come.

Further learning points

There is straightforward practical information a recovering anorexic/bulimic needs from the helper that relates to bodily changes that take place as weight increases. One quite alarming but normal occurrence is that hair thins, sometimes very obviously, as any emaciated person gains weight. Sufferers who are already frightened enough by the weight they are gaining, who find their hairbrush or the bathroom sink full of hair each time they brush or wash it, will need to be reassured that this is usual and to be told that new stronger hair will grow.

Likewise, as weight increases to around 85–87 per cent AEBW, or, in the case of exercisers, to a weight adequate enough above muscle bulk, it is helpful for female sufferers to know that, even though they have reached the level where it is high enough for there to be the possibility of menstruating again, in practice this will not usually happen until they have held this weight consistently for about 9–10 months. Menstruation can be confidently expected only if they hold their weight at 90 per cent AEBW or higher, for fat cells are thought to produce minute amounts of a hormone that is essential to the reproductive cycle, and it takes 9–10 months for that hormone to have its effect on the functioning of the ovaries.[1]

At low weight sufferers will generally have avoided the colds and other minor infections that their family or friends have suffered, but as weight increases they will 'seem to catch anything going'. It usually reassures them to know this too is a normal and predictable, if uncomfortable, consequence of increasing weight, and happens when anyone who has been very thin regains weight. It is what the body's defence system manufactures in the process of responding to the infection that causes the symptoms, not the illnesses themselves. At low weight the body cannot spare the raw materials to make the antibodies to the invading organism. So though infection may be present, its symptoms, such as a fever or a streaming nose, are missing.

Withdrawing from therapy too soon

At 85 per cent AEBW sufferers are still underweight but, because they are looking more viable, the whole world assumes they must feel better, and indeed be better (see Chapter 6). There will be little credit forthcoming for the effort they are making to hold their weight at this level. They are likely to find everyone encouraging them to act as if they are fully recovered.

Since there appears to be nothing obviously wrong, all the usual expectations and obligations flood in: the expectation that they will get down to school work, complete the training, obtain the degree, take up a challenging job 'appropriate for a person of your intelligence', that 'uses your qualification'. There will be the anticipation that they will make friends, fulfil social obligations, find a partner, have children; that they will get back on the road to success in whatever way others see as appropriate. Since they appear to be so much better, it is also generally assumed at this stage that no further help is needed.

Meanwhile, even though they feel swamped by them, sufferers are only too likely to accept these assumptions as valid, and 'right'. This is the stage at which they typically tell themselves they ought 'after all this time' to be able to manage on their own. 'I don't look as though I need help. I feel such a fraud, continuing to have help' is a view they often voice. They can feel very uncomfortable about taking up any more time, or resources, even though they know they need the help still. They can be full of guilt about having 'taken enough'; about not deserving any more; they ought to keep everyone happy; the family will be happy if they are better, so they ought to do their best to seem better, and so on. Thus they will put up their old appearance of coping whilst still feeling inadequate and a failure, knowing that in their process of disengaging from anorexic illness they still have ground to cover.

It is where such pressures and obligations are felt that sufferers may at this stage withdraw, or be withdrawn, from therapy. Not yet secure or confident enough in themselves, not yet liking themselves enough to be sufficiently self-directed to avoid getting caught up again in the same conflicts and the same confusion, they will be unable and/or unwilling to say they feel swamped, unable to cope. They will find it impossible to say 'I am still stuck, I do still need help', or say so loudly enough. So they stay stuck, drawn in the swirl of the same insidious vortex, held in its spin, knowing they are still in danger one way or another of being drawn in tighter, and sinking again.

Where sufferers are clinging to food restriction their sinking will be obvious because their weight will fall again. Depending upon how long their anorexic thinking has been in place, and upon their history during the illness, they may be unaware that they are sinking, or they may be fully aware and openly admit: 'I feel such a mess. I know I still need help. But if I get fat (i.e. allow myself to be a bit nearer a normal weight) I won't get it. So I can't get fat.' Where male sufferers, emerging from a lower weight, are alarmed and humiliated at their literal descent into a 'female illness' they may rapidly spin into exercise: 'It was odd I hadn't realised I'd got into starving, I lost so much weight. I got help though. I eat regularly now, and changed my job. That was good. Came here as sports coach. It keeps me on my toes. Yes, it's still there really.'

Far from being deceitful, sufferers are usually as honest about themselves as those around them will allow them to be. What is so painful and causes them so much despair is that, however honest they may be, they still feel utterly helpless, stuck and powerless to change.

Alternatively, the fact that a sufferer might be sinking will not necessarily be obvious to others because 'the conflict and the mess is all there behind the scenes', because cover is taken behind various facades, all with equally unhappy consequences.

> They thought I was better, so I thought I'd better be better. I put up a good show. But I got worse. I had this continual feeling of being totally out of control. I ate and ate and ate, then made myself sick. Vowed I wouldn't eat and did. Felt dreadful and guilty. So I'd vomit again, or clean the chemist out of laxatives. But it wasn't just about eating. I was out of control over everything. Everything was total chaos. A never-ending nightmare. I'd run anywhere, constantly running, do anything, sleep with anybody to get away from it. Anything to block it out.

Sufferers can be painfully aware of the plight they are in, as their off-hand remarks can show: 'I'm just a circus . . . a ring-load of performances.' Equally: 'It's all the same, isn't it? It's all part of the costume-shop'; their despair is there to be heard.

Acting out the chaos

Despite weight being more viable within this range, sufferers still perceive everything in black-and-white, all-or-nothing terms, including ideas relating to food and body control. As they think in extremes, dramatic changes in behaviour are the common pattern throughout this transition stage. They are common too in the band above this, where sufferers are at or around their average weight, and in the overweight bands and beyond.

Because the chaos they experience is greater at this stage, swings into the 'absolutely bad' category are likely to be bigger, more violent. Feelings and behaviour are in every respect more impassioned, more 'wild', and can result in actions which are humiliating to the sufferer, and alarming to others. However violent or dramatic these shifts, they are still a consequence of the way the sufferer is thinking and feeling, even at this stage. They are part of the illness, and not to be considered a sudden deterioration, or some new kind of problem. A helper will need to bear this in mind to remain steady; to be able to continue to accept a sufferer as he or she is at this point too, even possibly in the face of events that will be traumatic to the sufferer and devastating to relatives.

Where their frantic behaviour, shifting from one extreme to another, serves as a focus for others' despair or disapproval, their conviction that they are worthless can become the harder to bear, and to the same degree sufferers punish themselves more stringently, or try more determinedly to keep their mask intact. It is where these strategies fail that a sufferer may perhaps come for help for the first time, after years of being at a more viable, regained weight and hiding disordered eating.

Help and care at viable weight

Sufferers attain a more viable weight as they move towards levels at the top end of this transition stage – from 83–85 per cent AEBW onwards. It should not be assumed that it is no longer necessary to check their physical position – or that it will no longer be necessary to keep a check on this in the following band, i.e. when they are in the band of weights between 85 and 100 per cent AEBW. As we have indicated, the possible range of problems is greater as sufferers move through this particular stage than when weight is lower and food is being successfully avoided, and when evidence that there are problems can be difficult to detect. The range of problems is as great when they move beyond the 85 per cent level. In relation to this, the following is a useful checklist a helper may bear in mind.

Patterns of food and body control

Here the task is to ascertain:

- the sufferer's current weight and whether it is stable or not. If not, at what rate is it rising or falling?
- the current pattern of food restricting. Is this constant, or does control break down? If so how often? How much food is consumed in one episode? How much money is spent on food, or on food avoidance? Can the sufferer afford it?
- whether, and with what frequency, the current pattern includes vomiting and/or purging and/or using diuretics. If purgatives or diuretics are being taken, in what quantities and combinations?
- what forms of exercise are routinely or sporadically undertaken, and how much? Are there, or have there been, any performance-enhancing or other drugs used?

Stealing

Sufferers may have found themselves stealing – usually money or food – from members of their household. They may also have shoplifted.

Seeking oblivion

The helper should check with sufferers whether and to what extent they resort to alcohol and/or other drugs – prescribed or otherwise – to escape from unbearable feelings. It is also helpful to check whether, and how often, they have felt so despairing as to have actually overdosed to escape into temporary oblivion, or whether, more seriously, they have explicitly wanted or tried to commit suicide.

Self-harm

Sufferers may try to limit the overwhelming effect of their feelings by cutting or burning themselves, scratching or gouging their skin, pinching themselves, hair pulling, banging their head against the wall or otherwise deliberately bruising themselves. So visible marks should be taken seriously, and the possibility entertained that there may be damage, such as radiator burns, hidden by clothing. It is helpful to ask how any such hurt occurred and give them the opportunity to talk about the need to resort to self-harm, and how this need relates to feelings or emotions and the intensity of these.

Using sexuality

A helper should be open to the possibility that sufferers, male or female, may be desperately sleeping around. This can be a means of escaping from their own company. It can be a guard against night-time eating, or a guard against the fear of this. It may be a combination of all of these.

Alternative ways of restricting food and obliterating feelings can occur at lower weights, but behaviour of the above kinds is more likely as weight becomes viable.

Practical responses to the consequences of chaos

It will usually be a relief for a sufferer to find a helper who knows and can accept that none of this is unusual, who knows that spinning off into all kinds of behaviour is part of the pattern of the illness, and who is aware that it is possible to feel so hopeless, and to be so desperately out of control. It will also be useful if a helper can provide, or point the sufferer towards, any further practical information, advice or assistance that may be needed. For instance, a visit to their general practitioner could be a sensible step for some. Since it is not possible, simply by looking at someone, to tell what degree of biochemical disturbance is being created by regular vomiting, purging, or use of diuretics, it is essential that this is medically checked. Low levels of potassium in the body are dangerous. Hence routine blood testing for electrolyte levels can be requested from the doctor.

Just as it is important to increase food intake by gradual degrees at very low weight so the body has time to adjust, it is equally important that a sufferer who is using laxatives reduces these by small steps, thus modifying any imbalance in body chemistry gradually and more safely. It is useful if both helper and sufferer understand in general terms how the body progressively adapts to laxatives and the hazards that sudden change can bring.[2]

Sufferers may experience a welcome release of tension as a result of gorging food, then making themselves vomit. It can achieve a sense of 'at least resolving something'. But as well as the profound guilt and self-disgust they feel, a binge–vomit session is usually followed by lethargy, fatigue and patchy concentration. This is the result of switching on the parasympathetic nervous system, along with activating normal digestion processes. Severe and prolonged fatigue and muscle weakness can also build up if frequent vomiting leads to a drop in potassium levels.

While they provoke feelings of being useless and ineffectual, these experiences are no more evidence of fundamental worthlessness than the effects of food avoidance or underfeeding are evidence of being virtuous. But bulimics will castigate themselves for their ineffectiveness and for their inability to be lively, active, clear-headed. So, equally here, assistance will be needed in disentangling the physical basis of their feelings from sufferers' interpretations of them, and from the implications these interpretations have for self-esteem.

The task here is more complicated than when there is mere food restriction because biochemical changes are intermittent, depending upon what a sufferer is doing to himself or herself, and their effects are less predictable. Whether their eating/eliminating is routine, chaotic or ritualized, whether it is interspersed with exercise or total starvation, or not, sufferers at this weight level may despair of the mess they are in. But, particularly from the mid-point of this transition stage onwards, they will be more able to listen and to talk.

A helper can begin by providing information. For sufferers will probably be unaware of the extent to which vomiting and purging and alterations in food intake are affecting their moods and feelings. It is also useful for them to find this out for themselves in practical ways, such as noting how they are and what they are feeling before, during and after these episodes. The effects may also be apparent in a person's diet. Talking to them may reveal they are drinking orange juice, or taking potassium-rich foods such as tomatoes or a banana after vomiting or purging. Thus they may learn that without realizing it they have, in this way, been compensating for the imbalance they have created in their body chemistry.[3]

Knowing that feelings, emotions, and even behaviour in terms of the kind of food they reach for subsequently are affected by vomiting and purging can give sufferers a new perspective on their set response of self-devaluation. As at low weight, it can help them to learn to separate their feelings and sensations from their moral judging. Information alone is unlikely to 'cure' their very low opinion of themselves, but providing them with this information may enable them to peel off at least a first layer of self-recrimination and this way take a step forward.

Mixed addictions

Where sufferers are using or abusing alcohol and/or other drugs, the physical picture becomes even more complex and there is the danger of further addiction. These additional substances tend to create swift and frightening mood changes which exacerbate the confusion sufferers feel anyway, confirm their belief that they are useless, reinforce their feelings of disgust and self-hatred, and easily lead to their justifying further self-harm.

Priority must be given to reducing the complexity of a sufferer's situation generally. This is the first step on a path towards more productive conversations. Communication is easier when there is only one 'layer' of altered thinking to get through; that is, where there are only the changes brought about by starvation/underfeeding instead of unaccountable possible variables in mood and experience as a result of the biochemical changes brought about by the elimination of body fluids and/or the ingestion of various kinds of psychotropic substance in any combination including, often, medication. So many variables acting together produce a picture which is beyond a helper's ability to assess, let alone adjust for in communicating with the sufferer. Meanwhile the sufferer is the more likely to remain hopelessly locked in the resultant chaos, because its roots are too many and too complex for anyone in the midst of it to sort out by themselves.

Giving control back to the sufferer

Where sufferers variously have patterns of bingeing and vomiting, laxative using, stuffing and starving, using alcohol, using other drugs, or any of these activities in combination, a useful strategy is for the helper to provide such direct practical assistance as will enable them to regulate food at best in quantities that will at least keep their weight stable. Helping a sufferer to establish or re-establish a routine of eating and exercising, appropriately modified to fit current individual needs, has the advantage of reducing the complexity of the physiological picture. For some multi-substance abusers this process can be started only in a residential setting.

The approaches outlined in Chapters 11 and 12 for creating appropriate measures of safety and predictability will still be needed. Establishing a routine breakfast of agreed amounts of pre-arranged food is still a useful first experimental step towards achieving a sense of organization. Likewise three days on liquid food can break cycles of stuffing and starving, or bingeing and vomiting. Sufferers will usually feel better about themselves where they can begin to alleviate such recurrent degrading and humiliating episodes. By going through the practical detail of regulating food and eating, it is possible to enable a sufferer gradually to re-establish the control that has been lost. There is a need to regain some sense of autonomy first in this albeit very limited sphere. For although weight may be viable – or, through bloating, or as a result of muscle bulk, appear so – food/body control still has an absolute hold. It is still central to existence. Where sufferers are thus helped towards safer self-regulation, they are likely, over time, to resort less to bingeing, vomiting and laxative abuse as a way of feeling in control; or to drugs or alcohol as a way of obtaining oblivion and getting out of 'the whole confusing mess'.

Tackling every problem at once does not usually yield progress. Thus it may be useful to encourage a sufferer to concentrate first on stopping drug use absolutely, whilst not changing anything else. Any measure of autonomy they see themselves as achieving can generate some confidence, and create in them some faith that change is possible. The success of giving up heroin by 'cold turkey' tactics has strengthened the resolve of a number of drug-using anorexia nervosa/bulimia sufferers in such a way as to enable them to go on to free themselves from their original anorexic illness. Their attitude, as expressed by one of them, was: 'If I can get off heroin, I'm not going to be beaten by anorexia.'

Unless injury enforces this beforehand, they will also, as they begin to feel differently, gradually come to spend less time exercising.

Overdosing and potential suicide

There is no point in the helper assuming or pretending that a sufferer will not already have resorted to calculated oblivion through overdosing, or will not have brooded upon or attempted suicide, in this or any other way, as a means of solving his or her problems. Helpers who close their eyes to these possibilities because they are disconcerting, because they make them uneasy, are falling into the same trap as the anorexia nervosa/bulimia sufferer and will certainly be the less helpful to them. The expression of self-destructive thoughts needs to be allowed, and the feelings that give rise to them acknowledged, without judgement, criticism or blame. It is as important to the development of a person's sense of self to acknowledge their suicidal feelings as it is to acknowledge any other aspect of their being.

Enabling sufferers to allow suicidal feelings into the open is not only therapeutic in itself, it also enables the helper to work with them on the content of these feelings. Unlike the global despair of some potential suicides, the anorexic/bulimic's anguish will usually tend to focus around a particular instance of losing control over food or weight. In their panic they will see *all* as lost. Here, as at lower weight stages, it is helpful to bring into focus the progress sufferers themselves have acknowledged at other points in time, and the less despairing moments they have experienced, thus reintroducing more intermediate positions. These are the intermediate positions now more available to them as their weight becomes more viable, but which they still very easily – though now usually temporarily – lose sight of.

Open expression of suicidal feelings also enables a helper to judge the level of desperation that is being experienced, how committed a sufferer seems to be to the intention of dying, how specific the plans are that have been made for killing himself or herself, and to respond accordingly. It is appropriate to increase the frequency of appointments. Explicit instructions or invitations to phone the helper to maintain contact between sessions provide another anchor. A sufferer may not take up the invitation, but can find support in knowing the helper is available should he or she need the contact. A helper can encourage the sufferer to alert sympathetic others who are close to them or responsible for them. Or it may be necessary for the helper to do the alerting, preferably with the sufferer's prior knowledge and agreement, otherwise this is the only time when breaches of confidentiality can be contemplated. If the risk of suicide is immediate and detailed, it is in the sufferer's interest for the helper to mobilize more help.

Knowing overdoses are possible, it is sensible to assess what is available to the sufferer at home or at work to overdose with, act to remove the drugs that are most dangerous, and keep other drugs in smaller quantities. Anti-depressants can be helpful for a time, possibly to give sufferers some respite from the turmoil or despair they are in, and hospitalization may be necessary in some cases.

Anti-depressants and tranquillizers are not only useful for their pharmacological effect, but also for the way they influence the form an overdose may take. Sufferers who plunge into their extreme 'bad' category may well, as a result of their extreme thinking, swallow all the pills they currently have, yet be prevented by their inability to make decisions from taking any more action at this instant. Providing he/she is adequately informed, their general practitioner could take the precaution of not prescribing the more risky kinds of drugs and will take care not to supply quantities large enough to be lethal, while ensuring that such patients still have something they can take to deaden their unbearable feelings. In some cases this strategy may be adequate to contain a sufferer through a suicidal period. The alternative, as chaos and desperation increase, is that sufferers might resort to the more dangerous of the pain-killing drugs that are obtainable over the chemist's counter, so it is always appropriate to watch discreetly. Time can be crucial when it comes to caring for a person who has overdosed. Should hospital treatment be necessary, staff should bear in mind that the patient is anorexic/bulimic. Though a stomach pump may have been required, this patient will also need to re-establish feeding.

Stealing

For the starving anorexic who shoplifts, or the bulimic who takes food from a supermarket prior to a binge–vomit cycle, there can be an effective defence to a charge of theft based on the absence of a prior dishonest intention. In lawyer's language, many sufferers lack the necessary 'guilty mind' or *mens rea* because of their biochemically altered state.[4] Sufferers need to know that in law taking goods by itself does not establish that a theft has occurred.

Their very low self-esteem ensures that they feel bad and deeply guilty anyway, so they will assume that, having taken the goods, they are therefore proved guilty. These preconceptions render them the more vulnerable to a verdict that will provide them, and their families, with yet further evidence of how low they have sunk.[5] Their attitude is likely to be similar to that of the bulimic university student who automatically pleaded guilty, having been found taking food from a department store. When she came before the court, she was asked by the magistrate whether she knew what her guilty plea meant.

Student: It means I took the food. I must've done. It was in my bag when I was stopped. Nobody else could've put it in there.

Jp: No, it means you set out from home intending to steal. That you went to the store thinking how to take goods without being seen.

Student: Oh, no! I had no idea I'd even gone into the shop. I meant to go swimming, but the fitness centre was closed.

The magistrate in this case refused the student's plea and referred her to the duty solicitor. He advised her to plead not guilty, arranged for an informed medical report from a psychiatrist experienced in working with patients with eating disorders and, once the court had the full facts, a verdict of not guilty was returned.

Debt

Whether debt is mounting as a result of credit card spending or whether financial resources are being improperly drained in any other way, sufferers are not helped by a blind eye being turned on their being out of control in this respect either. They may see it as 'no bother', ignoring their accumulating debt, or it may be increasing their kaleidoscoping anxiety. Either way it is appropriate for the helper to point out where they may find additional help. Organizations such as the Citizens' Advice Bureaux can be a useful first step in providing this extra practical assistance.

Sexuality and 'relationships'

Sexual behaviour will generally follow the same all-or-nothing pattern that marks every other aspect of sufferers' activities. Everything to do with sex may be completely avoided, or rushed into. They may also swing between the two extremes, from celibacy to sexual binges. Where sex is not explicitly avoided, the pattern again can be equally extreme, from remaining with one partner to engaging indiscriminately with any number of contacts; 'the whole world'. While their sexual behaviour may look chaotic or impulsive, it can be a form of control: 'It's safer than being with food.' Sufferers may see their behaviour as promiscuity, in which case they are likely to consider it as all part of their worthlessness. On the other hand they may see it as achievement, as sexual scoring.

Where sufferers do not avoid sex, their uncertainty, confusion, despair and self-hatred mean that they are generally very vulnerable, which warrants a helper identifying issues of sexually transmitted infections, possibly injury, and the possibility of pregnancy.

Some girls and women can still be menstruating, even at weights lower than 80 per cent AEBW. Others may not. The absence of menstrual periods at any weight level throughout this transition stage, or in the stage above

85 per cent AEBW does not mean that conception cannot occur. It can. Few are aware this is so. Contraception is relevant, and sufferers need to know this. While children might ultimately be wanted, for many sufferers the idea of looking after a child while they are so clearly unable to look after themselves fills them with horror, and they express as much.

Just as sexuality can be used as an escape from chaos and as a fix in itself, so people can be used in other more general ways, inadvertently or otherwise, to escape from private unbearable confusion and turmoil, or for the buzz the crowd can give. The idea of having a 'special relationship', or finding a partner, or 'having friends' obtains much of its appeal in the same way, and much of its desperation. No fixing really works, however. The 'relationship', like any other form of fix, will eventually or repeatedly crash, or persist as a ritual and a pretence.

References

1 Slade, R. (1984) *The Anorexia Nervosa Reference Book*. London: Harper and Row, 36–7.
2 Ibid., 55–9, 64–6.
3 Ibid., 65–6.
4 Welbourne, J. personal communication, 'Do bulimics really steal?'
5 Slade, R. (1984) op. cit., 70.

fourteen

Moving towards a real sense of self

At weights around 85 per cent AEBW and above it is possible to reach a sufferer most easily and work with the existential malaise that lies at the root of the illness. This has, of course, been the aim throughout the preceding chapters where the suggested interventions have consistently been those designed to enhance a sense of autonomy rather than destroy it. But within this band of weights all a sufferer's faculties will be present, so therapy can be more wide-ranging and progress may be more rapid.

It is still appropriate to keep watch on patterns of food avoidance, eating, vomiting, bingeing, exercising and so on, and as part of the whole picture to note fluctuations in weight. But the main task here is to continue working with the underlying lack of self endured by all those drawn into food/body control by the need to feel that, at least in some way, they are author of their own life.

The problem thus identified, it might be assumed that therapy can now be a relatively straightforward matter of using techniques that have been found generally to be helpful in assisting personal growth and change. Yet while these may be a useful source of ideas, they are not applicable to anorexia nervosa/bulimia sufferers in any simple way.

The main difficulty in their use lies in the fact that, even when the physical effects of starvation recede, even when sufferers are then consistently fed and obtain adequate rest, their sense of self remains one that has been formed through food and body control. There is still the belief that in their food/body-regulating 'self' is the only solution to the question of how to live. Others may know this is an aberrant solution that can destroy a person physically and psychologically, but for those whose mindset is anorexic it is still the only solution they know, and they may still simply not believe any alternative is necessary. Conversely they may be keenly aware that a different way of living is needed, but have no faith that there is or can be any alternative. Either way they cling to the belief that, if only they were totally controlled, all their difficulties would permanently be resolved.

We have been to some lengths to show that food/body control is far more efficient than most people realize at providing anyone who lacks self with a feeling of direction and autonomy. Thus while control routines are in place, sufferers will still come across as strong, powerful, effective people, and this will still create difficulties.

Those, professional or otherwise, who are new to the task of working with anorexia nervosa/bulimia sufferers do not realize how very limited is the sense of their own being beyond their food/body control. Their apparent effectiveness encourages a helper to assume that the person he or she is meeting must benefit from the experiences that therapeutic approaches are designed to generate; that there will be a process of learning and change.

The reality is, however, that even at this stage it can be difficult to make real connection with sufferers. They are so conflicted, so fragmented and confused, so wound up with the anxieties and the frustration this brings, so preoccupied with the calculations involved in sustaining or regaining their control routines, there is no easy flow of thought or ideas. They have little or no capacity to accommodate or engage with new experiences. They are too overwhelmed, too readily humiliated, mortified even by the would-be therapeutic experience (see Chapter 6). As they involve acting out roles, approaches such as gestalt, or psychodrama are likely to be frustrating for sufferers. They will feel like empty games, and highly uncomfortable, since they see themselves anyway as 'ungenuine', and as 'just so many performances'. Such techniques easily seem like invitations to stage more acts, indulge in more theatre, put about more lies. Similar problems bedevil assertion training. It is difficult to assert a self that does not exist (see Chapter 8), and the rigid, food/body-control self they have, they are already very well practised at asserting.

To allow a focus upon any part of this 'self' meanwhile is a threat. As they shy from this, the likelihood is that they will staunchly deal with the whole painful, embarassing experience in the same way as the rest of the tortuous confusion: 'box it up, put it away'. Hence the therapeutic endeavour itself can increase fragmentation, add to the turmoil, bring fuel to the conflict that already torments them; that strings them out at this weight level. Indeed this is the kind of experience they standardly respond to by fixing, by 'doing something to make it better'. So unless a helper can facilitate something else here, events that might otherwise be therapeutic will become 'integrated' with the established patterns of the food/body control 'self' and effectively reinforce the absence of real self.

It is easy for helpers to remain unaware that they are engaging the mechanisms of therapy, but not with the person. It is easy to miss the fact that they are meeting only the mask, engaging only with the sufferer's ability to go through the motions. They cannot easily know there is no mesh here, but those trapped in the illness will know something is wrong. They will know that therapy 'whatever it is', or 'whatever it is supposed to be', is not touching them. In this there will also be huge relief, even glory. For in remaining untouched, their control also remains safe. Yet there will also be huge disappointment, at least for some, and the sense of being at a complete loss to know what to do about 'this help that doesn't seem to help'. They will see themselves yet again as being a fraud, useless, even 'a failure at therapy'.

Whatever form food/body control is taking, help will need to begin at a much more fundamental level. The task is not to strengthen the 'self' they have, but the more delicate process of enabling sufferers to rediscover whatever self there once was, however incipient, however frightened, enraged, sore, conflicted, confused. It is a process that involves reaching through the sufferer's protective façades and sharing the terrifying space, the sense of nothingness or 'not being' that lies beyond them and taking the time for all that this means. It is about listening accurately, informing correctly, enabling perspectives to be obtained that give coherence, organizing basic experiences from which selfhood can grow. It is by these means that the sufferer's genuine, if as yet still fragile self will emerge, and may have the space to develop, and eventually supplant the need for anorexic, bulimic or related body control – or the need for any other altered state, inadvertent or designed.

Choice, decision and selfhood

A crucial part in creating self is choice and decision making. Unable to choose or decide for themselves, sufferers cannot bring about any action or achieve in any way that provides them with a sense that they have any existence of their own.

Thus the helper will need to focus on the finest detail of the sufferer's choosing and deciding. Again, few realize how very minute the choices and decisions are that they have difficulty in making. Few realize the extent to which they rely upon externally derived routines to get anything done; routines provided by work or courses of study, by other people's requirements, or the needs or routines of pets, or other animals. It seems highly implausible that, when left on their own, a successful first-year medical student, or psychology undergraduate, a lawyer or an efficient staff nurse in a busy surgical ward should be unable to make a decision to move from one point in the room to another, or take their coat off, or, having managed to make a cup of black coffee, to drink it. Yet this is the degree of indecisiveness that sufferers endure. It is at this minute level that the capacity to choose and make decisions eludes them, that their ability to function is paralysed. It is at this level that they have no traction on the world.

Where therapy attends to the minutiae of choosing and decision making, particularly to identifying *who* is doing the choosing and *who* is doing the deciding, then sufferers will usually, even if painfully, begin to gain the traction they need. They will gain a sense that they have a self. They will gain the sense that they have the ability to initiate action that springs genuinely from their own will, or volition – quite distinct from action that is the product of willpower – and so gradually develop the confidence that they exist for themselves. Effective choices, no matter how minute, are affirmations of self that can be built upon.

Constituent parts of choosing and deciding

Feelings and sensations are important for making choices and decisions, for these are the source of the wishes and wants that are the basis of personal preferences. Without prior wishing or wanting that comes from our self, the self that is authentic, choices and decisions cannot be made. This especially is the case when external demands conflict, which is the overwhelming experience of those who become anorexia nervosa/bulimia sufferers.

Equally important on the other hand is accurate knowledge of the world; that is, how the world *really* is rather than how it *ought* to be. Judgemental and non-accepting of themselves as they are, sufferers also characteristically deny themselves 'value-free' information about their world. Everything *must* be 'positive', no matter what distortion of reality this entails. Yet accessing accurate information in a straightforward way about the world 'out there' beyond oneself is essential if choices and decisions are to connect with other people, events and situations in a way that is real, down to earth.

When wishes and wants are freely felt, and experiences of this personal kind are combined with an understanding of the world grounded in how that world really is on the evidence of current testing, then effective choices are the more likely. The actions that follow from such choices will be satisfying and rewarding too, and so contribute to, rather than detract from, a person's sense of self. As moments of ongoing and constructive reciprocity between self and the world, they enhance confidence and build self-esteem.

Learning to live in the present

Decisions and actions take place in the present. It is in the present that the feelings occur upon which preferences for action are based. From what is taking place 'at present', a great deal can be learned about what bears upon the person who is deciding, or making a choice. Thus providing the place and the time to focus on the minute detail of moment-by-moment experience is a potent means of helping sufferers gain leverage on their problem.

Staying in the present moment, sufferers may be invited to allow themselves to be aware of, and possibly express, feelings, wishes, thoughts, images, experiences as they arise. As a focused, experimental process, interacting with the helper within the prescribed world of the therapy session, a sufferer can explore direction, and choice, in a contained situation, explore how the process is paralysed, or how it becomes paralysed. Enabling sufferers to focus, to engage in the detail of directing attention to self in this way, is rather like providing them with an invitation to place themselves and the way they relate to the world under a microscope. Initially even a few moments of this process will provide considerable detail of experience for helper and sufferer to work on. Whether it is thought or image, emotion, feeling, whether it concerns physical self or the spirit of the moment, each experience that occurs, each aspect of self that surfaces, that the sufferer risks countenancing, bears on and connects with every other aspect of self. Although sufferers may not see it this way, there is a potential in this for them to be more present, more connected with self, and with the world. For to focus thus is ultimately to enable the *real*ization of self.

In Chapter 12 we illustrated how even when sufferers are starved and emaciated it is possible to help them identify their real wishes or wants, and by continually bringing their alternatives for action into focus, enable them to make adjustments to their actions to accord with these real wishes, so they have the greater chance of realizing them. At that stage the situation was one in which the sufferer was at risk physically and shut down psychologically, and the task of choosing was closely framed by the constraints these changes produced. The point of decision there was concerned with staying out of hospital. Facilitating their choosing and deciding is no different here, though since they are no longer low weight, sufferers will usually be able to access their feelings more readily at this stage. So they have greater potential to connect with them, for their decision making to become effective, and integral to their real-self experience rather than strengthening a food/body control self.

Discovering personal rules and core beliefs

The very suggestion that sufferers might stay 'in the here and now' will immediately bring to the surface the tangle of rules and beliefs that reflect their moral, rule-bound nature, their extreme sensitivity to the needs of others, their deep sense of worthlessness (see Chapter 6). These are the 'shoulds', 'oughts' and 'musts' that derive from, and are constantly reinforced by, their background and the culture of which they and their families are so much a part (see Chapter 7).

The exercise will conflict with the rule that 'one ought not to pay heed to oneself', and be disturbing, because of the belief that 'I am not worth the attention'. So the suggestion itself is likely to bring about immediate discomfort, and a typical response like: 'I can't sit here and just talk about myself.

Talking about me makes me feel guilty. There's no way I can avoid feeling selfish if we're talking about me.'

It will conflict too with other rules and beliefs which tie up with their pattern of looking to the future or to the past, and so work continually to prevent them from being aware of how they are *actually*, in the present moment. For instance, 'I am so bad [always in the past] I must strive to be better [in the future]', or 'I'm so negative [my total past experience], I must look to the future. I must be *positive* [I'm not "positive" yet, I've got to get there].' These prescriptions tie in with other fundamental beliefs, such as 'I alone am responsible for what I am', and 'I *must* get everything right.' (See also Chapter 7.)

As they are encouraged to explore the rules and beliefs they are attempting to live by, it will become clear how conflicted they are. They believe they ought to strive to be better in future, but they also believe they can only ever be worthless. Yet the value and purpose of striving is negated here at the same moment as it is being propounded. With strong beliefs thus in conflict, it is unsurprising that they feel so profoundly hopeless. We have also seen how, while they must be sensitive, caring, considerate of others' needs, they must also win. They must be the best. Less than absolute best is just not good enough. Yet as they win, they create hurtful failure for others, which is bad; 'the absolutely worst thing' (see Chapter 8). Meanwhile a helper's very attempt to acknowledge a sufferer is likely to bring to light rules about getting things right for others, pleasing others, being as others need them to be. If answers are not then forthcoming from the helper, and quite properly they will not be, here, a sufferer may even emit, exasperatedly: 'Tell me what you want me to do! How d'you want me to be? Then I can be it.' However, not believing it is possible to get anything really right *ever*, for *anyone* – which must also include the helper – and with no belief in this, even while asking for instruction to obtain it, conflict and confusion emerge here too.

There is in one way, therefore, no especial need for sufferers to delve into their past. For the conflict in their rules and beliefs that emerges with the exercise of staying in the present illuminates the paralysis that is being sustained in the present. It becomes evident how the ready possibility of resolving everything by doing 'the one right thing', that is food and body controlling, swiftly slips into place.

The variety of rules that emerges is quite limited, but every rule reflects the characteristic lifestyle. So that sufferers may become more familiar with their rules, and possibly look at where they might risk change, or note when they do risk change, a helper may invite sufferers, individually, to formulate their particular sets of rules and beliefs, for example: 'I must never be wrong. I must always be absolutely right/good/perfect'; 'Only the best is good enough'; 'I should put others' needs/feelings before my own, otherwise I am selfish'; 'I must be pleasing/acceptable to/liked by everyone'; 'I should think the right/ proper thoughts'; 'I must not have wants, I ought not to have needs of my own. I must give to others'; 'Emotional behaviour is wrong/disturbing to others and I ought not to upset/offend anyone'; 'Feelings are unreasonable/

self indulgent. I ought not to be unreasonable. I must not be self indulgent', and so on.

Each sufferer's own particular set of rules or guiding convictions will be present in the way that sufferer responds to the helper. The helper's careful drawing of attention to the mismatches and the conflicts as they emerge in this relationship may, therefore, be able to illuminate the way they are generating great discomfort for the sufferer even in the present moment. Furthermore, not only is this the discomfort that unresolved conflict always generates, but the rule will also be that, like every other feeling this too must be ignored. As it is ignored, supressed or cast aside, it is of course a banishment of exactly that kind of information within self that would enable the individual to obtain some sense of what is actually wished for or really wanted or what would be liked. Sufferers would usually very much like to feel less discomfort, if they would allow themselves to acknowledge even that.

Becoming aware of the way their rules and beliefs are involved both in creating their discomfort and intensifying it, and how the process of their choosing and deciding is thwarted at every turn, may provide some insight into the nature of their entrapment and how their sense of worthlessness and ineffectiveness is continually being reinforced. It would be a mistake to assume, however, that just because some insight may be gained, sufferers will, or can, alter their approach. Clear access to feelings is necessary to this, as is greater confidence in their perceptions and practice in remaining connected with the detail of their moment-by-moment living. All this takes time. There is a long and painful journey between insight and real change.

Acknowledging the rest of the iceberg

Attending to the fine detail of the decision-making process may itself create shifts, bringing about small and tentative adjustments in a sufferer's approach to life, though helpers meanwhile will often find themselves attempting to communicate with someone who is markedly unresponsive. Sufferers often refer to themselves as 'a very private person' and they are right. Little information emerges on how they are thinking or feeling. They give away little of what they are experiencing, even to themselves. In the early weeks, and probably months, helpers will frequently have to rely on their knowledge of the condition to keep the therapy session alive.

Sufferers, as we have said, may reject outright as unnecessary, indulgent and selfish the suggestion that they pay heed to themselves, though rules such as 'I ought not to cause trouble, or make difficulties', or 'I shouldn't offend' will prevent open disagreement with the helper, on this or any other matter. Characteristically they would rather not come back to another session than state their disagreement. Bad as they feel about themselves, they cannot afford to be disliked or looked down upon by anybody. Discomfited as they are by disagreements, they cannot afford to make enemies, or create situations in which they may have to assert any aspect of themselves that may result in their feeling worse about themselves than they do already.

On the other hand, they may be confused by the invitation to pay heed to themselves, disturbed and uncomfortable at the idea of going against principles they have grown up with, or at doing something they believe is not right or proper or that, morally, feels bad. Again anxiety and guilt at failing to please if they do not go along with the suggestion complicates everything further and adds to the confusion.

It is also likely that among these conflicts there will be stipulations about the importance of clarity, the necessity of being intelligent, and how inferior it is to be muddled, inadequate, stupid. Certainly, they should not be confused. They *ought* to know what to do. They *should* know what the answer is. So they will go round endlessly on a dizzy carousel of feelings, obligations, tensions, confusion, with no way of stopping the spin; no way of halting its clatter. So they panic, or end up totally blank. Yet they reveal nothing of this either in their inadequacy and shame; not to the helper; not to anyone.

Saying nothing is also a way of considering the helper's feelings. It can nullify the effectiveness of self-assertion exercises too, as the sufferer demonstrated who dismissed a manual on assertion training with the comment: 'I see what they mean. But I don't think people ought to behave like that. It just seems exceedingly self-centred and inconsiderate. It wouldn't be very pleasant to be like that.' Being assertive over righteous causes is more acceptable, however, and characteristically so. This kind of assertion is justified because it is on behalf of others: people, things, animals. They will often stand up for justice and fairness on account of another, but the idea of taking a stand for their own sake they will perceive as selfish and morally wrong.

It is important to let sufferers know that these ways of thinking, feeling and responding are typical of the person who is anorexic/bulimic, and that they are by no means unusual in other people either. This can be particularly important where a sufferer is mute, or recalcitrant. By indicating that these experiences are shared, and understandable, a helper may make it safe enough for thoughts and feelings to be brought into the open. They may indeed be 'very private', but some sufferers will admit they feel under siege. Yet, as gradually they become less defended, the more perspective they gain on themselves in real individual terms, which itself generates further constructive change.

While enabling them to become more expressive and more accurately aware of themselves, it is crucial for a helper to remain attuned to the fact that, in every case, the sufferer's real self is tentative, fragile, lacking the resources to cope with the most minor intrusions. Harmless as it may seem to anyone else, even mere talking can leave them feeling invaded, exploited, coerced, controlled. So it needs to be made equally clear that it is also entirely acceptable to keep their thoughts, feelings, whatever they are experiencing to themselves. They do not have to share them with the helper, and it is important a helper does not create an obligation, unspoken or otherwise, that they should. The very private person that the sufferer is needs still quite explicitly to be respected.

Making it clear that it is genuinely acceptable to say and do nothing, and acknowledging that time can be given as needed for them to have a sense of whether or not they want to open up on any point, it may also usefully be suggested that they themselves notice what stops them expressing their feelings. Becoming aware of the issues which they habitually censor or points at which they stall can tell them a great deal, even though they may not yet be ready to let those aspects out into the open. It can also be acknowledged that the world itself may be an issue here, either generally, in terms of how the world is, or specifically, since the reason for sufferers remaining closed on any point can lie in the person of the helper.

Allowing feelings and emotions

While freer access to their feelings and emotions is needed if sufferers are to make choices and decisions effectively, this is problematic. The prospect of allowing what they feel, or even that they feel, is frightening, painful, embarrassing. This can seem unbearable in so many ways. In actually allowing feelings, the fear is that they will be overwhelmed. 'If I do that I might cry' is the often unspoken statement, or they may say explicitly: 'If I let myself cry I'll never be able to stop', or 'I'll get angry and then it'll get unreasonable. Everything'll get out of hand', or 'I hate myself and I know I hate myself, so what's the point? Just hate, hate, hate – so it's not worth going on. I might just as well kill myself.'

Should they be overwhelmed by feeling, they are afraid of being unable to cope with themselves. They are certain that others will not be able to cope with them either, and this includes the helper, and they are afraid of that too. Or they are afraid that, as a result of expressing the real self in this way, they will jeopardize whatever fragile relationship there is with the helper, and this will leave them more isolated than ever. Again such fears may be grounded, and yet, even where they are not grounded, sufferers' experience is such that it is hard for them to trust others or themselves on emotional or any other issues.

Hence the helper will find that sufferers skid and slide, this way and that, diverting, distracting into anything, or anybody – especially anybody else who appears to need help – rather than focus on who *they* are, or connect with how *they* feel, or attend to what *they* themselves are about, right here, and right now. When they are asked about themselves, about their own feelings or experiences they will, for instance, often reply in terms of other people's feelings and others' experiences. Where the helper holds the focus, sufferers may discover for themselves how readily they 'disappear' or 'merge' with someone or something else.

> *Vee*: I can see what I'm doing. I just go blank every time. I noticed I looked out of the window just then, when you asked me how *I* was feeling. I disappeared. Completely cut off.

Helper: From?

Vee [Pause]: Attention.

Helper: My paying attention to you?

Vee: I suppose so. [Pause] But that's silly. Because I always thought I wanted attention. But it seems I don't.

Helper: I'm attending to you now. How does this make you feel?

Vee [Pause]: Scared.

Helper: You're scared. Of?

Vee: What you might notice.

Helper: What are you scared I might notice?

Vee [Pause]: How unconfident I am.

Sufferers typically struggle to say, simply, 'I want' and 'I need' without adding 'oughts' and 'shoulds'. It may be possible to experiment with being in the present and making such statements without adding 'oughts' and 'shoulds'. This might also provide practice at sharing current feelings, admitting current wishes, acknowledging how they are rather than stipulating how they ought to be, and, in relation to their actual feelings, identifying preferences and making decisions on the basis of priorities that are their own.

These things are easy to talk about, but much harder to effect. It can take months of regular sessions before sufferers who are tightly controlled will risk humiliation by revealing their 'weakness' in crying for instance, or risk 'letting themselves down' by showing annoyance, or being irritated or angry, or admitting the fears they have. There are those who may be more emotional, but they will usually be less ready to admit to feelings that one woman described as 'the more twisted and shameful ones' such as jealousy, or resentment, or black hatred. Generally they are less ready to touch the unbearable pain of disappointment or sound the frightening depths of grief, often specifically the grief at the loss of so much of their life to the illness. 'It's when I think of what I've lost . . . the waste, ten years of my life [her face distorting with emotion] like this . . . I could cry . . . but somehow I can't. It feels too deep.'

To allow the emotion that wells when realities are even quite lightly touched is to allow a tension to be released, and the real person to begin to mend. This is distinctly different from the release of emotion or feeling that provides some relief, but which does not result in sufferers moving from their conflicted and paralysed position. It is possible to be unaware that there are other feelings beneath or beside the emotion that most readily erupts. It is quite possible to cry, or rage, or indeed talk whilst omitting to acknowledge, or whilst remaining less aware, that there are other feelings at other levels, and, at these other levels, remain unconnected with self. Emotionality by itself does not resolve conflict, and may provide a place to hide.

It is possible also to emote and, at the same time, ignore or be unaware of an underlying script that runs: 'I'll let myself cry, because this is what this therapist wants me to do. So I must respond accordingly.' It is possible also to be unaware of a received sense that expression of emotion generally will gain a certain helper's approval. 'Feeling' of this kind will leave sufferers in the same whirlpool position as before, however.

Likewise, being pressured to 'feel', or encouraged to let to the surface more than can be accommodated will, if it does not reinforce the sufferer's defences, merely add to the chaos and complicate even more the tangle of feelings, and thoughts, and rules that she or he is already failing to cope with. The danger in encouraging sufferers merely to 'express feelings' is that they will be left with the same sense of wheelspin as they ordinarily endure, analysing, criticizing, intellectualizing, endlessly thinking themselves round in circles. They will be left with the same sense of pointlessness and frustration, but this time by 'making a big noise and going nowhere'.

Relating to the world

In their turmoil, sufferers will have lost any of the little confidence they might ever have had in their ability to make sense of the world, and relate with it. Though they may be out in the world at this stage, they will not readily feel part of it. The helper will need to give attention to this essential aspect of selfhood too.

Their lack of confidence is in large part rooted in their experience within a family that, for its own historic reasons and often from the highest motives, has covered up its painful or difficult past by 'making everything right', or 'making everything better', thus denying the facts and the experience that would have confirmed the eventual anorexia nervosa/bulimia sufferer's sense that things were not as they were made out to be. Experiences at school, at work and in relationships beyond the immediate family will often have increased this lack of confidence. Specific instances of loss, or failure, or disappointment may also have shaken them, though, as noted earlier, such events may not appear significant to others whilst being critically important to the particular individual.

So sufferers will need time and encouragement to focus on their relationship with the world, with people and events; time to test their perceptions, to assure themselves of the extent of their accuracy or otherwise and, as they gain confidence in this process, so gain confidence in themselves. As with matters concerning food, exercise, weight and eating, straightforward information given by the helper can be useful here too. But even more useful is the affirmation of self that can be gained first hand.

> *Helper*: To me you looked angry, when I suggested you experimented with moving by moving physically – taking a few steps away from the chair.
> *Mel* [silent]
> *Helper*: Are you feeling angry now?
> *Mel* [silent]

Helper: I'm wondering what it is you're not saying.

Mel [still silent and looking more tense]

Helper: You don't have to tell me. I don't mind if you don't want to.

Mel [scowling]: I suppose I feel pushed.

Helper: You feel pushed. By me, now?

Mel [tight-lipped]: Mmm.

Helper: Yes. I am pushing you. My own feeling, as I sit here, is that I'm pushing you. Hard. [Mel looks up with an expression of surprise – and some relief] How do you feel at my saying that?

Mel [thoughtfully]: Relieved, I think . . . You didn't deny what I was feeling.

Thus in the immediate relationship between sufferer and helper there lies the foundation for establishing or re-establishing the sufferer's relatedness with the world.

To help a sufferer connect the present moment to her or his experience of self in the world outside, as well as encourage experimenting further, the above conversation might continue in the following way.

Helper: I wonder if feeling pushed is a familiar experience for you?

Mel: Yes, and it always makes me angry.

Helper: Try looking at me and saying 'No! I don't want to move away from the chair.' [Pause] Try it as a way of pushing me back.

Mel: I can't. [Long pause] It's hard to look at you. I feel ashamed. [Pause] I ought to be able to move away from this chair. [Pause] I feel angry with myself. I do want to! I want to be able to move from here, but I feel stuck. I *ought* to be able to do such a silly little thing. But this is what happens when I'm on my own, when I've got time and space to myself, I just can't move!

Helper: You can't move. [Affirming her statement] I'm wondering whether there's a thought or a feeling in you now that goes with that sense of 'I can't move!'

Mel: I mustn't get it wrong!

Helper: You mustn't get it wrong. [Pause] Who for?

Mel: Me. It's got to be right. [Sounding irritated] Absolutely right. That's what I'm telling myself. Otherwise I won't do it. [Pause] If I move, it might not achieve anything.

Helper: And you've got to achieve something?

Mel: Always . . . And if I make any move I must know in advance what every little outcome will be.

Helper [nodding, and pausing]: Are you comfortable standing as you are now?

Mel: No. I feel stiff.

Helper: How about risking a move? Maybe see whether you can let yourself be a bit more comfortable?

Mel [silent at first, then annoyed]: I just caught myself then thinking, 'I don't deserve to be comfortable'. [Pause] That's how I put the stoppers on myself. Trap myself, all round!

It is important for a helper to assess a sufferer's readiness at any time for a particular exercise or experiment and make it clear that there is, as we have said, no obligation to do something just because the helper suggests it. Nor should the helper underestimate the degree of support sufferers need in order to be able to risk an experimental change.

They would like a magic wand, a miracle, anything that would give them an instant cure, and they can cling to the hope that there might be one: 'I thought if I kept on coming here, to these counselling sessions, I'd wake up one morning and it would all be all right.' Here again, of course, are instances of extreme, or polarized thinking. 'I want to (must) be better this instant! Otherwise I'll never be better at all.' The often cherished belief that, if they were 'normal', there would be no failure, no unhappiness, no discomfort and that even if a problem did arise it would be instantly resolved, is a belief in the same style.

When sufferers can begin to allow that 'normality' is not so fixed, and that there is no 'instantly achievable, once-and-for-all solution to everything, yesterday', they will already have made considerable progress. There is a real move in their beginning to accept that it is possible to 'win a bit, and lose a bit', and to find that there is no absolute necessity to strive or to win every time because the only other possibility is absolute failure. Their engaging more with life as a fluid and changing process that continually produces new challenges, and their taking practical steps that involve trial and error, and degrees of flexibility in response to these challenges, mark significant change likewise.

It will take many months of work, both in the therapy setting and in the course of everyday living, for sufferers to accept not only that there are such risks of trial and error to take, but that it is *they* who have to take them. Neither the helper nor anyone else can do this. No one else can say for them whether a decision or a choice feels right for them, either in the course of their therapy or elsewhere in their life, any more than another person can make decisions for them about eating and resting (see Chapter 12).

Long-term, even very long-term therapy is not an unusual requirement for anorexia nervosa/bulimia sufferers. For any individual, learning to live, and live effectively, may be seen as a process of a lifetime, and at any point personal therapy can enhance this. But anyone who is trapped in food and body control and who has a style of thinking that is anorexic will need longer time to move away from the security, and from the easy certainties this mindset provides.

Integrating the experience of self

Working with anorexia nervosa/bulimia sufferers who neither trust nor want the way they feel is a long and slow process. The greater the intensity of their self-hatred and the deeper that self-hatred sits, the slower the process is, and the longer time it needs to be allowed to take.

Help is often not so much a task of enabling them to access feelings, for they may already be too available, nor necessarily about sharpening their perceptions, for these are often highly accurate, though they have no faith in them. It is more a task of encouraging them to allow their rigidly held rules and beliefs to give a little, so that they can acknowledge and accept their thoughts and feelings and their perceptions, and use them more effectively.

It is the helper again at this stage who has to make the mental adjustments to ensure communication, and take the initiative to direct and structure the sufferer's experience. The process is one that requires the helper to be a person who is real, visible, authentic and non-intrusive. Sufferers need the security of being contained in this way, the safety of 'knowing where they are' in relation to the helper.

The task for sufferers is to connect with their own authenticity, however fragile it might be, or however ugly, confused, damaged, uncertain, knotted up, hurting. The courage required for this must not be underestimated. They will need time to learn to believe in, to trust, and to accept themselves, and to gain the confidence to find a constructive direction, and one that is their own. Where a helper enables them to become more aware of the moments where they *are* choosing, more aware of the nature of their choices, constructive or otherwise, confidence in their own authenticity will increase.

Helper: Listening to you I have the impression you've got a rule for yourself that goes something like: I ought not to be happy. Does that sound like you?

Kay: Mmm.

Helper: How about saying that statement for yourself. See if it really belongs to you.

Kay [Pause]: I ought not to be happy. Yes. I believe that. It's true, I've no right to be happy. That's for other people.

Helper: Happiness is for other people. So when you are happy, you *choose not* to have that feeling? You choose to follow your rule: 'I ought not to be happy.' And then make sure you're not? [Kay nods slightly] How about trying out something a bit different. See how you feel now saying 'I can be happy'?

Kay [tentatively]: I can be happy . . . [Pause] But I'm not! [Hunches herself up over her knees] I'm miserable feeling so stuck!

Helper [gently]: No. OK. You're not happy right now. I can see that. [Pause] There are times when you can be though. I wonder, d'you remember you told me a few months ago you'd gone for a walk and you'd felt happy just sitting by a pool in the fields near you? [Pause] How about trying out the statement another way. 'I can be happy sometimes.'

Kay: I can be happy . . . [Anxiously] But then I think straightaway I ought to be happy all the time. Everyone will expect me to be happy all the time. And I know I'm not. I can't be.

Helper: No. You can't be. [Affirming her statement] Because feelings are things that change. They come and they go, and they come again, if you let them. [Informing about the nature of feelings] Sometimes you feel hurt, angry, bored, guilty, disappointed . . . sometimes you feel happy.

Kay: It's too insecure, being happy. I'm scared something might happen to spoil it. So I rush on. Must keep going. Always on to the next thing.

An alternative movement might be suggested here.

Helper: How about experimenting? Allowing yourself a different choice: to feel whatever happens to be going on in you – happy when you're happy, disappointed when you're disappointed, hurt when you are hurting, even disgusting when you feel disgusting – without rushing away from those feelings. Without rushing into what might happen next. I'm not saying you'll feel comfortable that way. But those moments belong to you. They are your happiness, your disappointment, your disgust and hurt. It's hard, when right now they're all part of you.

Allowing time for experiences to connect, or integrate, and providing ways of opening sufferers to this possibility may be helpful. For example:

Helper: As you let yourself sense what's going on in you, try letting yourself see each experience of you as a fragment of a stained-glass window. So maybe your experience is 'I sense myself as cold, and somehow edgy.' Study the fragment closely, if you can, while it's in focus: 'Now my edginess is changing, to a restlessness . . .' or perhaps another feeling, or thought. Stay with that part of you while it's there, in your awareness. If you can't, notice that too. That part may be too much to face, too hard to bear at the moment . . . but at the same time be aware that all these fragments are joined. Held together, like a stained-glass window, with lead: your complete picture. This is who you are. Every part needs to be present. Every fragment of you is essential for your picture of you to be whole . . .

Kay: I like the idea. But I don't know if I'd be able to do it.

Helper: You like the idea. [Affirming her] You don't have to be able to do anything with it. Let liking the idea be enough for the moment? Allow yourself to focus . . . let it in. Just an idea you like – a constructive one, you know plenty about destructive ones – just an idea can be strengthening. It belongs to you. Like your happy moments. It's part of you. No one can take it away from you. It'll be there in you when you want it.

Kay [very thoughtfully]: I've never looked at it like that before.

Integration is a process that happens. Yet given the nature of the illness, enabling a sufferer to be aware of its being possible is helpful. Here the idea of allowing experience or thoughts to mull can be helpful. Mulling requires that nothing is done. This is likely to feel strange to someone whose rule is that they must 'do something'; that, if there is information, they must act on it. Confidence will be needed to stay with a feeling, or a thought, or an idea without analysing it, without taking it to pieces in a desperate attempt to 'make sense' of it, or find a meaning. This is the confidence illustrated by the former bulimic who found herself able to say, as she contemplated the week ahead: 'I'll be all right. It'll come together. Nowadays I just wait and see. I don't analyse so much. The ideas just connect. It feels much better. *I know where I am.*' As confidence grows, thoughts, ideas, images, recollections just fall into place, as in a jigsaw. Individual experiences and personal events come to make sense by themselves – they make sense to the individual, to the person to whom they belong.

Where a trusted helper provides clear, constant and pertinent affirmations, and provides them with the care and timing that enhances the possibility of their being assimilated, the sufferer will benefit as a person, becoming more sure, and eventually able to affirm her or his own self. Nor need such affirmation necessarily spring from conventionally pleasant episodes. One recovering anorexic gained a great deal from a moment when she found herself able to tell her parents, face to face, that she was angry with them. Still openly anxious about her calorie intake, she had suggested the soup she had just eaten had been thickened. Simultaneously her grandmother, who had made the soup, said that it had, and her parents said that it had not.

> I was angry, and suddenly instead of keeping it all to myself I said: 'I despise you! I've told you I'm still scared, and you were prepared to lie! I despise you for that.' Don't know how I came to say it, but I did! I felt very hot and cold afterwards. OK, they're scared I'll slide back, but it doesn't help if they lie about food. I know I'm not as panicky as I was. But I still get anxious, and I still need to know what I'm eating, because it makes me feel safer.

Hence change can be difficult for those close to a sufferer. 'It was when I began not to run so much, things started getting really nasty between me and dad. Then I realized I was sort of showing him up, and I felt awful about that. It became obvious he had a problem too. He had to run. He *had* to do all his sport. He couldn't stop.' Or, as another more genuinely confident 20-year-old remarked: 'I think my family's surprised how selfish I've become. Before, if I said I didn't want to go out with them, I'd have felt really guilty for a week. Now I feel guilty for about ten minutes!' There are many ways in which a sufferer's getting better can appear as 'getting worse'.

Signs and sounds of recovery

Accustomed as they have been to feeling and telling themselves they are bad, worthless and hopeless, sufferers will easily dismiss and forget constructive experiences. Again they will need time to alter this pattern and learn to take in compliments and expressions of care and affection, rather than push these aside in favour of the criticism, punishment and blame that are easier to absorb because they have so long believed these are all they deserve, and, as they are predictable and familiar, they are safer too. Yet as confidence is gained and the ability to believe good things about themselves increases, they will begin to feel, and even to believe they are, after all, 'at least a bit worthwhile'. These are not words that reflect polarized thinking. They are not about extremes. Notably, this comment itself is a moderated position.

There are often very minute shifts that suggest a change in attitude, that indicate a developing sense of self. It is useful for helpers to be able to recognize the signs and sounds of such shifts and to be ready to keep them in the sufferer's sights, to use them to hold direction when, for whatever reason, she or he is unable to.

Beginning to be able to express wishes, needs, wants, inclinations straightforwardly, without becoming paralysed by guilt or shame, without being tormented by an overwhelming sense of obligation or feeling it is necessary to justify, rationalize, explain, placate or apologize, is an important sign of change. There will be fewer global comments like 'I want to be normal', or 'I just wish I could be better now.' Though need always implied 'must', as in 'I need to (must) know exactly what's happening', 'I'd like to (must) know what everyone's programme is for today', now this will not be so inevitable. Statements generally are more likely to have reasonable connection with reality, to be grounded in what actually is the case at any particular time, rather than being cast only in absolutes and removed from reality. Wishes or wants are now more likely to be such that, with or without help, the sufferer can have some expectation of fulfilling them. This girl's weight is around 78 per cent AEBW, and increasing:

> I need a bit of encouragement sometimes. Not just with eating. Though I do want to get over this thing about I *must* eat on my own. It's when people drop in, and unexpected things like that happen. I need Mum and Dad to know how panicky it makes me when everything's not exactly as planned . . . I need them to understand, because when it gets panicky I lose confidence and just run away.

Sufferers who originally believed they ought not to take up a helper's time are progressing, not regressing, when they ask for support, as one woman did by asking for an earlier appointment in a week where her husband was going to be away. Unsure about coping on her own, she felt this would help her feel safer and avoid binges.

Often sufferers find they express themselves in terms of what they do not want, or do not need. In this they are making clear statements of their personal preferences. Yet so strong is their rule that they 'ought to be positive' or 'think positively', they dismiss or judge these as invalid because they are 'negative'. There is a positive side to knowing and expressing what is not wanted, or not needed, however. For when all these are peeled away, the number of options is diminished. So it becomes easier for sufferers to connect with what they *do* want.

Indications of acceptance of their real self, however this self might be, are a hopeful sign, and even more so when sufferers come to notice these signs for themselves. From a low-weight point of 68 per cent AEBW the 18-year-old here had refed herself gradually, in the way described in the preceding chapters. She made the following self-observation when her weight was around 74 per cent and increasing slowly, and her meals were still being carefully pre-arranged, but her attitude had significantly changed.

I can let myself just slump in the armchair now when I've eaten my meal. I know I'm going to be exhausted, and I can let myself just flop and be lumpy. I know it won't last for ever. Before, when I felt the least bit tired like that, it would immediately be the signal to get up and go out for a long run. I'd got to do something about feeling like that, otherwise I was lazy pig.

Any changes in routine that indicate a shift from what has been 'the rule', or the tightly held belief, are also hopeful. Such shifts will not be rigidly executed, they will not be rigorous or intense, they will not be frenzied or violent. They will not have the 'knee jerk' quality that marks them as being the product of impulse. They will be moderated, the product of a decision that has a certain ease, or that subtle quality which is spontaneity.

I was going out running – I still need that – and I got to the crossroads and suddenly I thought, just because I turned left yesterday that doesn't mean I've got to turn left again today. So I went straight on and round, back home by a different route, and I didn't find myself worrying because it was a bit shorter.

Similarly a helper may notice a sufferer has tied her hair in a different way, or happens to say: 'It was the first time I'd been out of jeans for months.' Such changes often coincide with changes in eating, or with the relaxation of an exercise ritual.

Small moments of spontaneity; a little flexibility: both are signs that a sufferer is beginning to feel differently. The less fear there is of not being able to cope with its consequences, the more likelihood there is of a sufferer being able to initiate his or her own action, being able to respond freely to others' suggestions for action, and respond in a way that feels satisfactory and rewarding not just to the other person but also, importantly, to the sufferer's new and developing self.

Further experiment, self-discovery and real development

When sufferers have genuinely begun to learn that needs and wants are allowable, that priorities can be ordered and that effective choice is possible, other ways may profitably be employed to strengthen the sense they will be beginning to have that they are somebody real.

Where there is now beginning to be a genuine self to assert, practice in asserting this self can be a way of sufferers enabling themselves to discover it is possible still to be sensitive, yet say no, and do so without the inevitable feelings of badness and guilt, and equally that it is possible to say yes without feeling coerced, overridden, leaned on, or used; to discover too that having once committed themselves by saying yes, that it is possible not to feel totally bullied, thoroughly burdened, contorted with resentment or frozen with terror. By the time, therefore, that assertion 'training' and other formal techniques can be constructively used, a sufferer will already have made considerable and painful progress, and progress of a particularly delicate and subtle kind.

It may be possible at this stage to experiment with psychodrama or other role play techniques on occasions, though their use will need only to be brief or incidental. Care in how they are used will continue to be required. They can be a powerful means of connecting with difficult realities. They can also, simply, be too much. Flooded with their own feelings, or by the feelings and emotional states of others, sufferers can be overwhelmed, become chaotic and potentially more at risk of harming themselves, or they can be swept into old patterns of masquerading, performing for others' benefit and otherwise shutting down. Whatever is the case, a helper will need to facilitate the process effectively. Where any sufferer is flung to either extreme, the helper will also need to look to their having a path back, finding the ground they had been on again, without recrimination, without humiliation and, at best, with the possibility of something having been learned from this episode.

Art, dance, yoga, music and other creative approaches such as guided imagery and working with dreams may provide a more gentle approach. But still, timing and the nature of the process is important. Art or dance may be imaginative, or creative exploration. They may be therapeutic in sustaining the developing self; key to its enrichment; inspiring in either of these ways.[1]

How any sufferer connects with them is of paramount importance, however. For while they can afford respite, a needed space of escape where a fragile self can rest, be safely absorbed, learn to idle creatively and re-emerge, they can equally and more dangerously be, in themselves, places from which re-emergence is difficult; or serve as a pass to that other place from which return is problematic, a path through to that haven which is food/body control. If these or any other otherwise therapeutic activities are not to be harnessed in the service of illness, both helper and sufferer together need to be able to keep an eye on the power and the insidiousness of the anorexic mindset in its ability to sequester them.

Finding out about the people in their past may help sufferers gain a perspective on their illness and a more rooted sense of who they are. The very high incidence of particular kinds of events in the histories of sufferers' families, the early deaths, rapid changes in social class, actual or threatened changes in economic status (see Chapter 7) gives a longer perspective on the problem. Often having happened before present family members were born, they are events for which none can really blame themselves, or indeed be blamed. Thus it can help alleviate the burden of guilt, the confusion and the paralysing sense of 'It's all my fault' that sufferers and members of their families feel about the illness. To the extent that it may explain or increase understanding, it may help defuse current anger and increase self-acceptance.

It can also integrate experience in other ways. Appreciating that certain kinds of situations, events, strong moral beliefs are so frequently present in the backgrounds of all sufferers that they may be seen as constituting a reason for their having become ensnared by the illness in the first place, and finding many of these in their own backgrounds, can be very reassuring to a person who badly wants to know *why*. Such information can provide some relief to people who are typically clinging to the rational, analytical approach to all problems, including their own, who will often ask in frustration and despair: 'But why should this have happened to *me*?' For it demonstrates that, at a historical and cultural level too, there is some order. Even here, there is some of the predictability that sufferers need.

As a practical task, many find discovering all that belongs to them in their past enjoyable for its own sake. It may also strengthen their relationships with members of the family in the present. For it usually involves inviting them, for better or worse – and often, as it turns out, for better – to talk about people, events and feelings that will usually have lain buried for years. 'It was a bit difficult at first. I wasn't sure Mum wanted to talk about her family, but then in the end she seemed really pleased, and relieved. I think it's brought us much closer. I enjoyed it too.'

This cultural perspective is also relevant to sufferers being able to sustain their emerging sense of self. For as they become less isolated and make more contact with the world, as they begin to explore the possibility of new friendships and need to find peers, they invariably discover that too many of the people they meet are stuck with the very beliefs and attitudes that have been so destructive in their own lives so far, and that they are still having to work to relinquish.

> I was glad when I got this job [at a garden centre]. But what's really hard is working with Betsy all day. She never eats. She has an apple at lunch. She might have a biscuit at five o'clock. She works late. Everyone says how committed she is and what a wonderful caring person, and what a way she has with plants. And I know what she's doing. She isn't stopping for meals, because she daren't.

They also find themselves mindful of the pull of the whirlpool in other ways. As they are aware that even at this stage they are still inevitably drawn by its force, they find they have to circulate with care if they are to provide themselves with opportunities for genuine friendship, and continue on their way out of the illness. They have to take care if they are to avoid becoming entangled with others who are not actually as available for real friendship or sharing as they might be because they are taken up by their drinking, their drug use or another similar preoccupation or 'commitment'.

Thus individuals who are emerging from the illness, who are attempting to release themselves from the hold food/body control has had on them, can experience a different kind of isolation at this stage, a different kind of loneliness. This can make it easy, especially where they have no continuing support in therapy, to falter in their newly found certainty in themselves and slip back into feelings of hopelessness, into not believing that there really can be a way through.

> I don't want to get back into anorexia again. I know I don't. But the awful thing is you begin to look around and everyone's into it. Everyone's into dieting, or eating the right food, or being vegetarian, or running, or doing work-outs at the gym, or into sport. And if it's not that, then they're into drinking, or smoking, or whatever; they're out of their head on something or other. And you just get to wondering, is there anything else?

A helper's own self-accepting attitudes and secure sense of self are crucial anchors for the sufferer at this, as at any stage.

While they may become clearer about themselves as individuals, more able to express their own preferences and be more effective in their relationship with the world, it is important that no one, neither helper nor family or friends, assumes that those emerging thus from food and body controlling will at this point always, or consistently, 'eat normally'. Their pattern of eating will alter, but change will be gradual, and may continue to be erratic at times. Relaxation over eating will still tend to follow after, or happen at the same time as, they begin to change in other ways. It will follow as they feel more confidence and trust in themselves, rather than precede these changes. It will take time before the fear of uncontrollable eating and weight gain, or indeed the gnawing guilt and anxiety about being an 'unexercised slob', entirely disappear. It will take time before they can say, as this woman did: 'Now when I hear that nagging voice telling me not to eat I don't take any notice. I know it's not the *real* me.' Fears about food and weight are usually the very last to fade, and of these, fear of weight will persist after fear of food has disappeared. But this too will fade as self-confidence continues to grow and the priorities of real living become established more securely.

> Of course, I don't want to be fat. But nowadays it's ordinary wanting. My life doesn't revolve around that. There are all sorts of other things I want as well that are more important. Like enjoying myself without feeling guilty, and deciding to do things on the spur of the moment. Yes, and being really able to laugh.

As the grip of anorexic thinking is loosened, therapy too becomes a different process: an eye to continued authenticity, the opportunity for the mending process to continue, and many discoveries still to be made. Choosing and deciding will become easier, though there will still be times of dither, and paralysis. Here at this stage, however, there is the potential for each crisis to provide opportunity for further learning, and for ongoing practice in becoming reattuned. It will become easier too at this stage for sufferers to find, or create, a balance between their own needs and wants and the needs and wants of others. With help they will gradually become more effective at sustaining a balance between self and the demands and exigencies generated by external situations and events.

They discover here that there is fun to be had that does not involve getting high, while facing, or denying, the inevitable crash. They learn to 'waste' time, or, as many describe it, 'spend a bit of time pottering'. Particularly, they learn to 'waste time' doing things that are meaningful to them personally. As at this stage there are even quite small moments of happiness, or real contentment, so these will hold the key to their own ingredients. With them the sense may emerge that contentment is a feeling that can be fostered, and genuine enjoyments are experiences that can be allowed to evolve. Even in such moments there lies the proof that it is possible to be happy in a way that is entirely different from that 'happy' which is being high. It also becomes possible to acknowledge the absence of enjoyment, rather than contriving a mask. It becomes possible to be free to be out of sorts instead of having to have everything sorted, and possible to be free to get things wrong, rather than having to be eternally right. So exploring being, rather than being in control, continues.

Reference

1 Ernst, S. and Goodison, L. (1981) *In Our Own Hands: A Handbook of Self-help Therapy*. London: The Women's Press. (This book provides a good introduction to a variety of helping techniques and suggestions for further reading.)

Appendix

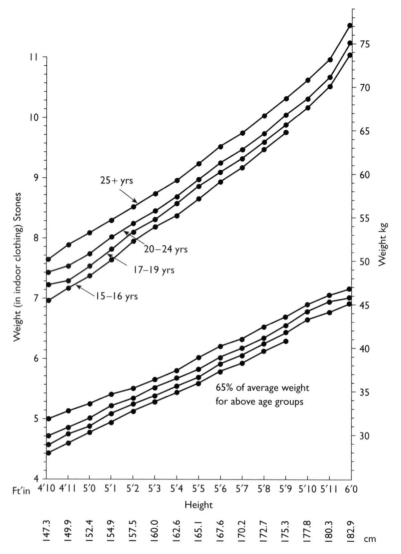

Average weight for women. *Height was measured in indoor shoes; it is suggested that 1 in. be added to normal height to read weight. Adapted from Scientific Tables from J.R. Geighy SA, Basle, Switzerland.

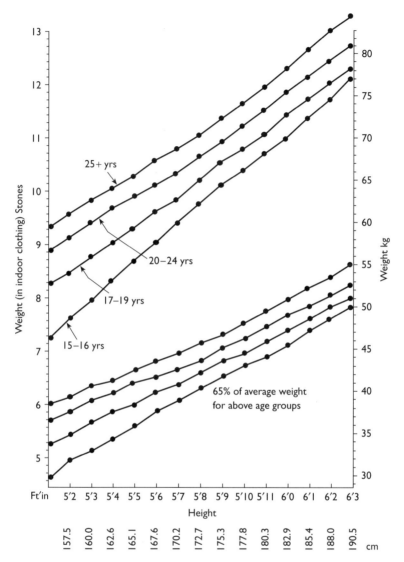

Average weight for men. *Height was measured in indoor shoes; it is suggested that 1 in. be added to normal height to read weight. Adapted from Scientific Tables from J.R. Geighy SA, Basle, Switzerland.

UNITS OF WEIGHT CONVERSION TABLES

lb	stone	lb	kg	lb	stone	lb	kg
56	4	0	25.4	86	6	2	39.0
57	4	1	25.9	87	6	3	39.5
58	4	2	26.3	88	6	4	39.9
59	4	3	26.8	89	6	5	40.4
60	4	4	27.2	90	6	6	40.8
61	4	5	27.7	91	6	7	41.3
62	4	6	28.1	92	6	8	41.7
63	4	7	28.6	93	6	9	42.2
64	4	8	29.0	94	6	10	42.6
65	4	9	29.5	95	6	11	43.1
66	4	10	29.9	96	6	12	43.6
67	4	11	30.4	97	6	13	44.0
68	4	12	30.8	98	7	0	44.5
69	4	13	31.3	99	7	1	44.9
70	5	0	31.8	100	7	2	45.4
71	5	1	32.2	101	7	3	45.8
72	5	2	32.7	102	7	4	46.3
73	5	3	33.1	103	7	5	46.7
74	5	4	33.6	104	7	6	47.2
75	5	5	34.0	105	7	7	47.6
76	5	6	34.5	106	7	8	48.1
77	5	7	34.9	107	7	9	48.5
78	5	8	35.4	108	7	10	49.0
79	5	9	35.8	109	7	11	49.4
80	5	10	36.3	110	7	12	49.9
81	5	11	36.7	111	7	13	50.4
82	5	12	37.2	112	8	0	50.8
83	5	13	37.7	113	8	1	51.3
84	6	0	38.1	114	8	2	51.7
85	6	1	38.6	115	8	3	52.2

UNITS OF WEIGHT CONVERSION TABLES

lb	stone	lb	kg	lb	stone	lb	kg
116	8	4	52.6	146	10	6	66.2
117	8	5	53.1	147	10	7	66.7
118	8	6	53.5	148	10	8	67.1
119	8	7	54.0	149	10	9	67.6
120	8	8	54.4	150	10	10	68.0
121	8	9	54.9	151	10	11	68.5
122	8	10	55.3	152	10	12	69.0
123	8	11	55.8	153	10	13	69.4
124	8	12	56.3	154	11	0	69.9
125	8	13	56.7	155	11	1	70.3
126	9	0	57.2	156	11	2	70.8
127	9	1	57.6	157	11	3	71.2
128	9	2	58.1	158	11	4	71.7
129	9	3	58.5	159	11	5	72.1
130	9	4	59.0	160	11	6	72.6
131	9	5	59.4	161	11	7	73.0
132	9	6	59.9	162	11	8	73.5
133	9	7	60.3	163	11	9	73.9
134	9	8	60.8	164	11	10	74.4
135	9	9	61.2	165	11	11	74.8
136	9	10	61.7	166	11	12	75.3
137	9	11	62.1	167	11	13	75.8
138	9	12	62.6	168	12	0	76.2
139	9	13	63.1	169	12	1	76.7
140	10	0	63.5	170	12	2	77.1
141	10	1	64.0	171	12	3	77.6
142	10	2	64.4	172	12	4	78.0
143	10	3	64.9	173	12	5	78.5
144	10	4	65.3	174	12	6	78.9
145	10	5	65.8	175	12	7	79.4

Index